A Handbook for Portuguese Instructors in the U.S.

Edited by

Margo Milleret
Mary Risner

ISBN: 099605118X
ISBN-13: 978-0996051187

Roosevelt, NJ

TABLE OF CONTENTS

PREFACE

WHY THIS BOOK?

Margo Milleret, Emerita
University of New Mexico

Mary Risner
University of Florida

This handbook is designed as a resource for all instructors of Portuguese in higher education who are engaged in teaching and developing their programs. Originally the two audiences for the handbook were beginning professionals, such as graduate students, and instructors who come to the U.S. from other higher education institutions, and who may not have familiarity with the skills and knowledge necessary to teach and grow a Portuguese program. In a pilot survey conducted in 2011, Milleret learned that 78% of the instructors contacted had not received any formal training in program development. Although many noted that the experience of teaching as a graduate student provided them with observation and participation in cultural activities, most indicated "trial and error" as the main source of learning as new faculty. The respondents were in agreement about what constituted program development. They consistently listed the following: developing curriculum, gaining support from the administration, recruiting students and organizing cultural events, advertising classes, collaborating with cultural centers and developing a study abroad program. Other tasks less consistently listed were sponsoring a language table or honorary society, sending out publicity, and conducting program evaluation. All of those contacted agreed that faculty needed formal training in program development and they suggested various venues and formats to accomplish such a task. A junior colleague said it best when she asked, "Why do we need to keep reinventing the wheel?" (*The Portuguese Newsletter*, Winter, 2012).

Much of the information presented in this volume is not new, but it was published earlier, or dispersed in journals, or presented at conferences, or shared between colleagues. For example, the founding publication, Bobby Chamberlain's collection *Building a Portuguese Program*, was published at Michigan State University in 1979. Many years passed before two journals dedicated a volume to the topic, *Luso-Brazilian Review* (Winter, 2003) and *Portuguese Language Journal* (Fall, 2010). Of note in all of these collections are the author's efforts to communicate their own experiences at specific institutions to their colleagues elsewhere in order to provide models and advice. The same approach is also true in this collection, although we have made an attempt to refrain from too many local references in order to provide examples and advice as applicable as possible to audiences anywhere in higher education in the U.S. Thus, our authors are passing along years of combined experience and materials that are now gathered into one place for the convenience of all instructors of Portuguese who need a reference or "how to" guide that they can consult easily.

Some of the articles included here could not have been written forty years ago when Chamberlain published his guide. For example, there are essays about using technology in the classroom, applying the National Standards for Foreign Language Learning to course design, organizing a community learning experience, and participating in professional development opportunities in person and on-line. In addition, research has led to a greater understanding of how to teach Portuguese to heritage learners and Spanish speakers, so those have been included in the book as well.

The handbook is organized into three sections that focus first on the entrance into the profession and professional development. The second section addresses the responsibilities of developing a Portuguese program in terms of advertising, curriculum, assessment and technology. The final section of the handbook offers more detailed information regarding the needs of heritage learners and Spanish speaking learners. Many of the essays include examples, tables of information, and lists of resources in order to facilitate further exploration and development.

Most of the elements of program development mentioned by the participants in the 2011 pilot survey have been addressed in this volume. We would like to see this handbook serve as a catalyst for the creation and implementation of university classes, websites, or workshops at future professional conferences. We hope that those who consult this handbook will find useful material that can be applied to their needs and challenges in teaching and developing Portuguese in higher education.

INTRODUCTION

PORTUGUESE INSTRUCTION IN THE U.S.

Margo Milleret, Emerita
University of New Mexico

In this introductory essay I will argue that all Portuguese instruction in higher education in the U.S., no matter where one teaches or how many classes one teaches, has at its core the important task of program development. I will suggest that there is not a final point to the job of program development. There are landmarks along the way, but those who teach Portuguese in the U.S. are always program developers. This is not a new idea but it is at the core of why this book was organized.

What is Portuguese program development and why is it necessary? The word "program" suggests that our goal is more than an offering of a few classes taught at an institution of higher education. Rather the goal is to build a whole curriculum of language, conversation, culture, and literature that prepares students not as tourists with a minimum level of communication skills, but rather as speakers of Portuguese with a high level of proficiency in language, culture and literature. The word "development" means growth, as in a maturation process that starts in infancy and progresses through adolescence and into adulthood. Thus, development means starting small with a few classes and then increasing the number of classes offered in order to attract more students, be more visible and have more influence on university or college campuses.

Multi-tasking in Portuguese Programs

To accomplish the goals of establishing and growing a Portuguese program, instructors must have many skills and must work longer hours than the majority of their peers who teach other foreign languages. Portuguese instructors are often hired to "develop" a program, not just teach a few classes. Thus, they are called on to exhibit a range of organizational, administrative, and marketing skills that are not expected of other instructors of the commonly taught languages, such as French, German or Spanish.

In order to develop a Portuguese program, instructors must know that enrollments determine the well-being of most university classes. Healthy enrollments are the numbers that the administration determines are needed to be of financial benefit to the university. Portuguese enrollment numbers are used to point to success, and therefore all instructors want to have strong enrollments in their classes. If any class does not have strong enrollments, administrators will cancel the class and interrupt the progress that students are making in their language learning. Trying to maintain healthy enrollment numbers turns instructors into marketing professionals who must do publicity and create events that will interest students and make them want to enroll in classes. Portuguese instructors visit classes and recruit students, they often teach extra classes in order to attract students from other disciplines of study, and they attend orientation sessions at the beginning of the school year to convince new students at the university to study Portuguese. Most instructors make contacts with colleagues on campus or with centers that might have an interest in Portugal, Brazil or the Lusophone countries of Africa. If there are Portuguese-speaking communities near campus, instructors will reach out to those individuals as well.

Finally, Portuguese instructors may get caught up in the politics of their campus or state, and may even feel an impact from national politics. At the departmental level, colleagues and the chair may not be supportive of Portuguese study because they feel it takes away from their languages or areas of interest. On the campus, the administrators may change and the new ones may be unsupportive of the Portuguese program. Thus, they will not provide funding, instructors, or political support when there is a need to keep a class with low enrollment, or to bring in a speaker, or pay for a conference trip. National politics and even international relations rarely focus on Portuguese-speaking countries, or the focus may be negative or uninformed.

Although the U.S., Brazil and Portugal have been friends and allies for many years, that friendship does not guarantee investments in Portuguese language teaching in higher education, because other languages and other language-speaking groups have been more visible and more powerful in representing their interests. Therefore, Portuguese instructors must be savvy about campus, state, and even national events that may have an impact on the perceived importance and need for Portuguese language study. They must build allies and support networks to help them protect their programs in difficult economic or political times. Finally, they must have enough visibility on campus that students will notice and complain if classes are not being offered, or if cultural events are cancelled.

Has it Always Been This Way?

This is an ambiguous title because it could mean "Has it always been a struggle to establish and maintain Portuguese on U.S. campuses?" or it could mean "Has Portuguese instruction always required multi-tasking?" or it could mean "Has higher education always been concerned with enrollments and politics?" The answer to all these questions is the same: YES. Instructors of Portuguese have always been concerned with their own and with other university programs. They have always wanted to see data that show the language is gaining attention among students. They have also been the first ones to make arguments about why Portuguese is an important language for study. Instructors in the U.S. have always worried about the health of their programs and that of Portuguese as a language for study nationwide.

According to my research, the first survey of Portuguese programs was published in 1925 by Eduardo de Carvalho of the Boston Consular office of the Portuguese government. Since that first publication, there have been numerous studies reporting enrollment figures and mounting arguments in favor of Portuguese study that have been presented in conferences and in scholarly journals. There are two that deserve a mention here. First, David J. Viera authored an annotated comprehensive study of over one hundred articles that appeared in print between 1940 and 1989. Second, Carmen Chaves Tesser explored the history of Portuguese teaching in "Brazilian Portuguese Language and Linguistics" which appeared in the collection *Envisioning Brazil: A Guide to Brazilian Studies in the United States*. There is a history of publications about Portuguese programs, Portuguese classes, and reasons to study Portuguese that is at least 90 years old. This history of publication speaks to the passion that Portuguese instructors have for their subject and to their perseverance in arguing for the establishment and maintenance of Portuguese language and cultural study nationwide.

Status of Portuguese Study in the U.S. Today

Portuguese has been taught in higher education in the US since the 1920s. At first, it was taught at highly selective universities like Harvard, Catholic University and Georgetown and it was taught as a grammar-translation course. Students did not learn to speak the language, but rather to read the great literary works by studying the grammar and then translating the content. The apparent ease with which Spanish speakers could learn grammar and translate Portuguese was first discovered in these grammar-translation courses. This interest in and study of Portuguese by Spanish speakers has continued into the 21st century.

The first big push to increase the number of institutions and classes where Portuguese could be taught came in the 1940s as a result of the alliances made during WWII and the Good Neighbor policy. The second push came as a result of the launch of the Russian satellite Sputnik. In the late 1950s and into the 1960s the National Defense Education Act supplied funding for the training of teachers and for the creation of textbooks. At that time, the research suggested that the audio-lingual method was best for learning a foreign language. The major sources for funding Portuguese in the 21st century are the U.S. Department of Education and the Department of Defense with Title VI, Startalk, and the Flagship programs. The communicative method is the favored pedagogical approach currently. Since the late 1950s Portuguese has been classified as a critical language of importance to national security and economic development. A visit to most state-funded universities in the U.S. or to the nation's most elite private colleges and universities, would reveal at least one instructor of Portuguese. The largest programs of Portuguese have three or more instructors. In addition to state universities that receive federal funding, the healthiest and best funded programs are in areas where immigrant communities have been present for many years and those areas are the Northeast and West Coasts. Originally, those immigrant communities were from the Azores, Cape Verde, and Portugal. Today, Brazilians are a growing presence in the existing immigrant communities and they have expanded into areas not previously settled, such as Florida and Georgia.

Nonetheless, in spite of the gains over the last 90 years, Portuguese is NOT considered to be a necessary part of foreign language study in the imagination of many faculty and administrators in public and private higher education. The most important second language in the U.S. right now is Spanish, and it is often the only language offered in primary and secondary education. The modern languages that have the longest history of being taught in the U.S. are German and French, and these two, in addition to Spanish, still dominate the language teaching world at all levels of study. When administrators decide to add a Less Commonly Taught Language to the curriculum, the preference often goes to Japanese, Chinese or Arabic unless the local community or faculty advocate for Portuguese. So, how can we summarize the status of Portuguese instruction in the U.S.? First, it is still a marginal language on many but not all of the campuses where it is taught, and it is not taught at all at some institutions of higher education. There is some good news to this picture, however. The enrollment figures are much better than they used to be some twenty years ago and additionally, the future looks good for continued growth.

Enrollment Figures from 2013

Now is the time for a short detour to look at enrollment numbers and what they can tell us about the study of Portuguese in higher education as of 2013. This information comes from the Modern Language Association, which began collecting and publishing data on English and Foreign Language enrollments in higher education in 1960.

- Students of Portuguese continuing their study into advanced classes are among the highest of all Foreign Languages, at 22.7%
- Graduate student enrollments increased from 434→514 (2009-2013)
- The overall number of institutions teaching Portuguese increased as follows:
  12 →29 (2009-2013) for two-year institutions
  129→207 (2009-2013) for four-year institutions
  40→41 (2009-2013) for graduate programs of study

These figures highlight growth in graduate student enrollments, indicate how many students of Portuguese continue their study beyond the basic classes (almost ¼), and demonstrate a growth in the number of institutions nationwide offering Portuguese classes. One figure that stands out is the small change in the number of programs offering graduate study. How is it possible to staff a growing number of classes at two-year and four-year campuses if there aren't more programs of graduate study? I don't know all the reasons, but here are two of them. First, the graduate programs at most research universities are small, but the faculty hesitate or are unable to increase enrollments because the market is not reliable enough to warrant expansion or to encourage other institutions to begin a graduate program of study. Second, many educational institutions hire Portuguese speakers from the community to fill the new job vacancies. Many of these instructors are either heritage speakers or are from Brazil and have a Brazilian higher education degree. Both of the reasons point to a continuing lull in graduate program growth.

Table 1 shows enrollment data since 1960. There is a healthy increase in the enrollment numbers starting in 1998. According to my survey research of instructors in 2010, the main reasons for enrollment growth were new pedagogical materials and curriculum redesigns. In addition, instructors mentioned growth due to media attention to Brazil, and the interest of Spanish speakers. As noted earlier, Spanish speakers have maintained a constant presence in Portuguese programs.

Table 1

Portuguese Enrollments from the Modern Language Association

Year	Enrollment
1960	1,034
1968	4,048
1980	4,894
1990	6,118
1998	6,926
2002	8,385
2006	10,310
2009	11,273
2013	12,415

The second table provides a comparison between Portuguese and other languages taught in the U.S., just to give an idea of how many students are studying and how many colleges and universities are offering language study in the U.S. As can be seen, Portuguese is not as popular as the other Less Commonly Taught Languages, except Korean, and is low in enrollments when compared to the traditionally taught languages of Spanish, French and German. According to the MLA, total foreign language enrollment numbers represent only 8.1% of all students studying at U.S. universities and colleges.

That is to say, that of all the students studying at institutions of higher education in the U.S., only 8.1% of them are enrolled in at least one foreign language class. Such a low figure could represent an opportunity for Portuguese instructors who might be able to recruit and build their programs among those who are not enrolled in language study.

Table 2

Data on Foreign Language Enrollments from the Modern Language Association 2013

Language	Enrollments in Higher Education	Number of institutions reporting
Spanish	790,756	2,226
French	197,757	1,606
German	86,700	1,074
Italian	71,285	665
Japanese	66,740	706
Chinese	61,055	866
Arabic	32,286	588
Russian	21,962	436
Portuguese	12,415	238
Korean	12,229	154

The Future

My crystal ball reveals that the number of students taking Portuguese classes at U.S. institutions of higher learning will continue to grow during the 21st century, although possibly at a slower rate than in the early years of the century. There are three main reasons for this continued growth. First, since the year 2000, language camps for high school and university students have been established in the U.S. and the U.S. government has provided more funding to support summer training for both instructors and students in the Flagship and Startalk programs. Thus, more students are being exposed to Portuguese at an earlier age in immersion programs and more instructors are being trained to teach those students. Second, there are more textbooks and online materials to teach Portuguese than ever before. In the not too distant past, instructors regularly complained about a lack of good pedagogical materials. It is noteworthy that some of the new materials contribute to the biggest need, advanced language learning, while others are easily accessible to students who want to study on their own. Third, Spanish speakers and for the first time Heritage speakers are having a positive impact on enrollments. Although Heritage speakers are limited to specific regions of the U.S., they are an increasing presence in Portuguese language classrooms.

Spanish speakers are everywhere in the U.S. and are interested in the language because it is a sister language of Spanish and because speaking Portuguese is a skill that is needed in business and government in the U.S. as well as in Europe and South America. There is a fourth factor that is more difficult to measure, but deserves a mention here. Both Brazil and Portugal have and continue to invest in the teaching of Portuguese in the U.S. at both the high school and university levels. In addition, all the countries that speak Portuguese have united around an agenda to have Portuguese recognized as an official language of international communication at the United Nations and in other diplomatic circles. These international efforts help to raise public awareness about the Portuguese language, but it is hard to know how direct an impact they have on language enrollments.

There are two concluding points to make and both of them are positive. First, Portuguese is a small, but growing area of language study in the U.S. with a widening support structure on the national, state and local levels. There are more high schools offering Portuguese study, while efforts to teach Portuguese at middle and elementary schools are expanding, especially in Utah and on both coasts. Second, in order for Portuguese to gain a greater presence in universities and colleges, that is, in order for Portuguese to become a necessary part of the foreign language course offerings, instructors must make it visible and vital to campus life. Program development in Portuguese can have an impact on language instruction in the community and therefore it is paramount to build strong Portuguese programs in higher education. I am asking instructors to grow their Portuguese programs so that students can develop strong language and cultural skills. These strong programs will contribute to the future of Portuguese as a meaningful language of study and expression in the U.S. when they are able to exercise influence in the communities and state around them.

References

Carvalho, Eduardo de. (1925). *A Língua Portuguesa nos Estados Unidos*. Boston, MA: Editora Empresa de Propaganda Patriótica.

Goldberg, D., Looney, D., and & Lusin, N. (2015, February). Enrollments in Languages Other Than English in United States Institutions of Higher Education, Fall 2013. *Modern Language Association*. Retrieved from https://apps.mla.org/pdf/2013_enrollment_survey.pdf

Milleret, M. (1990). Portuguese Program Development: Past, Present, and Future. *Hispania,* 73(2), 513-17.

Tesser, C. C. (2005). Brazilian Portuguese Language and Linguistics. *Envisioning Brazil: A Guide to Brazilian Studies in the United States,* 73-92. Marshall C. Eakin and Paulo Roberto de Almeida. Madison (Eds.). WI: University of Wisconsin.

Vieira, D. J. (1992). A Selected Annotated Bibliography on the History of Portuguese Language Teaching in the United States. *Hispania,* 75(2), 445-453.

PART 1

ENTERING THE PROFESSION

1.1 HOW TO NAVIGATE THE JOB MARKET

Robert Simon
Kennesaw State University

There are many challenges and opportunities in today's job market in Portuguese. On the one hand, according to *Inside Higher Ed*, as of 2015 Portuguese was one of the three lesser-taught languages with the greatest increase in enrollment. Data from the *MLA* report on enrollments in languages other than English show that this growth has approached 10% over the past decade (2). This means that more positions in the instruction of Portuguese language and Lusophone Cultures (particularly with focus on Brazil) may be opening in the near future. On the other hand, MLA statistics for tenure track (TT) and non-tenure-track positions overall do not tend to share such optimism. In its 2014 task-force report on the state of doctoral education in the Humanities, the MLA revealed that while the number of TT positions in English and Foreign Languages was steadily decreasing, the number of PhD holders graduating each year (which already outnumbered the positions available) remained steady (5). This indicates a glut in the market, making the chances of "landing" a TT job that much less a reality for the majority of PhD holders in Portuguese and other languages. Although the situation for non-TT positions (i.e., positions as "instructor" or "lecturer" in the US) is better, we cannot assume that everyone will be hired in a full-time position. So we need then to ask ourselves what we can do to make ourselves as competitive as possible for the positions available. The process really begins well before completing the thesis or dissertation, at home and in a moment of solace.

The Hard Look in the Mirror

Many graduate students have heard something like the following from our mentors in graduate school, "I think you'll be great in that tenured position at (fill in the blank with mentor's alma mater or dream school)." It is not that they want to set their students up for "failure" (or to believe we are failures if we do not meet their apparent expectations); in fact, statements like this one (as well as less altruistic ones) are pronounced out of faculty's fondness for their students and their dedication to those students' professional well-being. In essence, these well-meaning mentors simply want to see the student succeed in the way by which they have imagined success, i.e., achieving what they had achieved and landing a Tenure Track position at a major Research 1 university.[1] There is some truth to this – the Research 1 (R1) and Research

[1] It should be clear that not all graduate students will have the same experience, and not all dissertation advisors would make such a statement. I have drawn this section from my own

2 (R2) institutions do tend to offer higher salaries than at the majority of academic institutions and offer what may look like an "easy life" with a 2/2 teaching load (two classes per semester) and time for research. For your faculty mentors, anything else may have seemed like a case of misplaced priorities. It is common, for example, for Master's classified institutions to offer 3/2 or 3/3 teaching loads, with many others teaching anywhere from 3/4 to 5/5 and concomitantly lesser research requirements. The truth, of course, is not quite as simple, since at most R1 and R2 institutions the research requirements are rather difficult for many young faculty to meet, while the increased need for service (sitting on committees, leading curricular changes, or simply planning a student group event) can tend to occupy close to 20 hours a week to fulfill.

Beyond this there is also the reasoning behind earning the PhD to begin with. Any graduate student would need to ask him/herself why s/he decided to take on the task of completing a program of study. Would it have been with the intention of becoming the most powerful voice in your area of literary criticism/cultural studies/linguistics/etc.? Did you dream of spending time mentoring your own students in the ways of the beautiful world which literature has provided us? Or, did you always want to teach your love of Portuguese language to students whom you could then take to the country where the sights, sounds, and smells all woke up a part of you that you did not know existed before? Did something change for you during your program, or do you still hold on to one of these dreams, albeit a little modified from experience?

This is where the first step of your path needs to begin. At some point you need to look yourself in the eye and ask "what do I want from this degree?" "Who do I want to become?" "Where can I work to fulfill this dream?" The exercise feels uncomfortable at first; yet, in allowing oneself to answer these questions one will not only know yourself better, one will have had his/her "hard look in the mirror" moment – it will remind you (or tell you perhaps for the first time) what you want in your career. You may be surprised by what you find. Over a decade ago, when I took the time to do this exercise, I realized I wanted to teach and to publish my research, and that at the bottom of my heart I was not willing to give up one for the other. I also wanted my service to enhance my department and university. In other words, the more research-oriented and subfield-specific work performed at an R1, in the end, would not have been the best choice for me. More or less teaching, more or less research, more or less service, these are options which

experiences and observations, as well as those of many colleagues and students with whom I have had the privilege of communicating.

will become clearer to you each time. Just remember to be honest – it may aid in avoiding a lot of trouble and less-than-ideal experiences during years following graduation.

Preparation for First-Timers

The first thing you need to think about is your teaching. No matter what your preferred/ targeted institution type, you will need to teach at least two courses (if not four or possibly five) during your first several years on the tenure track. If you take a non-TT position, you may be looking then at a minimum of three classes but with no research requirement. In Portuguese programs this usually means smaller programs with fewer sections and, thus, more preparations than for those colleagues in French or Spanish. Speaking of classes taught, the nature of the job market today is one of multitasking; that is, you may be asked to instruct in more than one language/cultural area, and in some cases, in more than one department. You will not only want to know another language (preferably French or Spanish) and have at least some experience teaching it (i.e., a semester or two of 1st or 2nd semester language courses), but you will also need to be prepared to prove teaching ability in it. (This is where honesty is again a great policy – I know someone who once purported advanced-level knowledge of a language, only to have one of the interviewers begin speaking that language. When it was evident he did not speak at that level, the interview ended.) If your PhD program offers a "graduate minor" in another language area, you may consider taking the program up on it. Just to clarify – my own degree is technically in Spanish, despite my obvious leanings toward Lusophone Studies, since my alma mater did not offer a dual program in Portuguese and Spanish. In any case, this degree helped me to secure a TT position; my knowledge and experience in other areas helped me to found the Minor program which I coordinate, the topic of another chapter. If you are a specialist in non-Luso-Brazilian Studies in Portuguese, for most positions you will want to increase your knowledge of Brazilian literature and culture, since most universities are looking to increase their contact with Brazil (this, of course, will depend on the institution and the job ads that year – some even go so far as to advertise for "Brazilian Portuguese" speakers only). Any initiatives in which you have participated in on-line/distance learning (at any level), language "for the professions" (i.e., Portuguese or another language for Business, Human Services, Criminal Justice, Nursing, etc.) need to be included in your documentation and emphasized in your letter of application.

You will also want to hone your skills in areas of service (to the university and community) by taking part in, and or taking a leadership role in, extra-classroom activities (sitting on the board of graduate student organizations, volunteering to work in the community, etc.) This kind of experience shows you are not just focused on yourself but also would like to extend your knowledge to others. Given the pressures Humanities programs in general face in the wider world, departments tend to seek out such candidates as these, who may help to support both their mission and survival. On a less dire note, it also shows you to be a good steward of the department and college/school /"academic unit" to which your work pertains and to bring some experience in this area.

Research, although the last of the points I emphasize here, is certainly not the least. You will ***need*** at least one or two papers published in peer-review journals and presentations in regional or national conferences for both experience and networking opportunities. The papers do not necessarily need to find their way into A+ journals such as *PMLA* or *Luso-Brazilian Review*; however, without some sort of publication history the chances of being competitive for TT positions (and even in some cases non-TT positions) are slim. You will want to be close to completion of dissertation if not already completed and defended. Some universities are leery of considering incomplete PhDs, since they have lost candidates, and in some cases entire faculty lines, due to a finalist who upon hiring does not complete the degree in the allotted time. This last point is really the most essential, as without a completed dissertation a candidate will not have proven his/her ability to follow through with the kind of research tasks asked of faculty at all levels over the course of a career.

The CV, or Curriculum Vitae, will become an essential part of your application. Depending on the types of institutions which interest you (please refer to the "Hard Look in the Mirror" referred to above), you will want to create different versions of the CV, one for each type of institution to which you would like to apply. Study the institutions' profiles and try to get a feel for the direction in which the university wishes to go. Just because it is classified one way does not mean it has not begun a push toward another (many Master's-level universities are currently moving toward Research status, for example, meaning the focus on research is strong but not to the point at which teaching would become an area of more local importance). You should definitely look to tailor each version of the CV to this focus, meaning if applying to a university classified as R1 or R2 or to a position for which research will be a primary goal, you should place this section first. If applying to teaching-focused institutions, then the list of classes taught, pedagogically-oriented professional development, etc., should go first. Always follow your mentor's advice in this regard.

This brings us to another vital discussion, that of finding a good mentor. Really, you will want at least two mentors, one for research and one for teaching. If these happen to be the same person, then consider yourself fortunate. If your mentor for one is not a shining example of the other, then find one for the other. They will each have differing approaches to offer for how to prepare yourself for the job market. That is all right, as no one true answer exists for any of the questions the experience on the market will raise.

Applications

The first rule of sending a job application is to send what they ask for and no more. This seems easy, but when a university asks you to submit a short writing sample (usually the length of a term paper or article), you may feel the temptation to send your unfinished dissertation. From my own experience serving on search committees, I can assure you that nothing puts a committee off from an initial application more than not following directions. Also, triple-check your documents, the submission address, etc., before submitting. Many institutions now ask for a letter of application (very, very well proofread, and by more than two people if possible), a copy of your CV, unofficial or official transcripts (again, make sure you know which and can provide these), a sample syllabus, and a teaching philosophy. As for these final two entries, you not only want to make sure they are well-edited and spotless, you also want to ensure they pertain to the job advertised (as a committee member, it is rather pointless to be staring at a syllabus for a graduate-level course in Lusophone African literature when the job specifically states that "the successful candidate will instruct lower and upper-division Spanish courses, and lower-division Portuguese courses"). One other point – the aforementioned mentor (in teaching, of course) really should have the chance to look over your teaching philosophy and comment on it. Request the liberal use of the corrector's pen; you may not enjoy the comments you receive at the time, but you will enjoy them much more while sitting in your new office as a Lecturer or Assistant Professor a few months later.

Interviews

Now, let's say you have received that exciting call or e-mail to hold a phone, Skype, or MLA interview. Each of these formats is different but should be held in the same esteem. Dress formally, even for a phone interview – you will take it more seriously that way. Have prepared answer templates but do not prepare to give a canned answer – committees can see through the "my passion for teaching is evidenced by A, B, and C…" style answers and do not feel it shows either a real knowledge of department / institution or a true focus on the position itself. Answer questions quickly but thoroughly (30-60 seconds per response if possible, unless the committee has asked a more involved question or has requested more examples to underscore a previous answer). Prepare questions for the interviewers whose answers cannot be found on their website. You can also ask about the committee's timeline for a decision, assuming the committee does not volunteer this information beforehand. DO NOT ASK about salaries, course releases, or if you can teach in an area out of field/outside of the field advertised for the position.

This can be perceived as showing a lack of interest in the job itself and can sink a candidacy. For the best possible outcome, you may want to see if faculty at your institution will perform a mock-interview with you and give you feedback.

Another point about appropriateness is the type of job for which you are applying. While a discussion on your research is an excellent idea when interviewing for a TT position, when interviewing for a non-TT position ("Lecturer" or "Instructor," for example) the focus should always be on your teaching and service experience. You can always mention that you perform some research (particularly if you hold or are about to hold the PhD), but make sure not to dwell on it. Many a candidate has received no more contact from Lecturer search committees when their principle topic of conversation is their dissertation and how it will inform a generation of literary/cultural studies critics. For a non-TT position it misses the point, and the candidate misses an opportunity to start a career.

Once you have had your first interview, you will feel anxious about receiving word concerning an upcoming, on-campus interview. It is best, however, simply to allow the process to happen and not interfere, as sometimes the decision-making protocols can take upward of three to four months to yield any results. Assuming you are contacted for an on-campus interview (which can take from a single day to three full days and two to three nights, including meals with the committee and other faculty), here are a few tips. First, *be on your best behavior* from flight take-off to landing back home. There have been cases of "informal plane interviews" in which a faculty member from the target department just happened to be sitting next to a candidate on the plane. They struck up a conversation, and the rest was history. Know as much as possible about the campus and your potential new colleagues beforehand! Do your research on personnel, locations, useful acronyms, etc. Even if you do not plan on spending your career in a place, treat it as though you did. While on campus, do not speak poorly of anyone you are asked about, even if the one asking has their own opinion. Even if in jest, such speech can make a candidate look too "subjective" to want to bring on as a colleague. Conversely, you are interviewing them in a sense. Feel free to take mental notes on how you feel, and if you feel uncomfortable for whatever reason. A strange pang in the mind now may save you from years of torment later.

For the technicalities of the on-campus interview itself, you will most likely be asked to hold:

- a teaching presentation (either for an existing class, a mock class, or even for a room full of faculty pretending to be a class);
- one or two talks on your teaching philosophy, research agenda, service philosophy, etc. (again, the combination of these will depend greatly on the type of position and institution – at a teaching-focused

institution and / or for a teaching-focused position you will more than likely not be asked to give a talk on your research, while at a research-focused institution or position you may have little or no focus on service);

- individual conversations with a Dean, the Chair, the Provost (for smaller institutions), and perhaps even with interested graduate/undergraduate students.

A word on the teaching demonstration: always have a back-up method ready in case the technology does not work (I am telling you this from experience) and make sure to remain in the target language. Speaking of that language, if you are not a native speaker you will need to ensure your basic grammar is up to par and that, for both the teaching and other aspects of the visit, you can hold lengthy conversations in the language about a variety of topics (i.e., that you have reached what ACTFL calls "Advanced-High" competency in that language, although obviously "Superior" level is preferred). Your fascinating research will not matter if your conversational Portuguese sputters out in less than an hour.

When you return home from your visit, always send a thank-you e-mail to the chair of both the search committee and the department. It seems like a small task but it can make a difference in a hotly contested search.

The Offer

When/if you are offered a position, you have the option to negotiate salary, moving expenses, extra supplies for research and/or teaching, etc. Although I would encourage you to do so, please know that each institution may have limits on what, if any, may be negotiated, particularly if you are a "newly minted PhD." Also, you will want to study data such as the average salary for Humanities faculty at your soon-to-be new rank at that institution, cost of living, etc. Generally you can attempt to negotiate 5% above the offer; however, be prepared either to hear a "no" or to find that, with the increase in salary, some other aspect of the offer may be reduced (for example, you may be able to negotiate from $45,000 to $47,500, and find your moving reimbursement reduced concomitantly). Finally, despite the difficulties in reaching this point in the interview process, until you sign a contract you have the chance to back out. If you are not satisfied with the conditions of employment to the point at which you simply cannot see yourself working there, you can always say "no."

Having said that, the conditions for accepting a TT position tend to be different from those of a non-TT position. The former's salaries will always be higher, usually (but not always) with at least some moving expenses covered, and sometimes even extra bonuses or summer teaching opportunities. For the latter, the salaries begin around $10,000-$15,000 lower than for the former, with few if any perks added. I would suggest not letting this discourage you, since the majority of positions advertised recently will be teaching-focused, non-TT positions, and they are at the very least a good way to begin your career.

For Senior Level Positions

The market for Associate Professor and Full Professor positions is indeed very tricky. There exist fewer candidates but much more pressure in terms of expectations, which in all of the areas above are higher. Jobs at this level usually entail a heavy administrative load, and/or are themselves administrative positions. Networking is also more essential, since it is a much more comfortable situation if the search committee feels the candidates are well-known to them (and outside, since prestige is also a factor). Obviously, this kind of networking is not something you can do immediately in preparation for an application. Get involved in your profession now, and stay active.

Positions Outside of Academia

Finally, it is worth mentioning that not everyone will find themselves in a TT or non-TT job at a university or college. More newly graduated PhDs have found it ever more difficult to secure such a position, particularly if they have not been able to keep up their scholarship as time goes on. For those unable to do so there may be a feeling of failure; this is natural given the environment from which we come (5-10 years of graduate training, one-on-one mentoring by our supervisors, etc.)

The good news is that many positions exist outside of the academic setting which require candidates whose linguistic, writing, reading, editing, and presentational abilities would set them apart from the typical office worker. In fact, even the *Chronicle of Higher Education* (among other websites) offers a list of non-academic positions in a variety of fields.

Conclusions

You may have noticed the frequent use of the word "experience" in this short chapter. This is very purposeful, since the more you do, the more you will know and the better you will know how to market yourself. If the first year does not go as planned, take note of what you felt went well or not and do it again. If you feel you need to beef up the research/teaching/service portions of your portfolio, then take every opportunity to do so. If you feel your presentational skills need improvement, try presenting to colleagues/well-informed friends who will be honest with you about strengths and challenges they see you facing. Finally, non-academic positions in Portuguese exist in various areas in business, not-for-profit, and government. If you feel drawn to these, please give them a try. No matter what, I wish you all the success in the world. Good luck! Força!

References

American Council on the Teaching of Foreign Languages (n.d.). ACTFL Proficiency Guidelines 2012. Retrieved March, 6 2015 from http://www.actfl.org/publications/guidelines-and-manuals/actfl-proficiency-guidelines-2012

Flaherty, C. (2015, February 11). "Not a Small World after All." *Inside Higher Ed.* Retrieved March, 3 2015 from https://www.insidehighered.com/news/2015/02/11/mla-report-shows-declines-enrollment-most-foreign-languages

Goldberg, D., Looney, D., & Lusin, N. (2013, fall). *Enrollments in Languages other than English in United States Institutions of Higher Education. Modern Language Association.* Retrieved November 30, 2015 from https://www.mla.org/content/download/31180/1452509/2013_enrollment_survey.pdf

Modern Language Association. (2014, May). Report of the MLA Task Force on Doctoral Study in Modern Language and Literature. Retrieved March 3, 2015 from http://www.mla.org/pdf/taskforcedocstudy2014.pdf

1.2 IT TAKES A VILLAGE: PROFESSIONAL DEVELOPMENT IN TEACHING FOR FACULTY IN PORTUGUESE

Celeste Dolores Mann
Georgian Court University
Robert Simon
Kennesaw State University

Reasons for Professional Development

Teaching is an essential part of our career development, whether we work part-time or full-time, in a research university, a traditional teaching college, a "comprehensive university," or any other type of institution. At all levels, we instruct Portuguese language and content related to literatures, cultures, linguistics, etc. of or directed toward the Portuguese-speaking world. In all of these areas, we cannot stop learning about the instructional aspects of our careers, even after we have landed our first teaching job; indeed we need to embrace a philosophy and practice of lifelong development.[2]

No matter what the institution or individual area(s) of focus, possibilities for development in the area of teaching exist, as they do in related areas of mentoring and supervising students, both undergraduate and graduate. Even for graduate students, as well as part-time and full-time faculty, entities within and outside of the "home institution" may offer opportunities for growth as a teacher/instructor/classroom professor.[3]

Professional development, essential for those who are teaching in the classroom, is not limited to innovation in language instruction, but also beneficial for research, networking, mentoring, program development and growth of the Portuguese language (Checklist in Appendix A). The teaching of Portuguese language, and Lusophone literatures and cultures, as well as related second language acquisition, pedagogy and linguistics and applied linguistics research, is a collaborative effort—it flourishes when all contribute to the learning process. Everyone is both a learner and teacher in this process, with something to share with someone else. When master teachers are involved this raises the potential for the entire group. This exchange among scholars and teachers in Lusophone countries and the United States, and the

---

[2] It should be noted that this chapter will not delve into professional development opportunities related specifically to building a research portfolio, nor will it deal with development in the area of administration.

[3] It is in some contexts preferable to use the term "instructor" rather than "teacher" when describing oneself professionally on and off campus. The professional workload and implications within and outside of departments take on a different hue based on whether or not colleagues, administrators, and the general public see us as "language teachers" (equivalent to a High School teacher) or as "professors" (a position for which we must emphasize work in Research, Service, and Teaching, even if not necessarily in that order).

interactions among the most and least experienced, keeps the field innovative, the teaching cutting edge. In turn this makes for better Portuguese instruction, growth of departments, and more students learning the language and studying abroad.

Internal and External Professional Development

There are always exciting, internal opportunities for professional development, within the institution or the system to which it belongs (state or otherwise). University activities and events, for example, may provide a wealth of information and practical applications for new teaching resources and instructional/facilitative techniques. Most universities have some sort of center, or institute, for instruction which usually runs workshops or seminars on such topics as "Teaching and Learning in the 21st Century," "Writing Across the Curriculum," or "Technology and Instruction." The latter, by the way, has tended to be both popular and challenging for faculty in our profession, in the past few years.[4] Many will post announcements on their website and/or post on or around campus. If your campus happens to have an on-line announcement system, these will tend to show up there as well. One unique change which has infiltrated institutional initiatives in recent years has had to do with a relative surge in programs such as these dedicated to part-time faculty. As such, part-timers may also have opportunities available to them in order to hone their instructional skills. You can look into funding for part-time faculty if possible and/or applicable.[5] There also exist, albeit generally on a smaller scale, the occasional invited speakers or workshop leaders. These are usually offered either through centers or even individual departments. Some are advertised better than others, meaning you will want to keep an eye out for these possibilities as they may arise.

Here is as bit of advice specifically for graduate students: at least a few years before your planned graduation date, you should already be on the lookout for these pedagogy workshops at your institution. Plan on taking part in three or four, with one of them in an area in which you feel you have already a recognizable "mastery." This is so that, first, you can carry proof of knowledge in the area onto your CV, and second, you have the chance to learn something you may not have known before (remember that "mastery" is not an end-all; rather, it is the ability to move and flow within an area of

---

[4] Although it may be argued that using technology is an absolute necessity in the classroom (and, of course, if you are to offer hybrid classroom/on-line courses or even fully on-line classes), it will be your task to decide to what end technology may serve you and, on a more philosophical note, where the epistemology of high-tech teaching counters your own intuition on language, literature, culture, etc. instruction.

[5] Some institutions even have financial or other incentives available for part-time faculty who participate in professional development seminars and workshops, and/or who take lesser leadership roles in various areas related to instruction.

expertise, always looking to find out more). Holding fluency in both Portuguese and the vocabulary of instruction looks very good on a cover letter and even better in a department meeting because both are valuable and necessary job skills.

External opportunities for growth in teaching abound, and begin at conferences. In almost all cases there will be presentations and workshops at the major international, national, and regional conferences in Lusophone Studies and Humanities (see a list at the end of this essay), and in the Southeast: MIFLC, SCOLT, FLAG, and SECCLL.[6] A great way to find these is one of the most simple: look up the Calls for Papers (CFPs) associated with teaching at these conferences. There are usually multiple panels on topics related to instruction, as well as the more evident ones in your particular content field(s). We would suggest you first attend a few of these panels / workshops to weigh in on their usefulness and novelty, then try to utilize what you have learned. Send in an abstract for a paper on that area of teaching, and then present on it. (This is another area in which a CV will shine; by participating in discussions on the in-class facilitation of your content area, and not just in the content area itself, you show flexibility and a willingness to "branch out," all good characteristics in a job candidate or candidate for promotion).

Engagement with professional opportunities facilitates the development of an individual as a recognized "teacher-scholar" within the profession. This is a somewhat complex issue since instruction is a relatively localized phenomenon. Creating your network and maintaining your contacts is a great way to become known in the field of Portuguese-Speaking/Lusophone Studies and to ensure recognition for your work in both your content area research and your teaching (at all levels). As an example, at conferences make sure to obtain a presenter's card or contact information. Invite that person to talk more about their topic (most of us adore talking about our presentation topics). After the conference, write to them to say how great it was to meet them and how much you would like to know more about that particular area. This is a quick way to make positive connections within the field, as well as to begin the journey of participating in your area of study. It also opens the door to insights about the field which only experience can usually teach. This type of professional development based on researching both your content field and the instructional resources available will help in your efforts to inspire students to learn more.

Another significant exchange that can happen at conferences is between theorists and graduate students of Second Language Acquisition (SLA) and

---

[6] MIFLC is the *Mountain Interstate Foreign Language Conference*, SCOLT is the *Southern Conference on Language Teaching*, FLAG is the *Foreign Language Association of Georgia*, and SECCLL is the *Southeastern Coastal Conference on Language and Literatures*. Each holds an annual conference and publishes a peer-reviewed journal.

language instructors. Some of the graduate researchers still teach language, but others mainly educate and advise instructors, or teach more theoretical courses to advanced undergraduates and graduate students. Although they may be conducting research locally, attending conferences and discussing their ideas, or serving as master instructors or lecturers in workshops, helps transmit the theory to those teaching in the classroom. Their participation promotes a necessary interchange between theory and practice in the Portuguese classroom. We have already discussed the advantages of presenting at conferences for graduate students and entry-level faculty. Faculty researchers who work with graduate students can double these advantages by organizing a panel and including their students and part-time faculty–this mentoring role assists others in learning and getting a foot in the door and also promotes their own research agenda.

Conferences encourage us to hear and see what others are doing in the form of presentations and panels. Although they are less ubiquitous, longer programs provide more profound learning experiences such as practical teaching experience in the form of micro-teaching, observation/evaluation of colleagues' teaching and also hands-on experimentation with technology and hybrid/online classes. The Center for Advanced Research on Language Acquisition (CARLA), STARTALK and the National Language Research Centers (NLRC) offer these types of programs, which can make a lasting impression on one's teaching and understanding of pedagogical approaches.

Moreover, professional development opportunities are rich with possibilities for collaboration on future research projects, service learning, and community outreach. Some of these networks are established at conferences and internal workshops, but can also be inspired by the National Endowment for the Humanities (NEH) and the Council on International Educational Exchange (CIEE) International Faculty Development Seminars. Many opportunities also exist in order to build on collaborative efforts with the K-12 educator community. The STARTALK program, funded by the government for critical languages taught in K-12 and 4-year undergraduate study, is a good place to initiate and nurture a connection with Portuguese Community Schools and K-12 teachers (as well as part-time and freelance instructors). Brazilian and Portuguese community schools are region specific (they exist mainly in New England, New York, New Jersey, Florida and California) but they are a driving force in the keeping of Portuguese language and Luso-Brazilian cultures in US-based students' minds. It is helpful for university instructors and those who teach adults to understand how Portuguese is being taught to heritage language speakers and in the lower grades. This informs our university teaching and vice versa, and gives us insight to the growth of Portuguese in certain regions and what we may expect from heritage language speakers and high school students who eventually will end up in our classrooms. The articulation between high school and college is important so that secondary school teachers know how to prepare their students, and also for the sharing of ideas about pedagogy. Linkages with Portuguese speaking communities are essential in developing outreach and service learning projects, and also exposing our students to real people outside the classroom who speak Portuguese.

Extended programs such as those funded by STARTALK and Fundação Luso-Americana (FLAD) provide total immersion environments in the USA and in Portugal/Azores in which non-native speaker instructors can improve their language skills. Along with other programs and conferences overseas, native speaker and non-native speaker instructors can gain first hand cultural experience in different parts of the Lusophone world, further enriching their knowledge.

Mentors

Finally, and we cannot stress this enough, having a mentor or mentors with regard to teaching or instruction is in our view the most essential element of your professional development. These may be internal to the institution, or external, or both (if more than one). Such colleagues can aid you in avoiding traps and/or gaffes which could follow you throughout your career. They will be the colleagues you go to with questions about teaching, and who would be at least somewhat aware of existing teaching development workshops, conferences on teaching and other issues of importance. Internal mentors are particularly helpful in advising you on the culture of your institution, how faculty and students relate, student end of the semester evaluations, questions about approaches, grading and rigor that work with *these* students. Look for them among faculty in your own department, other departments, and in the Teaching Center, if your institution has one. Finally, as your career develops, these relationships may continue for years or decades.

In keeping with the idea that "it takes a village," and in highlighting collaboration and mentoring, here are some comments about professional development from colleagues in different areas/stages of their careers:

Professional development is especially important post-tenure, and particularly in a relatively 'young' field like [theoretical] linguistics, where there is ongoing (and multilayered) evolution of paradigms. In my case, I have used professional development resources to incorporate new instructional technology into my teaching and to redesign courses. For my personal teaching style, I'm always looking to apply more active learning techniques. I've also attended workshops that have helped me in terms of pedagogy in my discipline. In terms of research, I participate in conferences and serve as a reviewer on grant panels so that I benefit from the latest content knowledge in my field. I also participate in a writing group, where we share and comment on each other's manuscripts. (T., Associate Professor, R1, personal interview).

I continually seek professional development to stay connected with colleagues and stay on top of developments in the field. Feeds my interest, engagement; keeps me energized and committed to offer quality and meaningful learning experiences to my students. It's a worthwhile investment of time, energy—I look for opportunities that require low cost or are free such as STARTALK. (D., Part-time instructor, R1, personal interview).

Capable professionals are always training. This is even more important for a language instructor, and especially those who are teaching languages to foreigners outside the countries where they are spoken. I think and discuss a lot about the situation of professors of Portuguese as a Foreign Language, Second Language or Heritage Language, who don't have much contact with the Lusophone countries. Language is a living thing, constantly transforming. In order for us to teach it in a way that flows realistically, it's necessary for the instructor to keep herself up to date with constant training—in an individual sense or in a pair or group context. There's also the situation of native Portuguese speakers who are offered jobs teaching their own language. Normally these "natives" are not language instructors by profession, and therefore, it is essential that they be trained in how to teach languages. The same thing can be said of instructors without experience. Training in person or by distance learning should be routine for anybody who wants to improve/develop in the teaching profession. (S., Director of a language institute in Brazil, personal interview).

Conferences helped me to move forward on some of my research projects. When I was stuck, it was really useful to attend a conference, as colleagues would offer suggestions on texts to consult. It is important to meet colleagues and to find out what they are working on." (K., Visiting Assistant Professor, 4 year selective university, personal interview).

For those of you who are the only one, or two, teaching Portuguese at your institution, there are many people and sources available to help you find external mentors. In addition to those you meet at external conferences, workshops and programs, there are web sites for Portuguese instructors, such as *Fale Português*, which has over 4,000 members and Facebook groups, such as *Ensinar português*, with over 8,000. For example, the former, based in Brazil, holds a weekly online chat, facilitated by members, about aspects of teaching Portuguese, and its site has many materials, including breakout groups, videos and lessons to aid in your teaching. These are not the only groups—these virtual communities are a viable substitute for those who do not have access to internal mentors to keep up with developments in pedagogy and to meet and share with colleagues. More discussion of online professional networks is presented in Chapter 3.

Being Pragmatic and Keeping your Eyes Open

Particularly for younger, less experienced graduate students and new colleagues, you need to be on the lookout for predatory conferences and journals. These are entities which do not have much validity in our profession, yet purport their impact via flashy posters and e-mail bombardments. Many exist, and as such, we suggest you be careful when signing up for a conference or journal not associated with a recognized professional association, a particular university, or any reputable publishing house. Many do not share the same quality controls and will charge excessive registration fees for attendance (the journals in this category will usually charge to publish work per page). Having a mentor and conversing on this topic will aid you in avoiding these.

Also, you may wish to scrutinize wisely the teaching-related opportunities which may come about. It is tempting to leap on the newest discourse regarding teaching, particularly if it grandiosely claims to "rewrite teaching" or "make teaching easy." You would be advised to check the scholarship on certain topics to ensure quality peer-review or other measures are in place, and that there are no empty promises to "make your teaching perfect," or "bring culture back into the classroom." Many of these use hype and buzzwords to entice younger faculty into promoting what may not be very useful tools (or could simply rename something you already do). If an idea put forward seems to fit one of these bills, you may want to contact your mentor(s) to find out the back story and, ultimately, to see if this is a legitimate line of inquiry to follow, or if it is a fad, or a façade for a predatory journal.

Another source of potential confusion, and perhaps disappointment, is a lack of understanding about which types of professional development are valued at your institution. Depending on your position (part-time, non-tenure track, tenure track, tenured or freelance) and your particular college or university, specific forms of professional development may be encouraged or given more weight in terms of promotion, tenure or retention. For example, those with tenure track jobs must publish something, so publications and conference presentations and talks are prioritized in your evaluations and are absolutely necessary. For part-timers and non-tenure track faculty, publications are often not required, but excellence in teaching and demonstrated professional development in the form of teacher training and methodology might be. We believe that this should not be the only deciding factor in whether you pursue an activity or publication, since you can definitely learn something and improve your teaching/research/networking from any legitimate endeavor. However, you should be aware of how this activity or publication will impact decisions of tenure, retention or promotion. Ideally, you want to balance those opportunities that have primarily intrinsic merit, with those that offer you deep learning and networking experiences AND positive recognition in your department and our field.

Conclusions

Teaching and research are unquestionably endeavors that are not accomplished in complete isolation. Particularly in teaching Portuguese language and Lusophone Studies, we can benefit from our networking and collective expertise. Collaboration with our Portuguese-speaking colleagues around the world, "our village," bolsters and invigorates our community, and propels us to attain our individual and common goals. Despite the challenges, continuing your professional development in various areas will increase your visibility, chances for advancement, and ultimately, your career goals as an academic professional in Portuguese language and/or Lusophone Studies. By moving ahead with enthusiasm and a little bit of caution, you can keep up to date with new trajectories in research and teaching, and build on your reputation while getting to know others in your field.

Resources for Instructors of Portuguese

A. Professional Associations

For English and Foreign Literatures & Languages

Modern Language Association (MLA) http://www.mla.org

Midwest Modern Language Association (MMLA)
http://www.luc.edu/mmla
Northeast Modern Language Association (NEMLA)
http://www.nemla.org

Pacific Ancient and Modern Language Association (PAMLA)
http://www.pamla.org

Rocky Mountain Modern Language Association (RMMLA)
http://www.rmmla.org

South Atlantic Modern Language Association (SAMLA)
http://samla.memberclicks.net

South Central Modern Language Association (SCMLA)
http://www.southcentralmla.org

For Teaching Foreign Languages

American Council on the Teaching of Foreign Languages (ACTFL) http://www.actfl.org

Central States Conference on Teaching Foreign Languages (CSCTFL) http://www.csctfl.org

Northeast Conference on Teaching Foreign Languages (NECTFL) http://www.nectfl.org

Pacific Northwest Council on Teaching Foreign Languages (PNCFL) http://www.pncfl.org

Southern Conference on Language Teaching (SCOLT) http://www.scolt.org

Southwest Conference on Language Teaching (SWCOLT) http://www.swcolt.org

For Portuguese

American Association of Teachers of Spanish and Portuguese (AATSP) http://www.aatsp.org

The American Organization of Teachers of Portuguese (AOPT) http://www.aotpsite.org

American Portuguese Studies Association (APSA) http://www.portuguese-apsa.com/

Brazilian Studies Association (BRASA) http://www.brasa.org

North American Portuguese Teachers Association. http://www.appeuc.org

B. Resources for Workshops and Teaching

Resource Centers for Language Teaching Workshops

Center for Advanced Language Proficiency Education and Research at Pennsylvania State University (CALPER) http://calper.la.psu.edu

Center for Advanced Research on Language Acquisition (CARLA) http://www.carla.umn.edu

National Language Resource Centers (NLRC) http://www.nflrc.org/

Penn Lauder Summer Institute: Learning a Second Language for Business Communication http://lauder.wharton.upenn.edu/ciber

STARTALK https://startalk.umd.edu/

Faculty Development Seminars

Council on International Educational Exchange (CIEE) http://www.ciee.org/what

National Endowment for the Humanities (NEH) http://www.neh.gov/grants

International Study and Research

Fundação Luso-Americana (FLAD) http://www.flad.pt/

Fulbright (grad students, research teams, faculty exchange) http://www.cies.org/

Instituto Camões http://www.instituto-camoes.pt/

Links for Teaching Resources for Portuguese

Center for Open Educational Resources and Language Learning (COERLL) http://www.coerll.utexas.edu/coerll/

Facebook Group : Ensinar Português https://www.facebook.com/groups/ensinarple/

Fale Português http://faleportugues.ning.com/

C. Other Resources

The MLA Language Map https://www.mla.org/map_main

The ADFL/MLA Report on Foreign Languages and Higher

Education http://www.mla.org/flreport

The ADFL Statement on Junior Faculty Development https://adfl.mla.org/Resources/Policy-Statements/ADFL-General-Guidelines-for-Departments

Appendix A

Checklist for Professional Development

1. Access what you need:
   - ☐ Practical ideas/activities for the classroom
   - ☐ Portuguese textbook choices
   - ☐ Assessment ideas/training
   - ☐ The Publication of Articles
   - ☐ Presentations in your field / sub-field
   - ☐ Outreach/service learning connections
   - ☐ Research networking
   - ☐ Language enrichment/total immersion in Portuguese-speaking environment

2. Identify Current Programs:

3. Research the programs and identify their benefits:
   Does the program fit your needs in "1"? Is it reputable? Does it fit your schedule? Will this opportunity count favorably toward your promotion, retention or tenure? Does it add to your research agenda? Who can you help if you do this? (your own students, other participants?)

4. Funding: Make a budget for each potential conference/program and identify internal and external sources of funding.

5. Choose programs that give you the most or deepest learning/networking opportunities AND positive recognition by your institution. Note deadlines for funding and applications, and organize accordingly in your calendar.

1.3 PROFESSIONAL LEARNING OPPORTUNITIES FOR PORTUGUESE LANGUAGE EDUCATORS

Mary Risner
University of Florida

Professional development for faculty across disciplines is valuable to remain current in a particular subject area, but can be costly for language faculty in departments with limited funding. For junior faculty and those with a high teaching load, it can also be difficult to take leave from campus even for a few days. Fortunately, with today's technology options, faculty at all levels can stay informed and connected with colleagues through virtual spaces when conference travel is not possible.

The goal of this chapter is to raise awareness of options for Portuguese language professional development available through virtual networks and traditional professional associations. The topics to be addressed are: 1) What is a Professional Learning Network (PLN) and why participate?, 2) What virtual networks and professional associations are available for Portuguese?, 3) How does one engage in either type of professional learning network? The chapter will close with a discussion of the ways individuals at different career levels can contribute to and benefit from PLNs to enhance one's career path and strengthen the field of Portuguese.

What is a Professional Learning Network? (PLN)

PLNs connect educators to provide support, advice, and feedback to one another. These informal virtual or formal networks through professional associations help educators stay abreast of what colleagues in their field are doing. Both types of PLNs can be empowering and support the development of emerging leaders in a disciplinary field when people engage at their own pace and interact with individuals of all levels. As stated by Parker J. Palmer (1999, paragraph 12) and very relevant to PLNs, "a scholar is committed to building on knowledge that others have gathered, correcting it, confirming it, enlarging it."

Virtual PLNs are typically considered "informal" learning, but allow educators to collect and access information from the Web in one organized area so they can efficiently stay current on the latest teaching techniques or materials (Trust, 2012). Perhaps one of the most valuable aspects of virtual PLNs is the potential for collaboration and the building of professional relationships among individuals across disciplines, institutions, and national borders. They are an affordable and efficient way to maintain regular contact with colleagues between conferences and other professional gatherings. A virtual PLN can cover any topic and may range from participation in a

Twitter chat group, a Ning, a wiki (PB Works, Wikispaces), a Facebook page, or LinkedIn group. Activity, membership numbers, and participation vary across groups.

Harold Arche (2012), international consultant on workplace collaboration, suggests that professionals engage with web-based communities for informal learning opportunities to maintain professional creativity and be open to new perspectives in their field and others. According to Arche, in the network era, one's network is more important than one's current knowledge or expertise as fields of knowledge are constantly changing and growing. Professionals must continue to be learners themselves and consider moving away from the concept of subject matter experts to subject matter networks, a term coined by Mark Oehlert (2009). In a more complex information age, more can be achieved through collaboration and sharing of knowledge, rather than expecting one person to master everything. These points are relevant in the changing world of education in general and in the field of languages in particular, where debates are ongoing about teaching approaches and course content focus.

Virtual PLNs are not replacements for formal professional associations, though. Probably the most important benefit and factor that distinguishes a formal professional association from a virtual PLN is being part of a recognized group of professionals in a field. As a member of an official association you have the opportunity to share your work through publications, develop leadership skills by volunteering for committees or offices, and follow trends in your discipline. While there are varying fees associated with membership, most associations offer quality peer-reviewed journals, scholarships, awards of recognition, and discounted event rates to members. Associations have websites and are now offering more services online such as webinars, forums, and resource portals to members. Many offer lower membership fees and travel grants for new faculty and graduate students to grow membership and encourage new perspectives.

For scholars who may be concerned about how social media are perceived in the academy, George Veletsianos (2013) has been researching a variety of aspects of scholarly sharing at the post-secondary level. He examines online practices of scholars and how these align with the values of academic institutions. Through his research and experience in online networks, he suggests that social media sharing and engagement of faculty in digital scholarship is "a way to innovate higher education." Veletsianos promotes the integration of digital scholarship in graduate student research methods courses and has offered an open online course on the subject entitled "Networked Scholars." According to Veletsianos' (2014) homepage, the course addresses "emergent practice of scholars' use of social media and online social networks for sharing, critiquing, improving, furthering, and reflecting upon their scholarship." More courses like this from a College of

Education technology program would be beneficial to students in other departments, or better yet, having graduate students across disciplines interact within this type of course, regardless of where it is housed.

Both formal and informal networks have advantages and disadvantages. Face-to-face personal interaction is usually preferred for collaborating, but is not always possible due to distance or lack of colleagues in a particular institution or region. In the case of Portuguese where faculty are not as numerous and span large geographical areas, in–person meetings are encouraged, but virtual PLNs are extremely practical to maintain ongoing contact with other professionals. To grow a field and enhance individual growth, PLNs can facilitate e-collaborations regardless of geography and size of the academic community in question. Some features of each type of PLN interaction are listed below in

Table 1 *Informal Virtual or Formal Professional Networks*

Informal Virtual Networks	Formal Professional Networks
No membership fee	Membership fee
No travel expenses	Travel expenses
Continuous access to peers	Peer access at events
No travel necessary	Travel necessary
Ongoing communication	Communication confined to events
Connections beyond traditional national borders	Limited geographical areas
Archived discussions/resources	Fewer archived event materials (though this is changing with better technology)
Anytime, anywhere access	Usually on annual basis
Lack of "personal" touch	Rewards of face-to-face interaction

Whether it be through informal virtual networks or formally established professional associations, educators can benefit from both types of learning by connecting and sharing with peers in their field. Some examples are listed below.

- Research updates in the field
- Current pedagogical materials
- Event information and calls for papers
- Mentorship between colleagues of varying levels
- Discussion on topics of concern in the field
- Identification of colleagues for collaborative projects

Professional Learning Networks for Portuguese

As virtual platforms increase in quantity and in ease of use, the more variety there is from which to choose. The networks and social media venues specifically for Portuguese have been growing steadily. These virtual informal networks keep individuals connected at lower expense by supplementing the annual conferences typically organized by professional associations. The following section of this chapter is not exhaustive, but compiles a list of some professional development possibilities for faculty interested in Portuguese and are divided into: 1) Web-based collaborative spaces, 2) Traditional professional associations, 3) Newsletters in print or electronic formats.

Online Collaborative Spaces

There are many Portuguese language-related spaces throughout social media sites including Twitter, LinkedIn, Facebook, WordPress blogs, and more. To follow is a list of a few that may be interesting to explore as informal and free collaborative learning spaces. One extremely active Facebook page is *Ensinar português como segunda língua* established in 2009. The group serves individuals interested in Portuguese as a world language, with the objective of sharing ideas and pedagogical materials, job postings, and events to enhance professional growth. The group has over 9,500 members from around the world and continues to grow.

The **Ning Fale Português** offers information similar to that of the Facebook page described above. Nings began as educational networks and are less commonly used since other virtual platforms have become available. However, this Ning is a well-established and growing community of close to 5000 Portuguese instructors from across the globe focusing on Portuguese as a Foreign Language, as a Second Language, and Portuguese as a Heritage Language. It was established in 2010 with initial support from Editora SBS and current support from the Editora Galpão. It is a very active network offering discussion spaces organized by group topics, free webinars, videos, resource sharing, and face-to-face events that alternate venues around the world.

Brazilian Portuguese as a Second Language is another group with fairly regular activity on LinkedIn. This group currently has over 1,400 members. While lower in membership than the groups cited above, members post resources about Portuguese language in general and ask language-related questions seeking feedback from peers.

Wikis have been developed with the goal of compiling resources and encouraging contributions from Portuguese instructors. While some of these wikis may eventually become less active as new platforms and groups develop, the resources at these sites remain available. Two examples of Portuguese-based groups are through Wikispaces: *Ensinar Português como Língua Estrangeira (PLE)* and *Espaço PLE*. *Ensinar PLE* features pedagogical materials, academic publications, and professional development opportunities compiled from the *Ensinar PLE* Facebook page. The focus of *Espaço PLE* is primarily to share supplementary materials to the textbook *Ponto de Encontro*. It includes activities and lesson plans and ideas for classroom ice breakers.

The **Network of Business Language Educators (NOBLE),** established in 2009, is a professional learning community working to better prepare students for the global workplace through the integration of Languages for Specific Purposes (LSP) materials and teaching approach. While the group promotes the study of all languages and world regions, Portuguese faculty are encouraged to participate in NOBLE webinars, conference events, blog posts, and resource sharing. NOBLE features a special section with Business Portuguese textbooks and online resources, and an advocacy video of "Why You Should Learn Portuguese" (2012).

Finding Portuguese Social Media Resources

Other Facebook pages, Twitter accounts, and social media platforms pertaining to Portuguese language exist, but are too numerous to list here. The primary purpose of this chapter is to provide an initial overview of social media spaces aimed at building learning networks and interaction between instructors. Other networks or sites related to Portuguese language for other purposes can be searched using keywords. To find Portuguese-related groups on Twitter, one can begin a search with a broad hashtag like "#portuguese", "#portugues", to see the type of Twitter accounts that appear and decide which to follow. To search for groups on Facebook you can also use the search tool at the top of the page entering "Portuguese language" or "Portuguese groups" (in English and/or Portuguese) to see the multitude of options from which to choose. One usually has the option to "Like" a page or join a group.

For LinkedIn, you can also search at the top of the site page with the keyword or area you choose for focus. In one sample search using "Portuguese language" there were over 160,000 results including categories such as professionals working with Portuguese, groups for language learning, language companies, and jobs related to Portuguese. To join a group, you may have to wait for facilitator approval and you can choose how to receive alerts of posts. For most groups you may be able to view some information without joining, but to have full access to content and interact, you are required to open an account. As you join more groups or connect to individuals with similar interests in Portuguese, all of these platforms regularly make suggestions of new possible connections through individual or group accounts.

Professional Associations

As previously mentioned, formal professional associations are a valuable option for language educators to stay current in their field for a membership fee determined by each organization. The six associations with a focus on Portuguese language described below are based in the United States with the exception of the Sociedade Internacional de Português–Língua Estrangeira (SIPLE), which is based in Brazil. All of the associations hold regular or annual conferences in varying locations and some feature special initiatives through their organization which may or may not require membership or a fee.

The *American Association of Teachers of Spanish and Portuguese (AATSP)* was originally established as a Spanish organization in 1917 and Portuguese was added later in 1944. While over 95% of members represent Spanish, the Portuguese segment remains active through a variety of initiatives. Membership provides post-secondary instructors with the opportunity to sponsor a chapter of Phi Beta Lambda, the Portuguese Honor Society for students. At the secondary level, AATSP sponsors the National Portuguese Exam to promote the study of Portuguese for high school students. AATSP also publishes a bi-annual Portuguese Newsletter and the quarterly, peer-reviewed journal *Hispania.* A new and promising publication is the annual *Spanish and Portuguese Review (SPR)*, created specifically for graduate student professional development. The first issue of SPR was released in the fall of 2015 with at least half of the articles addressing Portuguese language or literature.

The *Sociedade Internacional de Português –Língua Estrangeira (SIPLE)* was founded in 1992 at the third Brazilian Conference on Applied Linguistics at UNICAMP. SIPLE holds most of its conferences in Brazil, but has also held the event in Argentina, Paraguay, and in 2015 the conference took place in Spain. Through the SIPLE website one can access issues of the "Revista SIPLE," information on past events, and other relevant news about Portuguese language around the world. SIPLE's primary partners are the American Organization of Teachers of Portuguese (AOTP), the Asociación Argentina de Profesores de Portugués (AAPP), and Casa do Brasil- Escola de Línguas.

The *Brazilian Studies Association (BRASA)* was established in 1992, and while its primary focus has been the broad study of Brazil through the humanities and social sciences, Portuguese language has now been encouraged, resulting in more BRASA conference sessions and participation that represent Portuguese language and linguistics.

The *North American Portuguese Teachers Association (NAPTA)*, also known as the *Associação de Professores de Português dos EUA e Canadá (APPEUC)* was established in 1994 to promote the teaching of the Portuguese language in the United States and Canada. The association has traditionally held an annual conference in rotating venues and provides a variety of news and resources on its website.

The *American Portuguese Studies Association (APSA)* holds a conference every other year in diverse locations. APSA promotes scholarly research on the Portuguese-speaking world, disseminated through the bi-annual peer-reviewed publication *Journal of Lusophone Studies*, (formerly *Ellipsis*). The journal is open access, but one must be a member to submit an article. In addition to the biennial conference, APSA also provides a job list on its website.

The *American Organization of Teachers of Portuguese (AOTP)* was founded in South Florida in 2007 with the goal of promoting the study of Portuguese and Lusophone culture. AOTP initiated the first annual Encontro Mundial Sobre o Ensino de Português (EMEP) conference in 2012 in Fort Lauderdale, Florida. The event has since grown and has expanded to various regions around the United States. AOTP aims to provide quality professional development at an affordable cost. In addition to the annual EMEP event, AOTP organizes other workshops throughout the year. The AOTP member website provides information on jobs, conferences, grants and professional development opportunities.

The *Portuguese Special Interest Group (SIG)* is part of the *American Council on the Teaching of Foreign Languages (ACTFL)* established in 2008. One must be a member of ACTFL and pay a small fee to join this SIG. It has special sessions allotted to Portuguese language during the annual conference, is run by its own board of officers, and provides a member forum through the ACTFL website. As a small group within a large association of over 12,000 members, it is an excellent way to connect more easily and immediately with Portuguese colleagues. The Portuguese SIG also increases the visibility of Portuguese in the largest language association in the U.S. ACTFL develops proficiency assessment and testing services and Portuguese is one of the languages available for the *Oral Proficiency Interview (OPI)* and the newly developed *Assessment of Performance Toward Proficiency in Languages (AAPPL)*. Information on both assessments are available on the ACTFL website with Frequently Asked Questions about how to offer these services to students.

Table 2 provides information "at a glance" on the year each group described above was established and where one can connect with the group through a website or social media.

Table 2 *Professional Associations with some focus on Portuguese as a World Language*

Association	Founded	Website	Facebook	Twitter
American Association of Teachers of Spanish & Portuguese (AATSP)	1917 (1944)	www.aatsp.org	Yes	@aatspglobal
Sociedade Internacional de Português – Língua Estrangeira (SIPLE)	1992	www.siple.org.br/	Yes	@siple2011
Brazilian Studies Association (BRASA)	1992	www.brasa.org	Yes	N/A
North American Portuguese Teachers Association (NAPTA/ APPEUC)	1994	www.appeuc.org	-	N/A
American Portuguese Studies Association (APSA)	1996	http://apsa.us/	-	@aportsa
American Organization of Teachers of Portuguese (AOTP)	2007	www.aotpsite.org	Yes	@infoaotp
Portuguese Special Interest Group (SIG)ACTFL	2008	www.actfl.org (under forums)	-	N/A

Newsletters/Journals

Mainly provided as informational resources to update educators in the field, the newsletters listed below in Table 3 share resources, but also solicit contributions from anyone wishing to share news, materials, and events relevant to the teaching and learning of Portuguese as a world language.

Table 3 *Portuguese Newsletter/Journals*

Newsletter/Journal Title	Frequency	Distribution
Hispania (AATSP) Articles primarily on Spanish and some on Portuguese	Quarterly since 1917, 1944 with Portuguese	www.aatsp.org (Under Publications tab. Also available in print)
Journal of Lusophone Studies	Established in 1996	http://apsa.us/ellipsis/ Online
Notícias PLE	Monthly since 2006	Electronic list-serve
Portuguese Language Journal (PLJ)	Annually since 2006	Online www.ensinoportugues.org
Portuguese Newsletter-American Association of Teachers of Spanish and Portuguese (AATSP)	Bi-annually since 2007	www.aatsp.org (Under Publications tab. Also available in print)
Revista SIPLE	Mostly annually since 2007	Online http://www.siple.org.br/
PLE Boletim	Monthly since 2014	Facebook: *Ensinar português como segunda língua*
Spanish and Portuguese Review	Annually since Fall 2015	www.aatsp.org (Under Publications tab)

How Does One Engage in a Professional Learning Network?

As seen in the aforementioned lists of formal and informal professional learning opportunities, there are many choices available for faculty to remain current in their field and continue learning at all stages of their career. When deciding which virtual network or professional association to join, one should consider a variety of factors. Some of these factors overlap between the type of network, such as the overall goals of the group, its reputation, and the quality of services or materials received through group interactions.

Participation at any level in a professional network through social media is important and having some kind of online presence with your background, teaching experience, and research interests is even more useful for others to locate and connect with you. The profile can be a page linked through your institution's website or through any other platform such as LinkedIn, Academia.edu, AboutMe, or your own blog. When choosing virtual networks in which to participate, one should consider which social media platform fits best with one's personal preferences and academic engagement style. Additionally, it is helpful to examine the degree of professionalism in member conduct, assess the quality of resources posted, and confirm that the group is being monitored to filter out unwanted spam postings.

Due to the large amount of virtual options, choosing which groups to join and how to manage the information received can be overwhelming. Most social media sites give the option of controlling frequency of notifications and from whom.

There are some options available to help aggregate the information through a social media "dashboard" tool such as Hootsuite or NetVibes. Dashboards help you monitor your media feeds such as Twitter, Facebook, LinkedIn, and others in one place. You can search for more options if interested in this possibility, as each dashboard offers different features that one can customize to personal preferences. Most dashboards are free for basic features and can be upgraded for custom services.

Some basic factors to consider before joining a formal professional association are how the group goals and mission align with your passion and interests, what the association offers to its members in terms of quality events and services, and cost of membership. Whether the association has chapters at the regional and state level for more convenient access is another factor to consider. Finally, Hamm & Cormier (2015) suggest that a key to successful professional development is finding the right combination of face-to-face engagement and online interactions with peers to meet the aspirations of individuals and advance one's field.

PLNs and the Future of Portuguese

Similar to benefits of balancing the formats of professional development with which one engages, there should be a balance in the exchange of knowledge and skills between entry level and seasoned faculty. Each brings unique perspectives on how far a field has come, current needs, and a strategy for the future of the field. Table 4 demonstrates how engagement in virtual networks and professional associations has the potential to enhance one's career at all levels and keep the field of Portuguese as a world language dynamic and progressive.

Table 4 *Value of Networks at Different Career Stages*

Activities Related to Professional Networks	Career: Entry Level/Graduate Students	Career: Mid-Advanced Level
Investigate and join professional associations	X	X
Investigate and join virtual network options	X	X
Follow innovators in the field of Portuguese through social media	X	X
Identify colleagues that share your interests in the field	X	X
Reach out to colleagues in the field for potential mentoring and advice	X	X
Share resources	X	X

Attend conferences to learn about academic processes	X	
Submit a proposal to conference	X	X
Serve on a professional association committee	X	X
Become familiar with Portuguese language journals and publications	X	
Submit an article to a Portuguese publication or other language journal		X
Serve on editorial board of Portuguese publication or other language journal	X	X
Seek out funding opportunities to build Portuguese programs, conduct research, or create materials		X
Give back by mentoring and empowering new Portuguese faculty		X
Serve as a mentor to graduate students	X	X
Encourage graduate students to participate in professional associations	X	X
Encourage graduate student engagement at your own institution	X	X

The increased presence of Portuguese in formal professional associations and the growing number of individuals using informal networks is raising awareness of Portuguese language initiatives around the world like never before. We hope that this introduction to Portuguese professional learning networks will contribute to strengthening the field by encouraging instructors at all career stages and teaching levels to harness the potential PLNs have to promote Portuguese as a world language.

References

Arche, J. (2012). Subject-matter networks. Retrieved August 13, 2015 from http://jarche.com/2012/03/subject-matter-networks/

– . (2013). Change agents worldwide. Retrieved July 7, 2015 from http://www.jarche.com/2012/03/net-work-skills/

Ferriter, B. (2015). Don't mistake simple sharing for collective action. *Literacy in Learning Exchange.* Retrieved July 15, 2015 from http://www.literacyinlearningexchange.org/blog/dont-mistake-simple-sharing-collective-action

Hamm, L. and Cormier, K. (2015). Meeting the challenge of infusing relevant PD in Schools. *Canada Education.* Retrieved July 30, 2015 from http://www.cea-ace.ca/blog/lyle-hamm-and-kevin-cormier/2015/04/4/meeting-challenge-infusing-relevant-pd-schools

Oehlert, M. (2009, December 16). Subject-Matter Networks: The Origin Story. *E-Clippings (Learning As Art).* Retrieved on January 15, 2016 from http://blogoehlert.typepad.com/eclippings/2009/12/subject-matter-networks-the-origin-story.html

Palmer, P. J. (1999). Good Reads. Retrieved on July 1, 2016 from http://www.goodreads.com/author/quotes/55813.Parker_J_Palmer?page=2

Trust, T. (2012). Professional learning networks designed for teacher learning. *Journal of Digital Learning in Teacher Education*, 28(4), 133-138.

Veletsianos, G. (2013). Open practices and identity: Evidence from researchers and educators' social media participation. *British Journal of Educational Technology*, 44(4), 639–651.

—. (2014). Networked scholars course website. Retrieved on July 20, 2015 from http://www.veletsianos.com/2014/06/03/networked-scholars-open-course/#sthash.1DoAE2wX.dpuf

University of Florida, Center for Latin American Studies. *Why You Should Learn Portuguese (2012*). Advocacy Video. Produced with funding from the United States Department of Education TVI Grant. Retrieved on January 12, 2016 from https://www.youtube.com/watch?v=BcZ2kDh7TSA&list=PLylrmGqeIordhEBilIFOV2iva2uSc7sfq

Additional Resources: Links Referred to in the Text

ACTFL Oral Proficiency Interview (OPI)
http://www.languagetesting.com/oral-proficiency-interview-opi

Assessment of Performance of Toward Proficiency in Languages (AAPPL)
http://aappl.actfl.org/

Brazilian Portuguese as a Second Language- LinkedIn Group
https://www.linkedin.com/grp/home?gid=4009299&trk=my_groups-tile-grp

Ensinar português como segunda língua Facebook Group
https://www.facebook.com/groups/ensinarple/

Ensinar Portugues como Lingua Estrangeira(PLE) Wiki to accompany Facebook group
http://ensinarple.wikispaces.com/

Espaço PLE. Wiki with supplementary material for *Ponto de Encontro*
http://espacople.wikispaces.com/

Fale Português Ning Group
http://faleportugues.ning.com/

Hootsuite
https://hootsuite.com/

Netvibes
https://www.netvibes.com/

NOBLE-(Network of Business Language Educators) Community for Language for Specific Purposes
http://nble.org/business/business-languages/business-portuguese/

Sites for Building a Professional Profile or Webpage

www.linkedIn.com
www.Academia.edu
www.AboutMe.com
www.WordPress.com

PART 2

DEVELOPING A PORTUGUESE PROGRAM

2.1 STARTING A PORTUGUESE PROGRAM FROM SCRATCH

Robert Simon
Kennesaw State University
Naomi Pueo Wood
Colorado College

Building a program where one did not previously exist can seem like a daunting task, given the limited positions and resources in the area of Portuguese language. Such a journey takes planning, fortitude, strength of heart, and almost no luck if you give yourself the time and patience this task requires. The first step begins at the time you accept a position. When joining a department, make sure you and your new department chair can both clearly articulate the expectations of the job with regards to the development of the Portuguese program and in terms of your contractual obligations.

Initiating the discussion of creating a program in Portuguese from the beginning of your contract helps to avoid many subsequent questions of split loyalty (which we discuss later on); if not during an initial negotiation, then it must be clearly stated somewhere in your job description that you intend to build a program. Having a transparent job description in writing and some basic guidelines from your new chair regarding review criteria for tenure/promotion with regards to your program building will make these processes clearer for both you and administration. If you have a mentor who has been through a similar process s/he can serve as a useful resource for reviewing your department's guidelines and expectations and confirming if the conditions set forth are fair to you or not. For example, if there are not concrete expectations regarding program building then, in your pre-tenure review, your Chair, or worse yet, a new Chair, could tell you that your efforts will be seen as a distraction from your "real job"; if you have something in writing concerning the original, approved plan this will facilitate later negotiations.

Challenges to Starting a Program from Scratch

Once you have secured a position at an institution and begin planning to build a program where one does not exist, you will confront a variety of challenges and negotiations. Here are just a few:

Concerning your position: Were you hired to teach Portuguese only? Is this a joint position between Portuguese and another language, entirely the other language with the "possibility" of beginning a Portuguese program, or not a language-based position at all? In each of these scenarios you will need to think about how best to incorporate this soon-to-be growing identity into your existing identity as a faculty member in a department.

Concerning the investment of the Department/College/University in a language/ minor/major program: What is the end goal of the institution? Are there other models on campus that demonstrate investment/commitment to such programs? Some institutions are more than willing to put resources (even if only minimally) into building a Portuguese program, while others may need some convincing. Establishing on-campus and local/national partnerships will be essential for supporting later requests for additional resources.

Concerning when it is the right time to develop a minor or major: The timing will vary greatly on your position, available starting resources, what support you may have garnered from colleagues and the institution, the institutional culture (whether it is open to exploring such an idea or not, how flexible the chair and dean's offices are), and, how it fits into the pre-determined contract and timeline as articulated in your job description. Ultimately, it may depend more on the program developer her/himself as s/he will be responsible for tracking and sustaining the curriculum. This commitment to sustain the effort may be the final determining factor.

Concerning the details of your position: If your position is shared with another department, you very definitely need to know if each of your affiliate departments supports the program's creation. You will need to ensure that all departments involved feel comfortable with this new partner with whom you will need to share your talents and your time.

Concerning the institutional investment: Finally, it is important to assess the short and long-term goals of the institution. Is the presence of a Less Commonly Taught Language (such as Portuguese) essential to the Spanish/Romance Languages/Foreign Languages Department? Is there a push toward greater connections with Portuguese-speaking cultures? The answers to these questions may help to support your claim for a need to develop a program, or to expand the one you may have been hired to sustain.

After establishing a plan of action, you are ready for the next step: achieving buy-in from colleagues and administrators. In order execute your program-building plan you will need to have the support of your colleagues and their chairs/deans. At this point you may need to develop a range of materials that will aid you in selling your idea to colleagues and administrators.

Developing Support for the Program

A typical and natural starting place may be the Spanish cohort (whether within a larger Foreign Languages or World Languages and Literatures department or just in Spanish). This alliance will be of value when recruiting students later, since the similarities between the languages will make these students your first, best candidates for recruitment.

A next step could be contacting allies in neighboring fields who specialize in Latin America and Brazil, Lusophone Africa, Portugal, Lusophone Asia and related topics in other disciplines including, for example, Africana Studies, Asian Studies, European Studies, Comparative Literature, Translation Studies, Religion, History, and Global Development/ Economics. As a general rule, in larger intuitions there is higher likelihood that faculty will have overlapping interests in the Lusophone world and, in particular, in the area of Latin America and Brazil; this intersection can happen at smaller institutions as well but is less probable unless a large Lusophone community resides nearby. By exploring *all* possible constituencies internally you have a better chance of establishing a base for support at an institutional level, rather than looking narrowly toward your own department. When discussing the potential for such a program, you may want to address colleagues about national growth trends in Portuguese, what constitutes a good number of students, and how the program will benefit their own work. This may also increase your visibility in an interdisciplinary way, allowing colleagues to speak for you across institutions and to build inter-institutional support within regional consortia.

Beyond finding support among colleagues, student involvement, in both courses and programming, will help build a case for further institutional support. In most cases enrollment numbers and participation in extracurricular activities (even if small) will impact administration more than well-argued proposals. Advertise in the student newspaper, speak with students who have shown interest, and make yourself visible to garner their support. Also, make sure that interested students understand what the Portuguese program can offer them (new linguistic abilities, connections with their major and future career, and possibilities for study abroad, for example) so that they are aware of the benefits of studying with you and other colleagues in Portuguese. (See "Marketing your program/on-campus opportunities" in this Handbook for more information on advertising to different constituencies.)

Finally, if possible, make contact with the local community, if one exists, and open a productive dialogue between these constituencies and your institution. By including your department chair, and perhaps even a dean, in the conversation you will help to build a coalition of support for your program and they will see the potential for community engagement and local collaboration that your program represents. Community leaders (possibly business or religious leaders) may be open to lend their support to you and thus to mutually benefit both groups.

Curriculum Development

Once you have gained the initial support from your chair, colleagues, and, possibly, the larger community, you will be in the position to begin the process of curriculum development and negotiation of institutional politics and bureaucracy. Filing the paperwork to initiate a major may be a challenge unto itself. Every university has a process for curriculum development and course and program approval. This can be a slow and tedious process full of unexpected difficulties. You will want to familiarize yourself with these processes, potential bottlenecks, realistic timelines, and the stages that you may need the most support, before proceeding.

Your early curricular decisions will greatly impact the development of your program. For example, you need to know if you plan to propose a language-only program (four semesters of language), or upper-level culture/writing/reading classes. These decisions will depend on your institutional culture – does the university prefer to start slow (language-only first, moving toward a larger program later), or is there a history of all-or-nothing proposals? You will need to determine which will be more effective given your and your department's goals. Also, you will need to consider the option of offering courses taught in English with a Portuguese-language component (i.e., a culture course for non-Portuguese speakers). In some institutions this is considered part of the Foreign Languages Across the Curriculum (FLAC); in others it is not. Some universities encourage such courses as World Literature/World Cultures within an interdisciplinary curriculum; others do not. Yet another issue you may face is that programs tend to enjoy having faculty instruct their assigned course-load (whether 2/2, 3/3, 4/4, or in some cases 5/5) before offering any Portuguese courses. The question of "can we spare you for this program" can emerge throughout various conversations and may result with you having to teach overloads (in many cases unpaid – more about this in the next paragraph). The discussion can quickly turn into a comparison of numbers of students "in seats," for which having data on national trends may also work in your favor.

Program Development and Vision

While the end goal of most programs may be the development of a major, Portuguese language study is most commonly incorporated into college and university curricula through a language-based or thematic minor program (i.e., Lusophone Studies, Luso-Brazilian Studies, etc.), consisting of anywhere from four to six regular (3 or 4-credit-hour) courses. In the former instance, students would be required to take four to six courses in Portuguese language and gain skills through the advanced level. Following years of program building, the entrance requirement for the minor could be set at the intermediate level and thus students would need to complete their minor coursework beyond those first two semesters. In the case of the thematic minor, students would be required to take some Portuguese language, perhaps through the intermediate, and would complete the additional coursework in affiliated departments that offer courses in Brazilian, Portuguese, or Lusophone Studies in some way. Depending on the size of the program and the options for cross-listed courses it may be necessary to brainstorm other creative configurations of the minor that best suit your students. A minor program offers students the ability to make their courses count towards a degree without burdening them with the course-load necessary for the completion of a major. Since recent trends show growth in Portuguese language programs and, in particular, increased participation and interest from Spanish-speaking students, a minor program offers students a way to integrate Portuguese language study formally into their broader areas of study without feeling the pressures of graduation or degree completion rates. Concomitantly, these programs also aid in increasing legitimacy for your program, since administrators and even faculty colleagues tend to view major programs more rigorously in terms of numbers of students completing the program; a minor is neither threatening to colleagues' programs, nor would it be called to task so readily, as deans and chairs feel the ever-growing need to cull smaller majors. Some may even find themselves unexpectedly contributing to the curriculum, particularly where the thematic based programs are involved and courses are not tied to a language component.

Balancing Program Development with Other Professional Duties

A somewhat painful reality of program building is that it may take years of extra, unpaid work in order to develop a program outside of the regular teaching load, and with little recognition for the efforts. This is true even if you were hired to build a Portuguese program, since, before the program is ready, in many cases you will be teaching in other areas. It is not uncommon for faculty in a 3/2 load, for instance, to be instructing a 4/4 load in reality, with several small sections "allowed to continue" for the sake of the program, but without remuneration. You will, if on the tenure track, also be required to fulfill your research and service duties equivalent to your fellow colleagues. Thus, it is possible for faculty in these sorts of positions to find themselves overburdened. This excess work can oftentimes go unrecognized and is often difficult to document within tenure/promotion files. Through maintaining an organized schedule and personal file regarding the time spent working on curriculum development and programmatic issues you can later make a case for yourself in your personnel file. On campus, you may want to keep a tight schedule and stick to it as much as possible. If the schedule does not work, re-write it to be more realistic for your short and long-term scholarly and career goals.

Negotiating time for program building and instruction can become a laborious and difficult discussion with departmental colleagues/chair/committee/dean, depending on the institutional culture. Make sure your chair knows of your workload issues and can see that you need both time and support for the program to become a success. Do not be shy in annual/bi-annual reports to express the number of hours and/or commitments to which you are obliged. Also, make sure these constituents know of the program's, and your own, successes. This communication and record keeping is a good way to garner support for future endeavors for yourself and your students. In this context, discussing failures or difficulties is also a way to acquire support and further understanding of the challenges involved starting a new program. Low-enrollment courses or low attendance at events, for example, are moments for reflection and sharing and should not be held by the program developer alone.

Particularly in the first years, you may need to defend yourself and your program from naysayers who, for whatever reason, do not feel it appropriate for you to teach Portuguese and/or for such a small program (usually relative to Spanish) to exist. Yet again, the concrete data on percentages of students moving through the program, growth (in percentage, not just raw numbers), and excellent support from your chair make a huge difference.

Program Expansion and Management

At some point the program may serve more students than one instructor can handle. Once it has become too big for one person, you may get support to hire part-time faculty to teach a class or two from your load. In conducting this hire, be sure you are aware of the protocols, rules, and laws of hiring and supervising part-timers. Also, be cautious of ideas of loyalty to a program as, when a colleague works for you part-time, s/he is not the same as one who has contributed to the development of the program. You cannot expect, for example, that a part-timer will have the dedication to take students on field trips *and* keep up with latest developments in foreign language pedagogy. It can be difficult to find dedicated and enthusiastic part-time faculty, and even more difficult to keep the good ones since they are usually seeking full-time employment. As such, supervising part-time faculty is both necessary and unique in that their positions are semester-by-semester. You should be prepared to perform observations, random spot-checks, and to meet one-on-one at least once a semester; and, to support their needs, and give criticism (and sometimes even non-renewal) when warranted.

You may also desire to delegate tasks when the workload becomes too much. Sharing with non-Portuguese department members, students, or interested/invested colleagues across campus will both support your success and that of the program.

Another option for expanding program staffing may be found through pursuing a Fulbright Foreign Language Teaching Assistant. These assistants are students with an MA in Linguistics or Second Language Acquisition who are assigned to colleges or universities that request them through International Education Exchanges (IEE) and Fulbright. They require some support from the college/university (like housing and a small stipend), but they are fantastic resources for both students and program developers.

In the end, there really is no “end” point. The program will always be with you, increasing in responsibility and complexity as numbers become greater and personnel grows. Ultimately, though, for our profession and for our professional development, building a program is one of the greatest achievements we can hold and the most profound way to impact our students, colleagues, and institutions.

2.2 MARKETING YOUR PROGRAM/ON-CAMPUS OPPORTUNITIES

Lígia Bezerra
Arizona State University
Cecília Rodrigues
University of Georgia
Ana Catarina Teixeira
Emory University
Naomi Pueo Wood
Colorado College

Marketing is essential to both establishing and sustaining a Portuguese language program on campus. In this chapter, we discuss different approaches and methods for maximizing the visibility of your program. Although each program has different needs, objectives, infrastructure, and internal and external support systems, we detail methods of advertising; assessment and data collection; and college, university, and nationwide partnerships that can aid in the dissemination of information and growth of your program.

The first step to developing a marketing strategy is determining the short- and long-term goals of your program. Are you, for instance, seeking to increase enrollment in one or more courses or increase knowledge of Portuguese-language study in general? For those starting a program from scratch, the previous chapter explains the process and challenges of starting a new program. The second step, which is essential, is to know your audience. This chapter features different strategies for advertising to students, colleagues, and administrators. And, third, it is extremely useful to reach out to the broader network of nationwide Portuguese programs to gain insight from past experiences. Our goal for this chapter was to address important questions for the growth of your program and offer suggestions for advertising at various levels and to a variety of constituencies. We focus on the following topics: (a) advertising your classes, (b) organizing and promoting events, (c) surveying students and collecting data, (d) starting and mentoring a Portuguese club, (e) identifying partners inside and outside your department and institution, (f) developing a website and managing an identity via social media, (g) using study abroad as a marketing tool, and (h) conveying to colleagues and administrators the value of increasing the visibility of your program.

Regardless of which of these proposed steps you take to develop your program, we strongly recommend that you document everything and, if possible, keep track of how many hours you spend on small tasks like replying to emails, making phone calls, and meeting with people across campus. If you document everything you do toward program development and track how many hours you spend on these tasks, you will have (a) solid evidence of the work that you have done and solid arguments for negotiating with your chair and (b) a clear sense of where your energy is going and whether you need to refocus to be more effective and efficient. For example, you may find that investing more time in some tasks rather than others may lead to the same—or even better—results and save energy toward other areas of your academic life, which is especially meaningful for those who are on the tenure track or who are adjuncts and lecturers planning to apply for tenure-track positions. In all of these cases, colleagues face the challenge of carving out time for scholarly work, which has become the most significant factor in tenure promotion or tenure-track hire even in teaching institutions. If you are on the tenure-track, it is crucial to provide a strong narrative in your tenure and promotion files to demonstrate to committees that the work you do is essential to your institution and cannot be put on hold while you are on the tenure track.

Advertising Your Classes

While framing your advertising strategy, there are many factors to keep in mind, not the least important being prior knowledge or stereotypical understanding that some students or colleagues have of the Lusophone world. Although many students have no knowledge of Lusophone Africa and may believe that Spanish is the national language of Brazil, there are other salient images, such as Brazil's fluctuating economic prominence, that can both help and hinder an advertising program. Before determining which strategies will best fit your department and campus, it is critical to assess the prior knowledge your students have about the Portuguese-speaking world. It may be a useful starting point to draw students into the program by relying on images of carnival, soccer, Rio de Janeiro, or the Amazon and then critiquing these stereotypes through course content and public lectures. Alternatively, your campus population may be more drawn to statistics of Portuguese as a growing global language and Brazil and Angola, for example, as growing global economies. In addition to utilizing this initial limited knowledge, it is important to introduce students to other elements of the culture that receive less media attention. Surveying colleagues and former students can help you determine the prior knowledge and dominant interests and ideas held by your constituents. After you have gained information about your audience of both colleagues and students, there are several factors to consider regarding the medium, timing, and content of your advertising campaign. These three concerns are the focus of the following discussion.

First, when advertising courses, you must assess the media through which students seek course information. If your department has a listserv, Facebook, Twitter, Instagram, or other social media platform, these may serve as easy starting points to disseminate basic information (See section "Developing a Website and Managing an Identity Via Social Media" for more information about using these tools). Beyond posters, flyers, and face-to-face announcements in courses, bringing in guest lecturers and hosting cultural events can serve as productive launching points for sharing information about new and existing courses. In addition, forming relationships with the study-abroad liaison and academic advisors, through both personal meetings and the creation and dissemination of a course brochure, establishes excellent on-campus resources. Beyond these natural partners, staff in the career center, diversity and inclusion offices, and dean of students office should also be well informed of the courses offered and the utility of Portuguese language study. Finally, departmental and affiliate colleagues provide one of the most effective means for course advertisement.

Second, the timing of advertising events, arranging individual meetings, posting to social media, and disseminating posters and flyers depends on the pre-registration period and the ongoing orientation of first-year students. After you have a core or network of committed students, you can charge these students with serving as introductory points to the course offerings and options for majoring or minoring in a related field. However, working closely with admissions and new-student orientation staff will provide you with the opportunity to identify entering students with related interests (e.g., Spanish and romance languages, globalization, development, African diaspora, and Latin American studies) and reach out to them directly at the start of their academic careers. Beyond outreach to new students, keeping a calendar of registration dates and study-abroad deadlines can help to determine the timing of campus-wide events, dissemination of visual materials, and classroom visits.

Third, the content of your advertisements, as previously mentioned, will vary depending on the prior knowledge of your students, colleagues, and administrators. After you have determined the campus-wide general interest and overall familiarity with Portuguese language study, you can shape your materials and presentations to both build upon and expand existing knowledge. The content of these advertisements may take the form of facts, statistics, rhetorical questions, images from the Lusophone world or student-related activities and experiences, or they can focus solely on informing students about course registration information based on the location and timing of the advertisement.

Beyond these principal concerns regarding the medium, timing, and content involved in advertising courses, the role and constraints of departmental and institutional funding and resources will affect your efforts. Again, partnerships with invested campus organizations (e.g., other departments, career counseling, study abroad) will be key to the sustained dissemination of your course advertisements. Because Portuguese is still considered a Less Commonly Taught Language (LCTL) by the U.S State Department, there are additional resources available for students and, at some institutions, for faculty to support the study and development of the language. In this area, prior students and invested colleagues are valuable resources for creating innovative advertising and forming cross-campus networks. Many Portuguese language programs rely on the work of one core faculty member with occasional support from adjunct or part-time instructors; thus, students and colleagues are essential to ensuring a wide-reaching advertising campaign as well as facilitating a sustained effort.

Organizing and Promoting Events

Hosting events is a terrific way to make your program visible on campus. Events are excellent opportunities to make the campus community aware of your program, especially if your event is announced via different means of communication such as posters, email, and social media. If you document your event well with pictures and videos, for instance, you can use these materials to promote your program after the event is complete. For example, you can post the materials on your program's web page or social media profile or group or decorate a bulletin board in your department. This material, along with sign-in sheets, can also become part of your program's history and, therefore, can generate useful data that may be relevant in two different cases: (a) if your program's existence is in jeopardy due to budgetary issues or other administrative shifts at your institution or (b) if you are in a position of negotiating another faculty line or requesting additional support. Events also provide opportunities to increase visibility for your institution through announcements to off-campus audiences such as colleagues in other institutions or within the local community. Whether your program is new or well established, you want it to have a presence on and off campus. Visibility is key to both starting and maintaining your program because it sends the message that your program is vibrant and has a valuable contribution to make to your institution, local community, and field.

There are at least two different types of events: academic and cultural. Academic events include lectures, symposia, and panel discussions. Cultural events include festivals; movie nights; game nights; and visits to local businesses, when available, where students can practice Portuguese. It is important to organize both kinds of events because they provide opportunities for the audience to find a connection with the field of studies through research interests and intellectual curiosity or an interest in cultural experiences. Events that are both academic and culturally rich are potentially the most rewarding. We have provided examples of advertisements for these events at the end of this chapter (see Appendix A).

How many of these events should you organize, and how big or small should they be? These answers depend on a number of factors, the most important of which is probably resources. If your program is well established, and you have a club, engaged majors and minors, graduate students, departmental support, colleagues inside and outside the Portuguese program who are willing to devote their time and energy, and several offices from which to raise money, organizing events is much less challenging than if you are the only Portuguese faculty member at a small institution with limited resources. Regardless of the size of your program, you may want to consider how to avoid potential scheduling conflicts with other events to ensure that you will have the greatest potential for a sizeable audience. You also want to make sure that the task of organizing events does not take away the energy you will need for other pedagogical and administrative tasks or the scholarly research that you and your colleagues may need to conduct. Although there is no maximum number, at a minimum, it would be ideal to organize one academic and one cultural event per year.

If you are part of a large program, defined loosely as a relatively established program with more than one faculty member and at least some upper-level classes, you should recruit students and colleagues and delegate tasks to them. Your colleagues can offer input on ideas for events and other major tasks such as securing funding, making room and technology reservations, and producing materials to announce the event. Undergraduate students who are passionate about Portuguese can be of great help, especially on the day of the event. They can help with logistics and unexpected developments such as when technology fails, and someone must locate a technician on campus to help or when you must speed up serving refreshments to a long line of attendees. Depending on your students' levels of involvement and experience, they can also participate in the planning of the event. All contributions are valuable, and you will be thankful that you can count on students for assistance. Similarly, graduate students in your department can gain critical professional experience by participating in the planning of events. The skills they acquire will make a difference when they speak about program development at job interviews and are trying to survive their first years at their new jobs. However, make sure that you protect their time so that they are not overwhelmed by service that will take away from their progress in completing their degrees. Creating a relationship with your graduate students based on open dialogue will help you determine the right balance.

If you are the only Portuguese faculty member, and the number of people you can count on for help is limited, you can still organize events, but you will need to be more careful while planning the details of your event. As you plan activities, always have a clear picture of the logistics involved in what you are planning. For instance, think about how difficult it may be to manage unexpected technical difficulties when you are the only person available to accompany a guest speaker on the day of a lecture. Reach out to colleagues whom you feel comfortable approaching and asking for help. Recruit students in your program who are reliable and passionate and work easily with others. Talk to students about the value of this experience and offer to write letters acknowledging their participation in the event should their experiences be relevant in the future and they need a recommendation. Another key piece of advice is to start small. If you have limited resources, you do not need to start with a full-day symposium or an out-of-town guest speaker; you can invite a colleague at a nearby institution or within your institution, but from a different department, to give a talk. Offer the audience coffee and cookies because light refreshments are always appreciated. If you cannot put together a festival, organize a 1-hr event or movie night with popcorn and a beverage. To make sure that your cultural event will also provide a learning experience for your audience, create an opportunity for the audience to engage with the theme in an intellectual way. For instance, if your event celebrates women in the Portuguese-speaking world, you can create a quiz about influential female figures and have the audience members compete to be the quickest to find answers online by using their cell phones. If the event is a movie night, choose a film that addresses a topic that is relevant to the campus community, prepare a short presentation that contextualizes the film, and then present it right before the screening or guide an informal discussion with the audience after the film. It is important, however, to keep these explicit learning opportunities limited. Remember that the goal of these events is to teach through experience, and there is value in learning about everyday culture as well as about high culture.

When should these events take place? Whether the event is academic or cultural (or both), it tends to work well if you can connect it with a seasonal celebration, a broad debate on campus, a current issue in the Portuguese-speaking world, or your audience's general interests. For example, if a Portuguese-speaking country is commemorating the anniversary of a historical event, invite to campus a scholar whose research is related to the event. If your institution's population is interested in migration issues that affect Hispanic populations, show a film that addresses migration and displacement in the Portuguese-speaking world. You can also tie cultural events to celebrations such as Carnival or Independence Day. Although events are easier to organize after you have accomplished them multiple times, it is advisable to avoid celebrating the same event every year in the same way. Your audience will benefit from experiencing different types of celebrations from different countries or different areas of the same country, especially if these areas do not receive media attention. Alternating events is an excellent way to increase knowledge, thus, showing the richness of the Portuguese-speaking cultures. Of course, you must keep in mind that celebrating certain dates will be more viable than others because of the availability of resources. Living in an area where there is a community of

Portuguese speakers could make a difference. For example, it will be much easier to organize a celebration when you can find restaurants that can cater food or immigrants who can teach students the steps of a traditional dance or give directions on preparing a traditional dish.

Regarding the timing of the event during the semester or academic year, if one of your major goals is to target potential students, consider holding these events—especially cultural events—a week before the advising period begins to help advisors and students remember that Portuguese classes are available on campus. To ensure that students learn about your program, take a few minutes to address everyone during the peak of your event. Distribute brochures to the audience to share information about the program (e.g., classes available in general and for the next term); refer them to your program's web page or social media group or profile; and tell them who to contact in case they have any questions. You can also briefly speak about how students from different areas of study can benefit from adding Portuguese courses to their curriculum. These events are valuable opportunities to educate not only students, but also colleagues and advisors about the practical applications of studying Portuguese for students' future careers. To avoid sounding repetitive, consider enlisting students to share this information with the audience. Students are often eager to hear about other students' experiences.

In addition to the support of colleagues, you will need funding to support any event. Sources of funding, depending on your institution, include your department; other department professionals who have an interest not only in Portuguese, but also in the theme of your event; international offices and organizations on campus, including clubs; and higher administration offices such as the Office of the Dean/Provost. Also, you may wish to reach out to colleagues at nearby institutions to see if they would be interested in co-sponsoring an event. Collaborations between institutions will be of special importance while organizing major events such as symposia or bringing in out-of-town guest speakers. If your institution is located in an area where there are associations of immigrants from Portuguese-speaking countries or entities, such as a consulate or a chamber of commerce, it is worth contacting them as well. Do not forget to give ample credit to those who support you by listing them as co-sponsors in any advertising materials and acknowledging them orally on the day of the event. You can also offer to share information with your students and colleagues about events sponsored by your partners.

Regardless of the type of events you organize, it is good practice to evaluate them in some way. Evaluation can be as informal as reflecting on what did or did not go as planned and what could have been done differently to avoid minor or major problems or as formal as a written evaluation form. This exercise may help you feel better prepared for the future. Evaluating the impact of the event on enrollment and visibility is a more challenging task. It would be naïve to think that events can work miracles in terms of enrollment and visibility when the truth is that enrollment and visibility depend on a number of other factors such as the current economic and cultural relevance of the countries where people speak Portuguese or general trends and policies in higher education that extend far beyond the boundaries of your program. However, it is probably safe to say that if you do not make yourself consistently present and relevant in some way for your community, other factors alone will not guarantee the growth and health of your program. (See Appendix A at the end of this chapter for examples of promotional flyers.)

Surveying Students/Collecting Data

Collecting data about your program is important for different reasons. First, it provides you with a picture of where your program stands and where there is potential for growth. Second, it allows you to evaluate your program and identify areas that work well or need improvement. Third, gathering data helps you build a case for administrators and colleagues anytime you are called upon to prove the importance of your program, defend it from changing policies that may put it in danger, or argue for the implementation of short- and long-term goals you may want to achieve.

The challenge with collecting data is that most of us have little experience with the design of surveys and analysis of statistics. Unless you have such knowledge or training, you will likely learn from your mistakes over the years and will edit surveys as you find out that some of the questions you designed did not produce the kind of data you needed. In spite of these difficulties, however, any information you learn about your program's growth, successes, and challenges is important and will be useful.

The first evaluation task you must accomplish is determining how you want to conduct your survey. Although conducting it online is relatively easy, you may want to consider visiting classes instead. It is easier to convince people to take a survey when they are, in a way, forced to provide results on the spot rather than prompted with an online survey that they may easily miss in the midst of hundreds of emails. The best opportunity to conduct a survey is probably in a colleague's class or your classes. If you choose to conduct a survey in person, start by identifying which classes are likely to have the student population you want to target. For instance, if you want to identify the potential for offering a course in Portuguese for Spanish speakers at your institution, try to visit first- and second-year Spanish courses. If you are trying to recruit freshmen, identify required general courses (e.g., freshman seminars, first-year writing courses) or ask the Office of Admissions staff if there are opportunities during orientation to conduct a brief survey. After you have identified the classes, start with colleagues who have shown support for your program. Unfortunately, the reality is that you will probably find resistance from colleagues who may see you as a threat to their programs. Collecting data to show that you are not a threat to them, but rather a partner, may put their minds at ease, and you may be able to gain allies for future surveys and support. Regardless of the classes you choose for administering your survey, to the extent possible, keep your surveys short. You want to be mindful of your colleague's time, and you do not want the students to become impatient with answering too many questions. You may also want to target areas of study that students with a potential interest in Portuguese would likely choose such as, among others, Spanish, Iberian studies, Latin American studies, African studies, business, and international studies.

The type of data you collect will largely depend on what your goals are and in what stage of program development you are. If you are at an early stage of program development, you may want to start with basic questions about students' interests such as their interest in taking Portuguese classes, how many Portuguese classes they would be interested in taking, and what kinds of classes they would like to take in Portuguese. Also, it is essential to identify relevant demographic data such as whether they are freshmen, sophomores, juniors, or seniors; their majors and minors; other languages they have studied and for how long; and whether they have had experience with Portuguese in the past. This basic data is extremely important in any survey you conduct. If you are targeting students outside the program, these questions will help you determine, for instance, if there is interest in Portuguese among students of a particular area of studies, other than the most obvious ones listed above, or which classes would better suit a student population. If you are surveying your students, the results will help you determine where else to recruit students or if you must recruit students at earlier stages so that they have more time to take coursework in Portuguese before they graduate.

If you have a more established program, you may want to conduct a survey to find out, for instance, why enrollment has gone down and what you can do to remedy the situation. You may also want to determine which classes need to be redesigned or replaced. Over time, you will find that data collection can help your program keep up with new job market demands, shifting interests inside and outside your institution, and a changing student population. Data from course evaluations may be great starting points to design your survey, especially if you learn information that raises red flags about possible misalignments between course goals and students' professional and academic objectives. Likewise, informal conversations with students and colleagues may help you design your surveys. Keep in mind that the idea is not to simply give students what they want. It is, rather, to make sound pedagogical and administrative adjustments from which both you and your students will benefit. Although you may find your students' suggestions less than helpful, you will also find useful insights about issues that you would not have otherwise considered. What is most important is to keep an open mind and understand that whatever problems the data may uncover, having this information will provide you with the valuable opportunity to make changes to your program. (See Appendix B the end of this chapter for a sample survey.)

Starting and Mentoring a Portuguese Club

A Portuguese club is a place for students to not only practice the Portuguese language, but to also learn about Lusophone cultures in a casual setting. One club option is to start a campus chapter of Phi Lambda Beta, the national Portuguese Honor Society, under the auspices of the American Association of Teachers of Spanish and Portuguese (AATSP). Phi Lambda Beta comprises undergraduate and graduate students who have shown outstanding achievement in the study of Portuguese language, culture, and literature. Information about starting a **Phi Lambda Beta chapter at your institution is available at the AATSP website.** Portuguese programs at institutions that already have French and Spanish honor societies could benefit from these existing models. For students, adding *Member of Phi Lambda Beta, the National Portuguese Honor Society* to their resumes is something to which they can aspire. Additionally, a student's membership in the honor society would not preclude his or her participation in a language club, allowing an institution to develop both. Because not all universities and colleges can support an honor society, this section focuses on the organization and management of a more informal language club.

A Portuguese club is different from a conversation group or language table because it focuses on practicing the language through hands-on cultural activities. The advantages of hosting a Portuguese club at your institution are, from instructors' perspectives, promoting and increasing visibility for your program and, from the students' perspectives, practicing language skills learned in a classroom setting, actively engaging with cultural topics, developing awareness about other cultures, and building community.

To promote an autonomous and participatory learning environment, you should encourage undergraduate students to take on leading organizational roles such as president and vice-president of the club. In the beginning, it would be advisable to have an instructor oversee the implementation of the club as well as facilitate the transition into a more independent and student-centered project. At some institutions, a mentor must supervise the students' work throughout the year. One way to inspire students to take on leadership roles is to point out the importance of such experiences during the years of their undergraduate education. In fact, a Portuguese club could be a highly beneficial addition to students' resumes under the category of service. It is smart to talk to students about the value of the skills they will develop while forming a club and conducting its business; these are skills that they will be able to use in their future careers and include, for example, working as a team, conducting business meetings, organizing events, preparing budgets and proposals, providing leadership, and solving problems. Instructors should use the first meeting of the club to make a selection of appointed and self-appointed potential leaders. Before the first meeting, instructors can also approach their students who have leadership potential and invite them to run for positions on the club's board. An election should follow so that the organizing committee is established during the first meeting.

To encourage student participation, instructors could build the club into the syllabus; this can be done in different ways such as requiring students to attend a given number of meetings per semester or, alternatively, by designing an assignment or project in conjunction with the club. Another possibility could be for instructors to give extra credit for attendance.

At the beginning of the semester and before making decisions about the club's calendar, instructors should informally survey students about ideal days and times for the club to meet. Choosing an agreeable time can boost attendance. Regarding the frequency of meetings, the club could meet once or twice a month during the semester depending on the timing of cultural activities. If meetings become elaborate and time consuming, limiting them to once a month would be a wise idea. On the other hand, if the cultural activities do not require a lot of planning on the part of the organizers, then meeting twice a month could be feasible. In terms of the length of meetings, they could be anywhere between 1 to 2 hrs, which would also depend on the nature of the accompanying activities. The space on campus where the club's activities can take place should be welcoming and ample and should include technology for, among other activities, playing music, showing movies, and using the Internet. The space should be comfortable and big enough for several different activities, including dancing, to take place. If your institution does not have such a space available for the entire semester, consider using different spaces for different activities to help make the club and, therefore, the program, more visible across campus.

The organization of the calendar could revolve around popular holidays and traditions in the Lusophone world. For example, in February, students could have a Carnival celebration where they would learn to sing Brazilian marchinhas and make masks, and in April, they could learn about Easter. Possible themes and activities include cooking classes, popular games, traditional dances, karaoke, movie screenings, enactments of soap operas and theater scenes, conversation tables, game nights, and guest speakers discussing a variety of themes such as current events, politics, or music. Guest speakers could be native speakers, professors from different departments, visiting scholars, and a variety of people from within the academic and local communities. One time each semester, club participants could bring a friend who does not speak Portuguese. Not only does this exchange make

Portuguese students proud of their knowledge, but it can also build interest on campus in studying the Portuguese language.

Advertising the club can happen at the beginning of the semester soon after the calendar is finalized. Instructors and teaching assistants could invite students by visiting Portuguese classes with information about the club, including the calendar. In addition, posters could be prepared and hung around campus, emails with the poster could be sent to listservs, and an invitation could be posted on your department's website and your program's social media profile. It may be a good idea to send out reminders via email before each event, especially if your campus has many activities scheduled for the same time.

The process of the organization of the club described above is ongoing and must be repeated on a semester basis. For instance, students who were leaders for a semester may or may not continue in their roles. It is necessary to recruit new students interested in the club before the beginning of the following semester to ensure continuity from year to year. In addition, club organization and development is a learning process in the sense that each subsequent semester will require reformulations and improvements based on the evolving student population and the knowledge that is gained each year. Perhaps some activities will be more popular or will work better than others, and new leadership roles will need to be created. One effective way to communicate with club members as well as evaluate the effectiveness of the club could be through social media, which could work as a forum where participants make suggestions and recommendations. An alternative would be to dedicate a final business meeting at the end of the semester to evaluate the activities of the club.

Identifying Partners Inside and Outside Your Department/Institution

Identifying and establishing mutually beneficial relationships with colleagues in different departments is key for both the short- and long-term success of your program. Colleagues in your department and faculty in leadership positions can aid you in compiling a list of those teaching and conducting research about the Portuguese-speaking world. If these initial contacts do not yield results, consider a basic online search. Most departments feature on their websites a list of faculty members' research interests, and, at times, faculty members are listed by geographical area. The most common disciplines in which you may find partners are history; international relations; science, technology, engineering and mathematics (STEM); area studies such as Latin American and African studies; and various language programs. Consider looking into postcolonial reading and writing groups as well as thematic programs such as gender and sexuality studies, race and ethnic studies, environmental studies, performance, music, film and media studies, and urban studies.

After you have identified colleagues, you should begin establishing relationships by attending and recruiting students to attend lectures or events in other departments related to the Portuguese-speaking world. Invite your colleagues to be guests in one of your language courses or speak at an event such as a lecture, panel discussion, or less formal setting like a Portuguese weekly conversation hour sponsored by the Portuguese program. Always look for ways to co-sponsor events. Not only will you be able to share costs, but you will also attract a bigger audience and amplify your presence on campus. Also, make yourself available to participate in other programs' activities whenever possible. Slowly, you will demonstrate how your expertise can be an asset to other programs on campus, which will, in turn, foster unexpected collaborations.

After you have begun establishing working relationships with colleagues in other departments, consider how the courses they teach can contribute to the Portuguese program. Ask for copies of syllabi for courses they teach and consider whether these courses could fulfill requirements or function as electives for the Portuguese/Afro-Luso-Brazilian studies major or minor to free up some of your core curriculum teaching responsibilities and allow you to teach other courses more closely related to your research interests. This may also be a good way to start a minor if you are the only Portuguese faculty member on campus. Individuals who find ways to match research and teaching interests will inevitably place themselves in more advantageous positions. For example, a course on the history of the age of discoveries or the history of Brazil nicely complements literature courses about Portugal and Brazil. Some institutions offer one-credit courses in Portuguese designed to accompany courses related to the Portuguese-speaking world. Students who speak Portuguese can take this additional one-credit course and complete and discuss readings in Portuguese as a supplement to regular classes taught in an English setting. Although more common in history courses, this model could be easily implemented in environmental studies and race and ethnic studies courses, just to mention a few. Some institutions not only accept, but also encourage cross-listings. While drafting your syllabi, consider how the content can meet the needs of other programs and submit them for cross-listing approval. Cross-listings can attract more students into your courses.

As you get to know your colleagues better and begin to discover the ways in which your research and teaching interests intersect, consider developing a course that you could teach together. Although co-teaching a course presents a set of challenges and requires support from at least two departments and the higher administration of your institution, it can be a rewarding experience for both faculty and students involved. The possibilities for interdisciplinary courses related to the Portuguese-speaking world—from freshman seminars to graduate courses—are endless. Examples are *History and Fiction in Latin America*, *Narratives of Race in the U.S. and Brazil*, *Representations of Iberian Feminisms*, *The Military Dictatorships in Argentina and Brazil*, or *Franco and Salazar: Iberian Dictatorships in the 20th Century*.

As you strive to create partnerships with other departments, do not forget to establish and foster allies within your department. Most Portuguese programs are housed in Spanish and Portuguese departments or in modern- or foreign-language departments and are inevitably smaller programs with fewer faculty members and, overall, fewer resources. You should follow the same steps that you have taken to create positive and mutually beneficial relationships with faculty members in your department who teach a different language but share similar research interests. Ask for advice and suggestions about how to strengthen the program and engage your colleagues at multiple levels. Invite colleagues to events, partner in initiatives whenever possible, and consider what you can add to their programs. If your institution has other small language programs, talk to the directors of these programs and learn from them about their experiences. They may be able to help you understand which program development strategies work best in your institution and where you can find potential partners in strategic offices on campus.

In addition to finding allies both inside and outside your department, it is important to consider which types of activities and events will garner the most support and recognition from the administration. You should identify which types of initiatives are sponsored and implemented at the college level and consider how the Portuguese program can contribute to the success of these initiatives. Pay close attention to announcements that encourage interdisciplinary approaches and take advantage of opportunities to make your program more visible. Invite staff and administration members to attend certain events related to their interests whenever feasible and appropriate.

Another important step for strengthening your program profile is to establish both informal and formal links with colleagues who teach Portuguese at other institutions in your region. If you live in an area of close proximity to other institutions, you can organize many events to foster inter-institutional collaboration (e.g., co-sponsored lectures, shared film screenings, opportunities for students to engage with peers at other universities, pedagogical workshops). Identify shared areas of interests and how you can support each other in accomplishing mutual goals; this is imperative for faculty members in small programs who are eager to find a space to discuss program development initiatives and curriculum concerns with others in similar positions and with familiar profiles. Consider formalizing the relationship by creating a consortium of Portuguese instructors between the various institutions. By doing so, you will also be in a better position to request ongoing support from the administration. If your institution is geographically isolated from others, there are still ways in which you can collaborate. You can, for instance, share the cost of international travel for a guest speaker.

Finally, if you live in an area with a significant Portuguese-speaking community, begin identifying key partners. Invite members of the community to speak at events on campus and encourage your students to attend festivals, exhibitions, or off-campus concerts. Plan an activity at a restaurant or at a market once a year or organize an excursion to a festival. Also, remember that engaged learning activities can provide students with unique opportunities to see practical uses for the linguistic and cultural skills they develop in the classroom. An example would be to find ways to pair your college students with middle or high school students from a Portuguese-speaking community. While the college student could serve as a mentor to the younger Portuguese-speaking student, the latter could help the college student by becoming his or her conversation partner. Another possibility would be to have students function as translators for parent-teacher conferences or at hospitals and courts. When well formulated, these activities can later develop into credit-bearing courses. (See Chapter 8 for more information about engaging with Portuguese-speaking communities).

Developing a Website and Managing an Identity via Social Media

It is of the utmost importance to develop a strong web presence to illustrate the vibrancy and fast-paced growth of your Portuguese program. The first step is to develop an interactive website that showcases the program's strengths. Considering your audience during this step is critical. In most cases, you will have to follow college guidelines and post information in a template. This does not mean that you cannot take advantage of the web presence to make your program stand out. Compliance with rules and creativity are not mutually exclusive. Some of the required website items are as follows: an introduction to the program with pictures and a list of reasons to study Portuguese; faculty names, profiles, and contact information; description of major and minor requirements; description of courses offered in the program; descriptions of courses currently taught and those that will be taught the following semester; and a calendar of events. After you have compiled all of the necessary information, consider what other information will attract people to your page. Always ask yourself, "What does the website say about my program?" To make your website more appealing to a broader audience, you may want to feature a list of resources, including popular newspapers, national and regional radio stations, podcasts, and well-read blogs or websites, for those wishing to study Portuguese. Consider posting a video of the faculty member introducing the program and post unique pictures that speak to the nature of your program. Instead of random pictures about the Portuguese-speaking world, consider submitting student pictures taken in these countries as well as pictures of events held on campus sponsored by the Portuguese program. If possible, include students' testimonials explaining why they have chosen to study Portuguese. Collect testimonials from a variety of majors and minors from across the college.

In addition to the website, consider which social media platforms will fit your program needs. In most cases, a Facebook page or group can be a useful tool for creating, sharing, and exchanging information, ideas, pictures, and videos. If your goal is to simply disseminate controlled information to students, staff, and faculty who may have a Facebook account, you should then consider creating a Facebook page, where you would encourage all of your friends, colleagues, and students to "Like." If your goal is to take advantage of Facebook to build a sense of a small learning community in which all members are encouraged to share equally, then creating a group may be a better option. You can assign multiple administrators so that you are not solely responsible for who is allowed to join the group. Although initially you will be the main creator of content for this group, there are ways to encourage participation from students, including encouraging students to share different interpretations of the topic you are discussing in class by posting on Facebook. For example, if you are discussing *Celebrações dos Santos Populares em Lisboa*, ask students to find pictures, videos, and songs related to the topic and post them on Facebook for others to see and invite them to comment. Ask students to share links to news articles related to the Portuguese-speaking world, especially on topics currently being discussed in class. Put students in charge of taking pictures of program-sponsored events or class activities and ask them to post the pictures on Facebook. Students will enjoy seeing themselves, and many of them will comment and share on their pages. If you notice that no students or only the same students are participating, you may want to assign points as part of participation or homework grades for this activity. If you turn your Facebook group page into a positive expression of your program's identity, students will begin to share their pictures, links, and ideas without direct prompting. These ideas can be easily applied to other social media platforms like Twitter and Instagram.

Although it may be difficult to assess outcomes from social media efforts, consider giving students a questionnaire at the end of the semester so that their responses can provide you with useful feedback about how they used and why they turned to the Facebook page or group. You can also evaluate the success of social media platforms through surveys you may want to conduct about your program. One simple way to collect this information is to include a question about how students have learned about your program, listing these social media as options for them choose. This will help you determine how much energy to spend on a particular medium in the future.

Study Abroad as a Marketing Tool

Study-abroad programs are an effective way of marketing your language or literature program and developing meaningful relationships between students and language learning. Nonetheless, because universities in the United States offer a variety of study-abroad opportunities to students, competition for student enrollment will likely present a challenge to establishing and maintaining your study-abroad program.

A compelling way to boost students' interest in a study-abroad program in Portuguese is to continually provide them with information not only about the relevance of the Portuguese language (it is currently the fifth most-spoken language in the world), but also about the growing importance of the Portuguese-speaking world to the global economy. Furthermore, Portuguese language skills serve students with an interest in pursuing theoretical questions related to postcolonial studies and careers in public health, environmental science, and international relations because this language facilitates travel beyond the better-known Brazil and Portugal to include Lusophone Africa and Asia. In addition, Portuguese is considered a critical language for economic development and national security by the United States federal government. All of these characteristics can translate into job opportunities for students in their future career paths, including, among others, employment in the federal government.

Another element of building a successful study-abroad program is word-of-mouth advertising. Instructors can benefit from enthusiastic returning students who can help encourage new students to participate in the program. Instructors may consider having students who are currently studying abroad communicate online with students in on-campus courses so that they can share experiences in real time. Study-abroad students could also utilize social media to share travelogues with instructors and students from different courses. In addition, instructors could incorporate exchanges into an assignment about cultural awareness. Another possibility for combining study-abroad and program advertising is to have returning students give presentations to current students during regular class times or at special information sessions targeting students outside the program. In this case, the study-abroad experience may serve as an incentive for students to take Portuguese classes in preparation for their future study-abroad experience. Likewise, returning students may feel more motivated to take more advanced classes in the program to improve and maintain their language skills. In addition, students who have studied abroad may find more concrete ways to apply the language to their careers, especially if they have the opportunity to do an internship or volunteer work while abroad.

It is essential to note that developing a study-abroad program requires a lot of skill and detail that go beyond those that qualify you to teach language and literature and cultural studies courses. Although the reasons for establishing a study-abroad program in a Portuguese-speaking country may eventually lead to the accelerated success of the program and retention of students, the excessive workload and demanding attention to detail may make it unsustainable for small programs or those that rely on only one faculty member.

With these challenges in mind, it may make sense to first partner with an already established language-teaching school within the host country and look for a platform program to provide infrastructure, such as host-families and field trips, while the program director focuses on recruitment, on-campus bureaucracy, and course instruction. This model allows the faculty member/program director to outsource the details involved with program design and focus on the advertising and selection process for student participants.

On the other hand, if such a partner organization or third-party institution is not an option, developing a multi-step process for the establishment of your study-abroad program may work. For this effort, it is advisable to first seek out colleagues who have previously developed and directed study-abroad programs and determine if they have materials that you could borrow or modify for your new context. In addition, identifying faculty on campus with some investment in Portuguese language study or research interests related to the host country will help the program leader to form an on-campus network of vested partners who may be able to participate in the program as directors at a later date. Next, it is useful to visit the host city with the program in mind, even if you are intimately familiar with the city, and form preliminary partnerships with local faculty, non-profit organizations, restaurants, and universities. The purpose of this visit is to develop the ideal arrangement and combination of on-site visits, local tutors, field trips, and potential sites for volunteer work. Each of these features, in addition to homestays or lodging and meals, must be itemized and crafted into a budget projected to serve a range of students. Having these defining characteristics will help you design advertising materials and gain support from across the college and university. Most faculty members and instructors have rudimentary training in crafting detailed budgets; however, a budget will become essential as you establish the total cost of the program fee and work to attract a range of students. The minimum enrollment will depend on your budget and staffing resources and is directly connected to the overall operating costs. Following the preliminary visit to the host city, the director will need to seek approval from both departmental colleagues and administration on campus. Again, the faculty director can rely on motivated students who are already dedicated to the program as well as classroom visits, social media, posters, and information sessions to gain student interest in the study abroad program.

Beyond the care that goes into program design and the selection of student participants and host-country partners or on-campus collaborators, faculty directors must also consider the time constraints and administrative demands that accompany coordinating and executing study-abroad programs. As previously noted, these trips may greatly contribute to the success and growth of the program; however, the work involved in their development often goes unrecognized by departmental colleagues or evaluating administrators, who may fail to officially recognize the program developer's workload and contribution to program and curriculum development. In addition, the study-abroad program will likely take place during the summer months and, therefore, constitutes a teaching overload for directing and teaching faculty. Although this may serve as compensated overtime, the time and energy spent being the full-time program director (with the 24-hr nature of that duty) cannot be adequately compensated through salary supplements. Like other program-building activities, responsibilities, and obligations, developing and leading a study-abroad program will positively contribute to program growth and success but may lead to faculty burnout. Establishing a study-abroad program that runs every other year both eases the stress on the faculty members and potentially ensures greater student participation. Of course, this means that you will have to inform students of the program dates well in advance. Consider finding a co-director in another department to share the organizational burden. It is essential to document the various steps involved in creating a new study-abroad program even when it initially relies on a third-party organization. The networking, reviewing, and organizing that goes into such a task is significant and should be included in review materials submitted for contract review, tenure, and promotion. (See Appendix C at the end of this chapter for more information about study abroad.)

Conveying the Value of Increasing Visibility of Your Program to Colleagues and Administrators

One of greatest challenges for faculty teaching LCTL is juggling activities such as those described above with the regular duties—namely, teaching, research, and service—of any faculty member. For our colleagues in large-language programs for whom recruiting efforts may not be an issue, it is often difficult to understand how much extra work is needed to get students through the door and into small programs. While our colleagues may be redesigning courses, we are often creating entire programs from scratch; while they have several colleagues with whom to share the organization of an event, many of us are lucky if we have one other faculty member teaching the same language that we teach; while our colleagues' students will come looking for their program and will bring with them a background from high school, the burden tends to be on us to look for students and educate them about the less-obvious ways in which they can benefit from learning a language with which they may have no prior experience. Another challenge small programs face is confronting the misconception that we represent a threat to our colleagues' programs. It is not uncommon to hear faculty members teaching

LCTL express their frustration with some colleagues' questioning of measures and plans that would perhaps hardly be questioned were they posed by more visible programs. Although there is a limit to how much anyone can change the minds of others, gentle, yet firm, argumentation becomes an essential part of the marketing strategies of small programs. It is important to keep in mind that many of the colleagues who are not as supportive as you would hope they would be probably have no idea of how much extra work you have to do because they never had to deal with that reality.

How can you turn them into allies? The key is communication. Essentially, it is another form of marketing. Perhaps the most important person who needs to be both aware and supportive of your work is the chair of your department. Schedule regular meetings with him or her and discuss your efforts and plans and seek her or his input. Be as detailed as possible and do not be afraid to present solid and honest arguments about why you think a given proposal could either benefit or cause damage to your program and possibly to the department as a whole. Remember, however, that your chair's time is just as precious as your time, so be prepared for each meeting: be succinct, state short- and long-term goals, and make specific requests. Remember that much of what a chair does goes unnoticed by other colleagues, so be sure to regularly thank him or her both in person and by email, especially during events. Your chair is certainly not the only person who needs to recognize your work, but he or she can help you, for example, decline certain requests. When explaining why you cannot accept another service request from a colleague at a given moment, consider sharing your list of responsibilities.

Depending on your department's culture, it may be worth it to also take a few minutes to send out emails to the department as a whole after an event you organized thanking those who attended or helped plan it. Take this opportunity to convey the success of the event and emphasize its value and the value of the hard work needed to organize it. It is not uncommon for colleagues to see a cultural event that you organized as unnecessary if they do not understand its importance for recruiting and visibility. Therefore, make sure that you know how to state that clearly. Focus on how the growth of the Portuguese program is truly an asset to the department. Embrace opportunities for reflection at the end of every semester and share highlights from your reflective practice with your chair, focusing both on successes and areas for improvement.

There is, unfortunately, no guarantee that what we suggest here will suffice to convince chairs, colleagues, and administration of the importance of our work. Sadly, the reality is that they may understand you, but budgetary pressures stemming from the business model that institutions of higher education are increasingly embracing may prevail. It is important to remember that many of us are going to be in vulnerable positions within our institutions. Adjuncts, lecturers, and tenure-track faculty have limited bargaining power and cannot afford to risk losing their jobs. However, we must continue to hope that dialogue, diplomacy, and a willingness to collaborate, negotiate, and understand the position of others will lead us in a positive direction. Otherwise, we run the risk of feeding into the very system that makes our job challenging.

The best advice is to remain engaged; focused; and, above all else, positive. Solicit advice when needed and foster a relationship of support with colleagues both inside and outside your department. Enlist your students whenever possible—their excitement for Portuguese classes and activities is certainly the most effective tool for displaying the vibrancy of your program.

Final Thoughts

To conclude, we would like to share a few suggestions related to what we wish we would have known about program development and marketing on our first days at new institutions. First, it is important to visualize your program as a jigsaw puzzle in which all decisions you make with respect to curriculum development, marketing, and establishing partnerships are intrinsically connected to one another and may have an impact on the whole of your program. Program development and marketing, therefore, require significant planning and careful consideration so that each decision you make will fit well within the bigger picture. To this end, having the support and expertise of colleagues both at your institution and other institutions will greatly increase your chances of success and sustainability. Developing the ability to perceive your program in this way requires time and experience, and mistakes are inevitable; however, it is important to try to be aware of the nature of this decision-making process from the beginning of your career. Second, it is helpful to delineate semester- and year-long goals. By focusing energy on a set of tasks, you can avoid feeling too overwhelmed by what may seem like a daunting to-do list. Always remember that you will have to establish priorities and work one step at a time. If you are the founder of a program and sole Portuguese faculty member on campus, start by scheduling meetings to get to know your colleagues, collecting data (both formally and informally), and learning about your department's and institution's cultures. Save more visible initiatives for when students are thinking about which classes they will take the following academic year. Also, at the end of an academic year, seek help from staff and faculty who work with incoming first-year and transfer students so that you can attract the type of student who has the most time until graduation to invest in learning Portuguese. This student often enthusiastically steps up to the challenge of studying something new. Third, carefully watch your enrollment numbers, but do not be discouraged if they are not what you expected.

Establishing and growing a program takes time and consistency, and enrollment depends on a variety of different factors, many times beyond your control. Numbers are not a direct reflection of your work, although, at times, it may become your job to explain those numbers to your colleagues and administrators. Finally, talk to colleagues, and do not hesitate to ask for their help or their thoughts while also being mindful of their time. Share your ideas, ask for advice, learn from others, and welcome opportunities to also mentor new colleagues. Always offer your support and help, especially to those who are just beginning the process of starting a new program; do not give less than what you hope to get in return. Although, at times, it may feel as though you are marketing yourself, if you are the sole faculty member in the program or the founding director, it is essential to locate yourself in a larger network of colleagues and to constantly check in with that wider community. Indeed, much of the passion and effort that goes into sustaining and building a Portuguese program centers on individual commitment and conviction. The collaboration involved in the creation of this handbook, for instance, is a testament to the importance of a network of determined individuals.

Appendix A

Sample Promotional Flyers

Lusophone Film Series

ANGOLA

BRAZIL

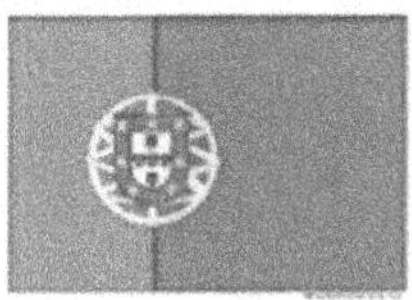

PORTUGAL

MOZAMBIQUE

o herói : Vitório has just returned from the front lines, where he lost his leg when he stepped on a land mine. He is stumbling (literally and figuratively speaking) in his attempt to build a new life for himself in the capital of Luanda.

DATE, TIME

LOCATION

WITH FREE PIZZA!

FOR MORE INFORMATION CONTACT (name of professor)
(email)

2nd noite cultural at name of institution

Join us for an evening of celebration of Luso-Afro-Brazilian culture!

Celebrate São João dancing to Brazilian rhythms with Brazilian dancer and dance instructor(name). Wear a plaid shirt and jeans if you would like to celebrate São João in traditional Brazilian style!

Date

Location

time

Learn! Play! Dance! Celebrate!

Learn about the successful women of the Portuguese-speaking world through a trivia competition (with prizes!) and enjoy Brazilian refreshments.

For more information contact Professor ( ).

Event supported by ( ).

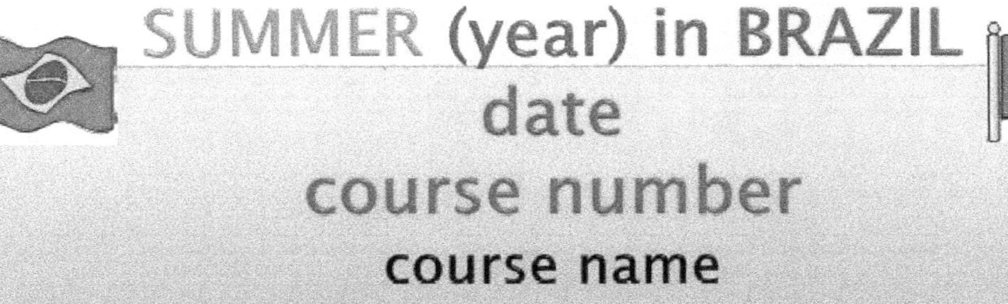

SUMMER (year) in BRAZIL
date
course number
course name

No prior Portuguese language necessary!
Informational meetings:
dates

Você fala português?
(Do you speak Portuguese?)

Portuguese can count towards your language requirement at (name of institution) or it can be a great addition to your knowledge of other foreign languages, especially if you already have knowledge of Spanish, Italian, or French. If you are testing into a higher level of Spanish or French for your language requirement, major or minor, consider taking Portuguese. If you have taken Portuguese classes elsewhere and/or have learned some of the language while living in a Portuguese-speaking country, you can take a placement test.

Portuguese classes offered in (semester):

(list of classes)

For more information, please, visit
(website)

Or contact:
(professor's contact info)

Why Should You Study Portuguese?

Portuguese is the fifth most spoken language in the world and the third most spoken language in the Western world. There are over 260 million speakers.

Everyday phrases in Portuguese:

Oi/Olá	Hi/Hello
Bom dia	Good morning
Boa tarde/noite	Good afternoon/evening
Tudo bem?	How are you?
Como você se chama/Qual é o seu nome?	What's your name?
Eu me chamo.../Meu nome é...	My name is...

Portuguese is an important language for the African Diaspora. It is spoken in countries such as Angola, Mozambique, Cape Verde, and Brazil. Learning Portuguese will give you access to a wealth of cultural and academic materials about these countries' history, literature, religions, and society.

There are many Brazilian communities in the United States, including Los Angeles, New York, Boston, Miami, Atlanta, and other areas (see the Language Map of the Modern Language Association www.mla.org/map_main). Learning Portuguese would allow you to serve these communities in your future profession, whether you will be a lawyer, a doctor, a psychologist, a business owner, or an educator.

Interesting Facts:

- In recent years, Brazil became China's largest trading partner
- Brazil hosted the World Cup 2014 and will be hosting the Summer Olympics in 2016
- Brazil's economy is the 7th largest in the world and it encompasses services, manufacturing, mining, and agricultural sectors
- Brazil is the 9th largest producer of oil and a leading producer of ethanol. It is also a leader in agricultural research
- The U.S. Department of State has declared Portuguese a strategic language

Appendix B

Sample Survey

Portuguese Survey (semester)

1. Why did you choose to study Portuguese at (name of institution)?

____

____

____

2. How did you learn about Portuguese at (name of institution)?

____

3. What are your major and minor?

____

4. Which year in college are you?

____

5. Would you be interested in doing a minor in Portuguese? If you are approaching graduation, would you have done a minor in Portuguese, if it had been available during your time at (institutions in your area)?

____

6. Do you speak or have you had instruction in any of the following foreign languages? If so, please, indicate the number of years or semesters you took of each of the classes in question. Also, please indicate where you took these classes (institution 1 (1)/ institution 2 (2)/institution 3 (3), at another university/college (AU), during high school (HS), abroad (AB). Select all that apply.

( ) Spanish, for ____________ ( ) 1 ( ) 2 ( ) 3 ( ) AU ( ) HS ( ) AB
( ) French, for ____________ ( ) 1 ( ) 2 ( ) 3 ( ) AU ( ) HS ( ) AB
( ) Italian, for ____________ ( ) 1 ( ) 2 ( ) 3 ( ) AU ( ) HS ( ) AB
Other language(s): ______________________________

7. Are you planning to continue to take Portuguese classes at (name of institution)? ( ) Yes ( ) No

8. If so, which one(s) of the following classes would be interested in taking
( ) (write list of courses)
( )
( )

9. If not planning to continue, what are your primary reasons for having made this decision?

____

____

____

10. Are you interested in study abroad in Brazil? What would you like to learn/experience in a study abroad program in Brazil?

____

____

____

____

____

____

11. Please, write any additional comments or suggestions about Portuguese at (name of institution) on the reverse of this paper.

Muito obrigado! ☺

PROGRAM SURVEY

1. Were you aware that (name of institution) offers Portuguese classes? If so, how did you learn about it?

____

____

____

2. Do you speak or have you had instruction in any of the following foreign languages? If so, please, indicate the number of years or semesters you took of each of the language in question. Also, please indicate where you took these classes (institutions in your area, at another university/college, during high school, abroad, etc.)

Spanish:______________________________________

French: ______________________________________

Italian: ______________________________________

Other(s): ____________________________________

3. Which language are you taking for your language requirement? Why did you decide to study this language?

____

____

____

4. Are you majoring or minoring in this or any other language?

____

____

____

5. Would you be interested in learning Portuguese if you could take accelerated courses for speakers of romance languages (Spanish, French, and Italian)?

____

6. Are you interested in study abroad in Brazil? What would you like to learn/experience in a study abroad program in Brazil?

____

____

____

____

____

7. Other comments or suggestions about Portuguese at (name of institution).

____

____

____

____

____

____

Muito obrigado! ☺

Appendix C

Questions to Consider While Developing a Study Abroad Program

General Concerns:

- What is the ideal host city/town?
- Where will students have access to spaces where they can practice their language skills? Will students be surrounded by tourists and English speakers?
- Are there faculty members on campus whose research concerns the Lusophone world who would be interested in collaborating?
- What is the college/university's policy on funding developing new abroad courses? Is there funding to support exploratory travel for program development?
- Do you need a second responsible adult to travel with you? How will you identify this person?
- Will you target elementary or intermediate-level students? What are the overall goals of the program?
- How frequently will you offer the program? Annually? Biannually? What is sustainable for the program director and realistic given the student population?

Working With a Partner/Third-Party Program:

- What does the third party provide (e.g., host families, classroom space, field trip transportation, orientation, course materials and teaching supplies, airport transportation, access to local organizations, guest speakers)?
- What are the options for scheduling? Are there limitations on arrival and departure dates?
- Where can you find references and testimonials for the program?

Developing a Program From Scratch:

- Do you have a budget template? What do you intend to include in the program fee and what will students be expected to cover on-site (e.g., transportation, meals, course materials, spending money)?
- How will you evaluate the success of your program in achieving course objectives within the abroad context?
- Where will students live?
- How do you develop a calendar that is rigorous but also allows exploratory time for students?

2.3 PLANNING A PORTUGUESE COURSE

Blair Bateman
Brigham Young University

> Alice asked the Cheshire Cat, who was sitting in a tree,
> "What road do I take?"
> The cat asked, "Where do you want to go?"
> "I don't know," Alice answered.
> "Then," said the cat, "it really doesn't matter, does it?"
> – Lewis Carroll, *Alice's Adventures in Wonderland*

Like Alice in Wonderland, first-time Portuguese instructors with the responsibility of planning a course may find themselves not knowing where to begin. Unfortunately, as the Cheshire Cat points out, if we start out with no particular goal in mind, we have no way of knowing whether we have reached our destination – or in other words, whether our students have developed the knowledge and skills that we want them to have.

I recall my first time teaching a Portuguese 101 course as a new graduate student instructor. A week before the beginning of Fall Semester I was handed a textbook and told, "Here's the book; go teach your class." I asked, "Is there a syllabus?" "No," was the reply, "you create your own syllabus." "Are there any instructional materials or tests available?" "No, you write those yourself." I remember feeling excited about the prospect of designing my own course, but also very much at a loss as to where to begin.

The purpose of this chapter is to share some of the lessons about curriculum planning that I have learned in 25 years of teaching Portuguese and studying and researching language education, partly in order to help newer instructors avoid mistakes that I and others have made. The chapter begins with a brief discussion of different types of Portuguese programs in the United States. It then introduces several important professional documents for language teachers, including the *ACTFL Proficiency Guidelines* and the *World-Readiness Standards for Learning Languages*, followed by a discussion on how to implement these documents in designing course-level learning objectives and assessments, selecting a textbook, and planning individual units and lessons.

Portuguese Programs in the United States

The demand for Portuguese courses in the U.S. is clearly growing. At the K-12 level, Portuguese classes have long been offered in a handful of states, primarily in New England, California, and Florida. An online search reveals bilingual programs in states such as Massachusetts and Connecticut for students from Portuguese-speaking families as well as specialized Portuguese schools in New Jersey. In recent years, Utah has established a number of

Portuguese immersion elementary schools. In addition, institutions such as the University of Massachusetts Dartmouth and the Portuguese Flagship Program at the University of Georgia offer summer programs in Portuguese for high school students.

In spite of this growing interest in Portuguese at the K-12 level, the vast majority of Portuguese programs in the U.S. continue to be offered at the postsecondary level. Many of these programs consist mainly of first- and second-year language classes at community colleges and universities, while a smaller number of programs also offer courses in literature and culture. Still fewer institutions offer courses in Portuguese linguistics.

Given that the vast majority of Portuguese courses in the U.S. are beginning and intermediate-level language courses, and that the instructors of those courses may not have had specialized training in language teaching methodology, particularly at the postsecondary level, this chapter primarily targets those instructors, although many of the principles discussed here may be applied to any type of course.

The ACTFL Proficiency Guidelines

In 1986, the American Council on the Teaching of Foreign Languages released the *ACTFL Proficiency Guidelines,* an adaptation of the scale used by the U.S. government for rating the proficiency of foreign language speakers. The ACTFL Proficiency Guidelines describe the performance of language learners at five major levels of proficiency: Novice, Intermediate, Advanced, Superior, and Distinguished. The first three levels, which represent the proficiency levels most often achieved by students, are further subdivided into Low, Mid, and High sublevels. There are separate guidelines for the skills of speaking, listening, reading, and writing. A summary of the speaking guidelines from Novice through Superior is shown in Figure 1; the complete version of the guidelines for all four skills is available online at http://www.actfl.org/publications/guidelines-and-manuals/actfl-proficiency-guidelines-2012.

Notice that speaking proficiency is conceptualized in terms of the communicative *functions* that students can handle, such as asking and answering questions, describing, narrating, and hypothesizing; the *contexts* in which they can function and the *content* they can talk about; their level of *accuracy* in language use, operationalized in terms of how comprehensible their speech is; and the *text types* they can produce, ranging from individual words and memorized expressions to sentences and strings of sentences, paragraphs, and then extended discourse.

Figure 1 *Summary of the ACTFL Proficiency Guidelines for Speaking*

Level	Functions	Context/Content	Accuracy	Text Type
Superior	Discuss topics extensively, support opinions and hypothesize	Wide range of general interest topics and some fields of special expertise	No patterns of error in basic structures; errors virtually never interfere with communication	Extended discourse
Advanced	Narrate and describe in all time frames; deal effectively with an unanticipated complication	Topics related to personal and general interest; some work-related and special interest topics	Understood without difficulty by speakers unaccustomed to dealing with non-native speakers	Paragraphs
Intermediate	Create with language; sustain simple conversations by asking and answering questions	Familiar topics related to daily activities and transactional situations	Understood, with some repetition, by speakers accustomed to dealing with non-native speakers	Sentences and strings of sentences
Novice	Communicate minimally with formulaic and rote words and phrases	Highly-practiced topics related to self and immediate environment	May be difficult to understand, even for speakers accustomed to dealing with non-native speakers	Individual words and phrases

The ACTFL Proficiency Guidelines can help instructors set goals for their students at various levels of instruction. For instance, at the end of one semester of college-level Portuguese, with classes meeting five days a week, students can typically reach the Novice Mid to Novice High level. As shown in Figure 1, Novice speakers are able to communicate minimally on familiar topics such as self and family using memorized words and expressions. In addition, the High designation in Novice High means that students are beginning to be able to handle the requirements of the Intermediate level, such as creating with language (e.g., going beyond memorized expressions) and asking and answering questions to carry on a simple conversation.

After two semesters of college-level courses, students typically reach the Novice High to Intermediate Low level; after three semesters, Intermediate Low to Intermediate Mid; and after four semesters, Intermediate Mid to Intermediate High. Thus, after two years of Portuguese study, students should be comfortable with the Intermediate-level functions of creating with language and carrying on conversations about everyday topics. They should also be starting to develop the Advanced level functions of narrating and describing in the past using the preterite and imperfect in paragraph-level discourse.

The World-Readiness Standards for Learning Languages

Unlike the ACTFL Proficiency Guidelines, which describe students' performance at different levels of proficiency, the *World-Readiness Standards for Learning Languages* provide a general outline of what students should know and be able to do as a result of foreign language study. Whereas the ACTFL Proficiency Guidelines are *performance* standards, the World-Readiness Standards (hereafter referred to simply as the *Standards*) are *content* standards -- that is, they provide guidance as to the actual content of language instruction. The *Standards* were first released in 1996 as a collaborative effort of the ACTFL, the American Association of Teachers of Spanish and Portuguese (AATSP), and other professional organizations. In 2014 the *Standards* were updated so as to include an emphasis on 21st century skills and other current educational priorities.

The *Standards* are divided into five goal areas, often called the five C's: Communication, Cultures, Connections, Comparisons, and Communities (Figure 2). The first goal area, Communication, regroups the four skills of speaking, listening, reading, and writing into three communicative modes: *Interpersonal mode,* which involves live two-way oral or written communication; *interpretive mode,* which involves understanding written or oral texts whose author is not present; and *presentational mode,* which involves preparing and presenting an oral or written text to an audience of readers or listeners.

Figure 2 *World-Readiness Standards for Learning Languages*

GOAL AREAS	STANDARDS		
COMMUNICATION Communicate effectively in more than one language in order to function in a variety of situations and for multiple purposes	**Interpersonal Communication:** Learners interact and negotiate meaning in spoken, signed, or written conversations to share information, reactions, feelings, and opinions.	**Interpretive Communication:** Learners understand, interpret, and analyze what is heard, read, or viewed on a variety of topics.	**Presentational Communication:** Learners present information, concepts, and ideas to inform, explain, persuade, and narrate on a variety of topics using appropriate media and adapting to various audiences of listeners, readers, or viewers.
CULTURES Interact with cultural competence and understanding	**Relating Cultural Practices to Perspectives:** Learners use the language to investigate, explain, and reflect on the relationship between the practices and perspectives of the cultures studied.	**Relating Cultural Products to Perspectives:** Learners use the language to investigate, explain, and reflect on the relationship between the products and perspectives of the cultures studied.	

CONNECTIONS Connect with other disciplines and acquire information and diverse perspectives in order to use the language to function in academic and career-related situations	**Making Connections:** Learners build, reinforce, and expand their knowledge of other disciplines while using the language to develop critical thinking and to solve problems creatively.	**Acquiring Information and Diverse Perspectives:** Learners access and evaluate information and diverse perspectives that are available through the language and its cultures.
COMPARISONS Develop insight into the nature of language and culture in order to interact with cultural competence	**Language Comparisons:** Learners use the language to investigate, explain, and reflect on the nature of language through comparisons of the language studied and their own.	**Cultural Comparisons:** Learners use the language to investigate, explain, and reflect on the concept of culture through comparisons of the cultures studied and their own.
COMMUNITIES Communicate and interact with cultural competence in order to participate in multilingual communities at home and around the world	**School and Global Communities:** Learners use the language both within and beyond the classroom to interact and collaborate in their community and the globalized world.	**Lifelong Learning:** Learners set goals and reflect on their progress in using languages for enjoyment, enrichment, and advancement.

The Cultures goal area of the *Standards* divides culture into three elements: practices (patterns of social interaction, customs, and traditions); products (books, food, songs, art, etc.); and perspectives (beliefs, ideas, attitudes, and values). The *Standards* emphasize that merely studying the practices and products of another culture without addressing the underlying perspectives yields only superficial cultural understanding, and may lead students to form erroneous judgments about the culture. For example, North American students who are accustomed to grabbing a sandwich or hitting the vending machines for lunch may be surprised to learn that Brazilians often take an hour off work to have lunch with colleagues (a cultural practice). Consequently, students may conclude that Brazilians do not work as hard as Americans. An examination of the underlying cultural perspectives, however, might reveal that the pace of life is different in Brazil, or that Brazilians tend to enjoy social interaction while eating, or that many Brazilians place a high priority on eating a complete lunch, whereas the U.S. tends to prioritize convenience, efficiency, and productivity. Understanding perspectives such as these can promote a more accurate perception of cultural practices and products.

The other three goal areas involve students in using the language to make connections with other academic disciplines, such as history, math, and science; in comparing the target language and cultures with their own; and in using the language both within and beyond the classroom to participate in global communities.

The 2006 version of the *Standards*, published in book format, contains a chapter specifically devoted to Portuguese, with sample progress indicators for students at grade 4, 8, 12, and 16 (the latter representing postsecondary education). For example, the progress indicators for Interpersonal Communication in Grade 16 include the following:

- Students exchange points of view on global topics (e.g., *a educação no Brasil; a ecologia; a política*).
- Students use Portuguese to discuss some aspects of their field with other students (e.g., *as diferenças entre o português e o espanhol; o português na medicina*).
- Students use Portuguese orally and in writing to communicate with people already employed in their field of study (e.g., *cartas pedindo emprego; entrevistas para o trabalho; opiniões sobre um texto literário*). (p. 414)

Over 40 states have used the five C's to create state standards for language learning at the K-12 level, and many university foreign language departments reference them as well.

In addition to the *Standards,* ACTFL has published a list of "Can-Do" statements that are intended for use as self-ratings by students, but are also useful for informing instructors about the skills that students at various levels should be developing. The statements describe what students at the Novice, Intermediate, and Advanced levels can typically do in terms of interpersonal speaking, presentational speaking, presentational writing, interpretive listening, and interpretive reading. It is worth spending some time looking over this useful document at http://www.actfl.org/sites/default/files/pdfs/Can-Do_Statements_2015.pdf.

Planning Course-Level Objectives

Armed with a knowledge of the *ACTFL Proficiency Guidelines* and the *Standards,* you are now ready to write learning objectives for your course. The process of starting with the end goals in mind and then planning how to reach those goals is known as *backward planning.* Unfortunately, far too many instructors fail to implement this process. If you find yourself tempted to do the same, imagine your students finishing your course and continuing to the next level. What will their new instructor have to say about the skills they developed in your course? Will they be prepared to continue their study of Portuguese? You don't want your students to be among the millions of Americans who say, "I took two years of foreign language in college, but I can't speak it to save my life." Articulating learning objectives can help ensure that your students leave your course with some degree of functional ability in Portuguese.

Since you may not know yet exactly what your course content will consist of, it is usually best to write course-level objectives in broad, general terms. Five or six course-level objectives is a manageable number. Keep in mind that first-year university courses typically emphasize the development of speaking and listening skills, whereas second-year courses generally include an expanded emphasis on reading (e.g., short literary and journalistic texts) and on writing short compositions. If you have already selected a textbook (see the next section of this chapter), the book can help inform your course objectives, although the book should *support* your objectives rather than *dictate* them.

Taking into account everything discussed so far, Figure 3 lists some learning objectives that I have used in first- through fourth-semester Portuguese courses. They incorporate content and skills that I believe are important, including interpersonal speaking, interpretive reading and listening, and presentational writing, as well as the Cultures and Comparisons goal areas of the *Standards*. The objectives progress from the Novice Mid through Intermediate High levels of the ACTFL Proficiency Guidelines. Feel free to use these objectives and adapt them to your context as desired.

Figure 3 *Sample Learning Objectives for First- Through Fourth-Semester Postsecondary Portuguese Courses*

First Semester	**Second Semester**
Students will be able to . . . • Communicate verbally in simple routine situations such as greeting people and becoming acquainted. • Understand the main ideas in simple conversations and messages about some familiar, concrete topics such as daily activities, likes and dislikes, family, and home. • Read short texts such as text messages, emails, posts on social media, and personal ads. • Write word- and sentence-length messages such as lists, biographical information on forms, and descriptions of people and things. • Identify basic facts about some Portuguese-speaking countries.	*Students will be able to . . .* • Participate in short conversations about some familiar, concrete topics such as self, family, friends, and daily activities. • Handle short social interactions in everyday situations by asking and answering simple questions. • Understand simple messages and conversations about familiar, concrete topics. • Read simple texts such as advertisements, travel brochures, and cultural explanations from the textbook. • Write short messages such as letters and emails. • Identify basic cultural products and practices from Portuguese-speaking countries.

Third Semester	Fourth Semester
Students will be able to . . . • Participate fully in conversations about concrete topics such as self and others, work, and school. • Handle straightforward transactional situations such as requesting services or making reservations. • Understand the main ideas from audio and video texts, such as commercials and news broadcasts, on familiar topics. • Read short journalistic and literary texts, such as articles and *crônicas*, on familiar topics. • Write short compositions in a variety of genres (résumés, theatrical scenes, poems, skits, etc.) • Discuss some differences between the cultural norms of Americans and Portuguese speakers.	*Students will be able to . . .* • Converse about some topics of general interest and tell about some past experiences. • Handle some situations with an unforeseen complication, such as resolving disagreements or customer complaints. • Understand the main ideas and some details from audio and video texts, such as TV and radio programs and films, on familiar topics. • Read medium-length journalistic and literary texts, such as articles and short stories, on familiar topics. • Write short compositions in a variety of genres (articles, short stories, essays, etc.). • Discuss some differences in cultural perspectives between Americans and Portuguese speakers.

You may notice that grammar is not explicitly listed among these course objectives. Although grammar is an essential component of communication, I prefer to address it at the level of units and individual lessons. Course-level objectives should focus more broadly on the communicative and cultural skills that students need to develop. After all, students do not enroll in a Portuguese course just to learn the imperfect subjunctive; they expect to be able to *use* the language for real-life purposes – which is precisely the purpose of course-level objectives.

Selecting a Textbook

Especially if you are a beginning-level instructor, the textbook you use will probably influence your curriculum. Depending on the context in which you teach, the textbook may have already been selected, but if you find yourself in the position of having to choose a book, the following information may be helpful.

As a less commonly taught language, Portuguese has far fewer textbooks available than languages such as Spanish or French. In recent years, however, the availability of Portuguese textbooks has increased significantly. A variety of textbooks are available for beginning and intermediate courses, with a few books also available for advanced classes, business Portuguese, and Portuguese for Spanish speakers.

An Internet search for "Portuguese textbooks" turns up at least a few dozen books, some of which are intended for self-study and others for classroom settings. Some of these books are published in the U.S. or the

U.K., whereas others are published in Brazil or Portugal; there are advantages and disadvantages to each. Books published in the U.S. and U.K. have the advantage of containing grammar explanations and translations of vocabulary lists in English, which allows the instructor to assign students to study these materials outside class. Books published in Brazil or Portugal, on the other hand, may feature more authentic language and cultural materials, although much of the cultural content may be implicit and need to be explained by the instructor. In addition, the organization of these books may differ from what North American students may expect in a textbook. Figure 4 lists some of the most commonly-used textbooks, based on a survey of university- and college-level Portuguese programs in the United States (Bateman, 2014).

Figure 4 *Portuguese Textbooks Commonly Used in the U.S.*

First-Year Textbooks			
Title	*Author(s)*	*Year*	*Publisher*
Ponto de Encontro: Portuguese as a World Language (2nd ed.)	Clémence de Jouët-Pastré, Anna Klobucka, Patrícia Sobral, Maria Luci Moreira, & Amelia Hutchinson	2012	Pearson Prentice Hall
Bom Dia, Brasil (3rd ed. of *Português Básico para Estrangeiros)*	Rejane de Oliveira Slade, Marta Almeida, & Elizabeth Jackson	2011	Yale University Press
Português para Principiantes	Claude Leroy, Severino Albuquerque, & Mary Schil	1993	University of Wisconsin-Madison
Novo Avenida Brasil: Curso Básico de Português para Estrangeiros	Emma E. O. F. Lima	2009	Editora Pedagógica e Universitária
Brasil! Língua e Cultura (3rd ed.)	Tom Lathrop & Eduardo M. Dias	2002	LinguaText
Intermediate-Level Textbooks			
Cinema for Portuguese Conversation	Bonnie Wasserman	2009	Focus Publishing
Para a Frente! An intermediate course in Portuguese	Larry D. King & Margarita Suñer	2004	LinguaText
Viajando através do alfabeto: A Reading and Writing Program for Intermediate to Advanced Portuguese	Clémence Jouët-Pastré & Patrícia Sobral	2010	Focus Publishing
Mapeando a Língua Portuguesa através das Artes	Patrícia Sobral & Clémence Jouët-Pastré	2014	Focus Publishing
Advanced-Level Textbooks			
Um Passo Mais no Português Moderno: Gramática Avançada, Leituras, Composição e Conversação	Francisco C. Fagundes	2010	Tagus Press (Univ. of Massachusetts Dartmouth)
Portuleiro: Língua, Cultura e Literatura (revised ed.)	Vanessa C. Fitzgibbon	2015	Linus Learning

Portuguese for Spanish Speakers Textbooks			
Pois não: Brazilian Portuguese Course for Spanish Speakers	Antônio R. M. Simões	2008	Univ. of Texas Press
Business Portuguese Textbooks			
Working Portuguese for Beginners	Monica Rector, Regina Santos, & Marcelo Amorim	2010	Georgetown Univ. Press

Some publishers will provide instructors with a free "desk copy" of their textbooks if you fill out an online form with information about the class you will be teaching. As you examine different books, the criteria in Figure 5 may be helpful. In any case, the most important factor in choosing a textbook is how closely it aligns with the learning objectives you have outlined for the course.

Figure 5 *Criteria for Selecting a Portuguese Textbook*

1. **TYPE AND LEVEL OF TEXT.** For what level is the book intended – beginning, intermediate, or advanced? Does it address all four skills, or is it intended mainly for teaching reading, conversation, or composition? Is it designed for a specialized purpose, such as business Portuguese or Portuguese for Spanish speakers? How many chapters are there? Is the amount of content appropriate for the time available?
2. **VARIETY OF PORTUGUESE.** Does the book emphasize Brazilian Portuguese, European Portuguese, or both? If it focuses on one specific variety of the language, does it make mention of grammatical and lexical differences from other varieties?
3. **ORGANIZATION.** What is the organizational basis for the text? Is it structured around themes (family, food, leisure activities, etc.), geographic regions, grammatical topics, or something else? Does this type of content match your learning objectives for the course?
4. **FEATURES OF CONTENT**. What special features does the book contain – e.g., an index, preliminary lessons, vocabulary lists, a pronunciation section, grammar summaries or verb charts at the end, a glossary, color photographs, maps?
5. **ACTIVITIES IN INTERPERSONAL MODE**. Does the book provide opportunities for students to use the language in a variety of real-life, meaningful contexts? Do the activities allow students to personalize their responses and express their own meaning in the language?
6. **ACTIVITIES IN INTERPRETIVE MODE.** Does the book include a variety of authentic texts from Portuguese-speaking cultures, including printed texts in various genres, as well as authentic audio and video texts? Are the texts accompanied by pre- and post-reading/listening activities? Are strategies for reading and listening comprehension taught?
7. **ACTIVITIES IN PRESENTATIONAL MODE.** Does the book provide a variety of writing assignments of different types? Does it teach writing strategies? Does it give suggestions for projects or oral presentations by students?
8. **GRAMMATICAL CONTENT**. Is the coverage of grammar topics appropriate for the level of the book? Are grammar concepts explained clearly, with sufficient examples and practice activities? Are they presented in contexts that illustrate their use in real-life situations? Is there a review built in for previously-learned grammar concepts?
9. **CULTURAL CONTENT.** What does the book's cultural content consist of? Does it focus on the culture of only one country or does it address a variety of regions? Does it encourage students to think about cultural perspectives as well as products and practices? Does it provide opportunities for students to compare the target culture with their own?

10. ANCILLARY MATERIALS. What ancillary materials are available – e.g., an instructor's edition, a testing program, practice activities in a student workbook or online, audio recordings, videos, an accompanying website? Are these materials included in the price of the textbook package?

Once you have chosen a textbook, it becomes a relatively simple matter to decide how many chapters you want to cover in a given course and how much time to devote to each chapter, and to distribute the chapters throughout the semester or quarter.

Unit Planning

Prior to beginning each unit or chapter, it is worth taking some time to think through the unit from beginning to end. This involves several considerations, including deciding on a theme or essential question for the unit, planning learning objectives, selecting materials to supplement the textbook, and planning how to assess students' learning.

Articulating essential questions. Most foreign language textbooks dedicate each chapter to a specific topic such as family, food, housing, clothing, or leisure activities. A chapter on housing, for example, might state at the beginning of the chapter that students will "discuss housing and household objects." Although this may be a valid communicative objective, it does little to expand students' cultural understanding or develop the critical thinking skills outlined by the *Standards*.

In contrast to a vocabulary *topic*, a *theme* is structured around an "essential question" that asks students to make cross-cultural comparisons or consider cultural perspectives. In relation to housing, for instance, you might ask questions such as "What is housing like in Portuguese-speaking countries? What differences exist in housing between urban versus rural areas, and between people of different socioeconomic status? How does this compare with housing in the U.S.? How do housing variables affect people's quality of life?" Any of these questions, or a combination thereof, can change a vocabulary-based topic to an engaging theme that can provide motivating content for students to speak, read, and write about in Portuguese.

Writing learning objectives. Having articulated one or more essential questions, you are better prepared to write specific learning objectives for the unit. Although some textbooks provide an overview of the grammatical and cultural content of each chapter in the introductory pages of the book or at the start of the chapter, this overview is often not in the form of learning objectives. As shown in Figure 3, objectives typically start with *Students will be able to* . . . Many instructors make the mistake of focusing on what they themselves are going to cover during a unit or lesson rather than what they want their students to be able to do. This tends to make for teacher-centered classes rather than learner-centered ones, with the result that the instructor covers the material but has little idea as to whether students have learned anything.

One characteristic of well-written objectives at both the unit level and the lesson level is that they are stated in such a way that students' learning can be easily assessed at the end of the unit or lesson. Continuing with our housing example, if your objective for a lesson is simply to discuss housing, you may end up with no idea whether students have learned anything from the activity. In contrast, the objective "Students will be able to describe to a real estate agent the type of apartment that they want to rent" can be easily assessed by simply observing students during a role-play or having them write a description of the apartment.

Compare the examples of effective and less-effective objectives in Figure 6. Which do you think would produce the best outcomes? Why?

Figure 6
Examples of Learning Objectives

Less effective objectives	**More effective objectives**
Learn the present tense of regular *-ar* verbs.	Students will be able to use the first person singular of regular present tense *-ar* verbs to tell what they do in a typical day.
Learn vocabulary for family members.	Students will be able to use family-related vocabulary to draw their own three-generation family tree and identify their relationship to each person.
Watch a video about *festas juninas.*	Students will be able to describe key elements of a *festa junina,* including typical dress and common foods and activities.

Learning objectives may be divided into various types. Among them are the following:

- ***Communicative objectives.*** These are the linguistic tasks or functions that students should master. Examples of communicative objective might be "Students will be able to make a plan with a prospective roommate on what type of apartment to rent" or "Students will be able to tell who does which household chores in their home."
- ***Linguistic objectives.*** Linguistic objectives often overlap with communicative objectives, but it may be helpful to consider separately the grammar concepts and vocabulary that students should learn. Examples might be "Students will be able to use reflexive verbs to tell about their morning routine" or "Students will be able to use prepositions to discuss where to place the furniture in a room" (note that both of these overlap with communicative objectives).
- ***Content objectives.*** This category of objectives refers to the subject-matter content that students are to learn. As shown in Figure 2, the Connections goal area of the *Standards* specifies that students should use the

language to learn subject-matter content from various disciplines. Examples of content objectives might be "Students will be able to locate the Portuguese-speaking countries on a world map" or "Students will be able to explain what *azulejos* are and tell how they are used in the construction of Portuguese and Brazilian churches and homes."

- ***Culture objectives.*** These may overlap with content objectives, since the content of units is often cultural in nature. Recall that the Cultures and Comparisons goal areas of the *Standards* state that students should learn about the cultural products, practices, and perspectives of the target culture and compare them with those of their own culture. Examples of culture objectives might be "Students will able to compare and contrast low-income housing in Portugal and the U.S." or "Students will be able to explain cultural imagery from the song *Uma casa portuguesa* and discuss the cultural values portrayed by these images."

Selecting supplemental materials. As you examine the reading materials, audio recordings, and videos from the textbook chapter, chances are that you will want to supplement them with additional materials that support your unit theme or essential question(s). An internet search engine can lead you to a wealth of authentic materials, or materials prepared by native speakers for other native speakers. In relation to the theme of housing, for example, you might find songs such as Vinícius de Moraes' *A casa* or Amália Rodrigues' rendition of *Uma casa portuguesa;* YouTube videos of Portuguese speakers giving tours of their homes; newspaper or magazine articles about the *déficit habitacional* in Brazil; blog posts by Brazilians visiting the U.S. and commenting on differences in housing; and *crônicas* in which someone's house or apartment plays a key role. As stated in the *Standards*, these materials can expose students to "diverse perspectives that are available through the language and its cultures." An added benefit is that authentic materials can be highly motivating for students as they discover that they can use Portuguese for real purposes in the real world.

Planning how to assess learning objectives. One of the most important steps in preparing an instructional unit is planning for assessment. Assigning grades is only one purpose for assessment; an equally important purpose is to inform students, instructors, and programs of the degree to which learning objectives are being reached. Following are some key points to understand about assessment:

- Assessments should be planned from the outset of instruction, along with learning objectives.
- Assessments should be aligned with learning objectives. Each objective should be assessed in one or more ways that informs you on how well students have achieved that objective.
- Assessments should mirror instruction -- that is, they should reflect the types of activities that students do in and out of class.

It is important to understand that *testing* is not synonymous with *assessment.* Tests are only one form of assessment; other forms include classroom participation, homework assignments, papers, compositions, oral presentations, portfolios, peer assessment, and self-assessment. The more you can incorporate various forms of assessment, the more complete your understanding will be of your students' learning. This is especially important given that some students simply do not perform well on tests.

Assessments may be either formal or informal in nature. *Formal assessments* include chapter tests, quizzes, and rubrics used for grading projects or compositions. *Informal assessments* might consist of observing students during pair or small-group activities, asking students to turn in some product of their pair work, or awarding points for participation. For example, an informal assessment of the objective "Students will be able to describe to a real estate agent the type of apartment that they want to rent" might be to observe students during a role-play in class; a formal assessment of the same objective might consist of an oral test at the end of the chapter where the instructor plays the role of the real estate agent, and students are assigned points for use of grammar, vocabulary, pronunciation, and overall completion of the task.

At the unit level, you will probably use assessments of a more formal nature, usually including an end-of-unit test. Daily lesson plans, in contrast, often incorporate more informal assessments (more on lesson planning in a moment).

Example of a unit plan. Figure 7 shows an example of a completed unit plan on the theme of housing. The first column lists the learning objectives for the unit, which are divided into communicative objectives, content/culture objectives, and linguistic objectives (including grammar and vocabulary), based largely on the content of the textbook chapter. The second column outlines the main communicative activities planned for the unit, categorized according to interpersonal, interpretive, and presentational modes. Again, the activities are taken partly from the textbook, but with the addition of authentic materials such as songs, videos, and blog posts.

Figure 7 *Sample Unit Plan*

Unit theme: *A casa e os móveis* (*Ponto de Encontro* Lição 5)	**Essential question:** How does housing differ by region (urban vs. rural) and by social class in Brazil and the U.S.?	
Learning Objectives	***Communicative Activities***	***Assessments***
<u>Communicative Objectives (tasks/functions/topics)</u> Students will be able to . . . 1. Identify and describe the rooms and furnishings in a house 2. Discuss who does household chores <u>Content and Culture Objectives</u> Students will be able to . . . 3. Discuss how housing differs according to region (urban vs. rural) and by social class within Brazil and the U.S., and between the two countries <u>Linguistic Objectives – Grammar</u> Students will be able to . . . 4. Use the present progressive 5. Express physical and emotional states with *ter, estar com* 6. Use *dar, ler, ver, vir* in present tense 7. Distinguish between *saber* and *conhecer* 8. Use demonstratives 9. Use reflexive verbs	<u>Interpersonal Mode</u> • Describe the "ideal" house • Discuss who does what chores in the home • Discuss renting an apartment with a roommate • Discuss regional and social differences in housing in the U.S. <u>Interpretive Mode</u> *(reading, listening, viewing)* Video from book: *Como é a sua casa? Quem limpa a casa?* • Readings from book: *Lugares para morar; O exterior e o interior das casas; Brasília e o Centro-Oeste do Brasil* • YouTube video: *Tour pela minha casa* • Blog post: *Diferenças entre casas brasileiras e americanas* <u>Presentational Mode</u> *(writing, presentations, projects)* Project: Work with a partner to interview someone in a Lusophone country online: - *Como é a sua casa?* - *É típica das casas das pessoas da sua região e classe social?* - *Que fatores influenciam os diferentes tipos de moradia no seu país?*	• Homework from My Portuguese Lab (1-2, 4-9) • Daily self-assessment of preparation and participation (1-9) • Oral test: Role play phone call to real estate agent inquiring about apartment for rent (1) • Chapter test: Listening: Dialogue – *Sérgio compra uma casa* (1) - Vocabulary: Identify household chores from pictures (2) - Grammar: *Dar/ ler/ ver/ vir*, *saber* e *conhecer*, present progressive; demonstratives; reflexives; *estar com/ ter* (4-9) - Reading: Ad for apartment for rent (1) - Writing: Email to Brazilian student coming to live with an American family, explaining differences between American and Brazilian homes (3) • Project: With their partner, students give a short presentation about the home of the native speaker they interviewed online (scored with a rubric) (1, 3)
<u>Vocabulary</u> • *a casa* • *os móveis* • *os eletrodomésticos* • *os afazeres domésticos*	<u>Change of Pace</u> *(songs, games, etc.)* Songs: *A casa* (Vinícus de Moraes), *Uma casa portuguesa* (Amália Rodrigues) Games: *Piccionário, Levante-se, Cesta de frutas*	

The last column outlines the plan for assessing the learning outcomes from the first column. The numbers in parentheses indicate which learning objective(s) are assessed by each assessment. Notice that each objective is assessed by one or more assessments; for example, Objective 1, "Identify and describe the rooms and furnishings in a house," is assessed through homework assignments, classroom participation, various segments of the chapter test, and a project in which students report on an interview with a native Portuguese speaker.

Lesson Planning

Having a prepared a unit plan makes it much easier to plan lessons for individual class periods. Like unit plans, individual lesson plans start with learning objectives and assessments, but in this case the objectives will outline what students should be able to do at the end of the class period rather than at the end of the unit, and the assessments will target these objectives. Again, many of these assessments may be informal in nature, such as simply observing students' participation or asking them to turn in some product of their work in pairs or small groups.

Other helpful elements to include in a lesson plan include the materials necessary for the lesson; a description of each activity along with the estimated time it will take (or the clock time to start the activity); and any homework assignments. Many beginning instructors find it helpful to write out a script detailing what they will say in Portuguese to introduce and conduct each activity. In addition, formal lesson plans generally list which of the *Standards* the lesson addresses, with a sentence devoted to each standard. Figure 8 shows an example of a completed lesson plan for a first-semester university Portuguese class.

Figure 8 *Sample Lesson Plan*

Lesson Plan: A casa *Ponto de Encontro* pp. 189-193
Purpose: Introduce house-related vocabulary and some differences between Brazilian and U.S homes.
Standards Addressed *Interpersonal communication:* Students converse about the layout and furniture of their home. *Interpretive communication:* Students understand and interpret a video tour of a house in Portuguese. *Relating cultural products to perspectives:* Students compare homes in Brazil and the U.S.
Communicative/Linguistic Objectives Students will be able to . . . • Identify the rooms and some articles of furniture in a house • Introduce the rooms in their house with *Aqui é . . . (a cozinha, o banheiro,* etc.) **Content/Culture Objectives** Students will be able to . . . • Identify some differences between U.S. and Brazilian homes

Materials needed	
PowerPoint slide reviewing pronunciation of the letter /*x*/; YouTube video *Tour pela minha casa* https://www.youtube.com/watch?v=3TMCc3D7BBQ ; simple drawing of floor plan of instructors house showing rooms and a few articles of furniture; two identical sets of index cards with vocabulary words for parts of the house for *Levante-se* game; Internet access for Google image search	
Time	**Activity**
9:00	• Boas vindas e anúncios: Daniel
9:02	• Warmup – Pronúncia da letra *x*: Review the four possible pronunciations and have students practice reading sentences aloud from the PowerPoint slide (e.g., "*Um aluno exemplar deve ter êxito em todos os exames*").
9:06 9:08	• Introdução ao capítulo: Briefly review the overview of chapter content on p. 189.
9:15	• Vocabulário: Project p. 192 from the e-text on the screen; model pronunciation of house vocabulary and ask, *Quem tem mais de um banheiro na sua casa? Quantos quartos tem? A sua casa tem fogão a gás ou fogão elétrico? Tem lareira?* etc.
9:22	• Atividade 5-2, p. 192: Have students tell what room each object is in and what they do in that room (model the first one).
9:32	• Vídeo – *Tour pela minha casa*: ○ Pre-viewing: Tell students, *Vamos ver um vídeo em que uma moça brasileira nos mostra a sua casa. Quero que você prestem atenção para descobrir (a) que cômodos são mencionados, e (b) que diferenças vocês observam entre a casa dela e as casas dos Estados Unidos.* ○ Viewing: Show the video starting at 0:37. ○ Post-viewing: Ask students, *Que cômodos foram mencionados? Que diferenças vocês observaram entre esta casa e sua própria casa?* Call students' attention to the *ladeira, grades nas janelas, guarda-roupa, azulejos no banheiro e na cozinha, área de serviço, tanque,* etc., teaching vocabulary where necessary. Explain each item. ○ Second viewing: Show a brief segment of the video again and ask students, *Como é que ela introduz cada sala? Em inglês nós dizemos "This is the kitchen." O que é que se diz em português? ("Aqui é a cozinha")* – write this on the board
9:43	• Atividade em duplas: A planta da minha casa Show the floor plan of your home and tell students, *Aqui é a planta da minha casa* (write *planta* on the board). Briefly describe each room and its contents. Then tell students, *Quero que vocês desenhem uma planta simples de sua casa, mostrando alguns dos móveis e objetos.* Allow 3 minutes for drawing, then have students describe their drawings in pairs (point to the expression *Aqui é . . .* on the board, and add *Na cozinha tem . . .*). Follow up by asking, *Quem tem uma casa interessante? Sara, como é a casa do David?* etc. • Jogo – "Levante-se": Divide class in two teams. Distribute two identical sets of vocabulary cards, one set per team, so that each student has one card (for example, one person on Team A and one on Team B will each have the word *cozinha*). With the projector turned off, do a Google image search for *cozinha*, and then project the images on the screen. Of the two students with that card, the first one to stand up, hold up the card and correctly pronounce *cozinha* wins a point for his/her team. Repeat with other vocabulary words.
Assessment	
Observe students' participation in the video and pair activities; have students turn in their drawing of the floor plan of their house	

Homework
Read pp. 194-199; do assigned activities in My Portuguese Lab

Additional factors to consider in lesson planning include the following:

Variety. Assuming that your course-level objectives include the development of speaking skills, every class period should incorporate at least one interpersonal speaking activity. Lessons should feature a balance between teacher talk and student talk, ensuring that students have ample opportunity to practice using Portuguese to communicate. In addition, lessons should regularly include listening, reading, and writing activities, with culture incorporated as often as possible. Again, this is much easier if you have a culture-related essential question to guide your planning.

Sequence. Every instructor has his or her own preferences regarding the sequencing of lesson activities. I like to start class with a warmup or review activity to link the lesson to previous material, assess students' retention and mastery of the material, and get them thinking in Portuguese. Next, I generally introduce new or more challenging material such as vocabulary, grammar, or functional skills, progressing from structured or controlled activities to more open-ended activities. Finally, I like to conclude with an activity that returns to a level at which students feel comfortable so that they leave class with a feeling of accomplishment and want to come back for more. Good wrap-up activities include games, songs, and communicative activities that involve the class as a whole.

Pacing. Pacing involves the timing of activities, which should ideally be neither too long nor too short. A good rule of thumb is that when 80% of students have completed an activity, it's time to move onto the next activity. With time you will develop the ability to estimate how long each activity will take.

Use of Portuguese. It goes without saying that the more Portuguese students hear in class, the faster they will learn the language. ACTFL recommends that instructors use the target language for at least 90% of class time. Of the hundreds of instructors I have observed over the years, the most successful ones make it a rule to conduct class almost entirely in the target language. As a Portuguese instructor, one of the best decisions you can make is to tell yourself, "I'm going to conduct my class in Portuguese, and I'm going to make sure my students understand me." There are many techniques you can draw on to increase students' comprehension, including the use of gestures, visual aids, examples, cognates and familiar vocabulary, and repeating or rephrasing rather than resorting to English when students don't understand. A little advance planning can help you keep your lesson in Portuguese and avoid the need for using English.

At this point you may wonder whether experienced instructors actually write out every day's lesson plan in this much detail. The answer is, usually not. Experienced instructors often rely on less detailed plans, partly because their experience enables them to make spontaneous decisions in the classroom with comparatively less preparation. For beginning instructors, however, I strongly recommend writing out daily lesson plans in as much detail as time allows, since more careful planning generally makes for better lessons. Even if you don't have time to prepare a detailed plan, at a minimum you should write down what you expect students to be able to do at the end of the lesson. I still follow this procedure after a quarter century of teaching, and I find that it often makes the difference between a successful lesson and a mediocre one.

Of course, having a detailed plan in no way limits your flexibility as an instructor. Skilled instructors frequently make spontaneous decisions to modify their teaching based on their students' response to a given lesson or unit. In fact, one of the main purposes of assessment is to allow you to gauge how well your students are learning and make adjustments accordingly. These ongoing, informal assessments of students' learning are known as *formative assessments* (as opposed to *summative assessment,* which is discussed below).

One last word may be in order here. I frequently counsel new instructors not to become discouraged if a particular lesson doesn't go as planned. Even experienced instructors find that their lessons sometimes go awry, whether due to misjudgments in planning or to factors beyond the instructor's control, including individual differences among students and the collective aptitude, personality, and motivation of a given class. One of the advantages of making detailed lesson plans is that you can make notes on what activities did and didn't go well, so that the next time you teach the course, you can make any necessary adjustments.

Summative Assessment of Students' Learning

The final step in the process outlined here is to conduct *formative assessments* of students' learning at the end of each unit and at the end of the course. This is where your unit assessments, as well as any culminating assessments such as semester projects or final exams, come into play. Many grading software programs, or even Excel spreadsheets, allow you to calculate descriptive statistics such as the average score and range of scores on a given assessment, which will give you a good idea as to how well your students have achieved the unit or course objectives, and in what areas you can help them improve. You may also want to look at the scores of low-performing students to determine exactly what they are struggling with and how best to meet their individual needs.

Conclusion

Having started this chapter with a quote from Alice in Wonderland, it seems appropriate to conclude with another quote, this one from renowned Brazilian educator Paulo Freire:

Ninguém ignora tudo. Ninguém sabe tudo. Todos nós sabemos alguma coisa. Todos nós ignoramos alguma coisa. Por isso aprendemos sempre.

Freire's statement suggests that as the instructor, you don't have to know everything. Your students will bring with them insights which, when combined with your own planning and expertise, will allow you to jointly co-construct learning experiences that will make every class period and every course that you teach unique. This is one of the most wonderful aspects of teaching, and one that I hope will contribute to your desire to keep returning to the classroom for many years to come.

Additional Resources

Bateman, B. (2014). Communication and other C's: A study of what Portuguese instructors want in textbooks. *Portuguese Language Journal, 8.* Available at http://www.ensinoportugues.org/

This article reports on a survey of 116 Portuguese instructors at 107 colleges and universities in the U.S. regarding what textbooks they use and what features they would like to see in an "ideal" textbook.

Center for Advanced Research on Language Acquisition. (n.d.). *Backward design.* Retrieved from http://www.carla.umn.edu/assessment/vac/CreateUnit/p_1.html

Brief webpage that offers a concise introduction to unit planning in language classes, including a focus on writing essential questions.

Montgomery, C. (2014). The transformative power of performance-based assessment. *The Language Educator, 9*(2), 42-46, 53.

This article provides a useful model as well as a wealth of practical ideas for planning unit objectives and assessments, with many links to online resources.

Wiggins, G., & McTighe, J. (2006). *Understanding by design* (expanded 2nd ed.). Alexandria, VA: Association for Supervision and Curriculum Development.

Although not specific to language education, this oft-cited book offers detailed guidance for K-16 instructors on the design of curriculum, assessment, and instruction, including a focus on backward design and key concepts such as essential questions.

2.4 ASSESSMENT: CREATING RUBRICS

Megwen May Loveless
Tulane University

For many students, families and teachers, "assessment" has taken on a negative connotation, particularly as the practice of standardized testing has become a major polemic across the nation. In reality, assessment is much more than simply quizzes and unit exams, and in a strategically-organized classroom, assessments are a tool to measure your own performance and stated goals as much as your students' performance. Well-designed assessment gives the instructor evidence to see if his/her learning objectives are coming to fruition.

As we will see in the world of assessment, mistakes can actually be a good thing. They are an intrinsic part of learning and can help both instructors and students zero in on how to improve. Still, making mistakes just for the sake of flopping is not good pedagogy. This manual is written by veterans in the field who have survived bumps and bruises along the way and would like to share their successes and failures in order to save new Portuguese instructors from having to make all the same mistakes we have already made. In this chapter I hope to provide useful tried-and-true resources for assessing your students.

After reading the chapter on lesson planning, you already know the importance of clarifying your learning objectives before creating your course syllabus, as well as the value of integrating course planning, teaching and assessment. This short chapter will focus on how to create a variety of assessments to gauge your students' progress across the curriculum. In particular, I will suggest ways to build a series of rubrics that can help clarify – for you *and* your students – what skills you prioritize in your classroom.

By now you are familiar with the term "backward planning," a term that suggests that instructors should start with their end goal(s) as they begin to think about how to structure a course. Part of backward planning is incorporating your assessments into the overall picture so you are providing yourself and your students with a "checks-and-balances" sort of system.

In some institutional settings, you will have considerable pressure to create certain kinds of assessments, in which you may have some tension between your teaching philosophy and/or methodology and your assignments and/or grading. But, as a rule, you should try to invest the time necessary to determine up front what evidence you hope to see that your students are indeed realizing the learning objectives you have determined for the course.

For example, if one of your outlined goals is for students "to communicate verbally in simple routine situations..." then a simple vocabulary quiz does not provide enough evidence that they have achieved this goal, and therefore is not an ideal assessment. Instead, you may want to have short oral interviews in which students speak to each other in a pair while you observe. If one of your outlined goals is for students "to identify basic facts about some Portuguese-speaking countries," then an oral listening exercise in which students fill in the missing word(s) does not provide enough evidence of their progress toward the goal, and therefore is not an ideal assessment. Instead, you may want to have students identify several images/statistics/etc. that you project to the classroom. Alternatively, you could use a multiple-choice test. If one of your outlined goals is for students to "show an advanced analysis of literary perspectives from across the contemporary lusophone world," then a true/false quiz will not provide enough evidence, and therefore is not an ideal assessment. Instead, you may want to assign a take-home essay asking students to compare and contrast three or more literary works from the course reading list.

Remember, too, that assessments can be informal or formal. Some assessments don't require a full-fledged rubric. Some might be better served with a "yes/no" rubric, or something far more simple than what I suggest below. One simple assessment, for example, that has been quite successful in my classroom is an "exit ticket," in which a student must create one "successful" linguistic phrase in order to leave the classroom. (I don't literally bar any student from leaving, but this can be a quick way to determine which of my students might need to follow up with me during office hours.) You may on occasion want to leave the assessment up to the student: some teachers have students flash "green" or "red" cards at regular intervals during lecture or class activities to ascertain if everyone has understood the material up to that point. Another take on this method is to distribute white boards and have students write answers and hold them up; this way the instructor can quickly see who is struggling with the material.

I particularly enjoy hosting "games" in the classroom, and these, too, can be an informal ways to assess how well students are performing on our course goals. For instance, in a linguistic relay race students might report a sentence to me with certain content; based on their delivery, I can determine how well each individual has learned the content. In a game of Taboo students attempt to use circumlocution to describe a word without using four key descriptors; based on his/her ability to participate, I can determine how well each student is learning strategic competence. In my classroom, I tend to use games to review material we have already learned, and I rarely use them for formal assessment, as I am wary of students getting too competitive with one another. But they can be a fun and energizing way in which to gauge the strong and weak areas of my class.

In the arena of formal assessment, more and more language instructors are moving away from the traditional exams that many of us remember from our days as students, instead embracing creative and collaborative projects and assignments. This new turn in assessment, while it can encourage active learning as well as cater to different learning styles, can present challenges in terms of arriving at a fair grade. How can instructors put a number onto an ephemeral performance or a collaborative piece in which several students contributed? How can we assign a grade for an oral interview between two students of different language levels? How can we arrive at a quantitative way to describe a student's daily participation over a 14-week semester?

The simple answer is to create a detailed rubric. Rubrics are beneficial to both teaching and learning, because they force the teacher to communicate his/her expectations clearly to students. The act of creating a rubric will actually help instructors determine what factors in an assignment are most important to them and by which standards they measure levels of quality.

In a perfect world, we would create rubrics and assessments alongside our course goals and regularly revisit each throughout the semester for consistency. In reality, we often have to cobble together course material on the fly. For that reason, and for new instructors who may have been thrown into the deep end without even a basic training course in assessment, I include several rubrics here that I have developed over the years as well as some basic things to consider when putting together a new rubric. I encourage all instructors to make changes to the rubrics below that reflect personal and institutional specifications, as much as I also urge both new and veteran teachers to create their own rubric(s), to enhance their understanding of their own expectations of student work.

For sake of ease, I will give a narrative of the evolution of a single rubric, the "composition" rubric. As stated earlier, this manual is meant to give new instructors the information necessary to avoid "reinventing the wheel," and hopefully these next paragraphs will help new Portuguese teachers get comfortable with better grading practices without repeating each step along the way. When I first started teaching an introduction to Portuguese language course, I graded written assignments for grammar and mechanics only. Over the course of the semester, students turned in four assignments (and four revisions) that were each 1-page double-spaced. I marked errors and took off approximately half a point for each error, then averaged the first version score and revision score for a final grade. This wasn't an atrocious system, but it made my grading relatively tedious, as there was no impetus for the student to create content that I would enjoy reading. It also didn't reward students who made an effort to write more or to write in more nuanced language.

So I changed the system somewhat. I started giving students two grades for each version: one for grammar/mechanics and one for content. This sent a message that I was interested in more than simply dictionary and agreement skills, and it did not make the grading much more onerous. It was difficult to justify numeric grades for content, though, and it still didn't encourage students to do much more than the minimum. In particular I felt frustrated when students came to office hours to ask how to improve their grades, since I couldn't tell them anything concrete or specific until reading over their paper a second or sometimes third time.

The next iteration was a formal rubric (Figure 1) inspired by a colleague's version,[7] itself inspired by a version in circulation at the University of North Carolina at Chapel Hill. This rubric was divided into two major categories with several subcategories in each (for content: originality, organization, sophistication; for grammar/mechanics: spelling, agreement, vocabulary, etc.). For the first version of the assignment, each subcategory was worth up to five or ten points (up to 80 total), and for the final grade, additional subcategories in the revision process added up to 100 points total. This system was great for showing students the areas they could improve, and it gave them a real sense that the revision contributed toward their final grade (Students would still have an 80 on the assignment if their first version was deemed "perfect" and they never turned in a revision, which was an excellent motivator for participating in the revision process). Still, this rubric simply told students what categories I was grading them on; it didn't describe my expectations. Too often we think that if we tell students they will be graded on "style," students will immediately know what we are referring to, or will think to visit us in office hours to ask. In fact, students don't necessarily know what "style" means, and it is part of our job as teachers to show them.

My rubric the following semester addressed this concern by switching to a narrative format. I had come to this format somewhat begrudgingly, because I was afraid that handing out a page with so much small text would discourage students from reading any of it. As it turns out, a student need only read one column of narrative in preparation for the assignment (the column that represents the grade s/he wants to receive), and several students told me this was their preference, so I finally acquiesced. Many instructors use this prototype as a "homework" rubric and simply include three categories: excellent, good and poor. For my class, though, I chose to create categories for A/A-/B+/B/B-. This would help students who were on the cusp of different letter grades, and would help clarify the difference between an A/A-/B+, which seemed to be the categories most fraught with student anxiety and concern. The narrative format took a long time to formulate, as I had to think very hard about what characterizes B grade style versus A grade style. Not only that, I wanted to echo the ACTFL "can-do" statements and use only positive language in each description. I struggled quite a bit with adjectives to describe what I was looking for in a concise manner. The time spent was well worthwhile, though, as it saved me quite a lot of time during

[7] Special thanks to Luis Gonçalves for sharing this rubric as well as countless classroom exercises, and his unrelenting enthusiasm for teaching "outside of the box."

office hours. Because I had managed to express the nuanced differences between grades in very clear and encouraging language, students felt they had more guidance about how to improve their writing.

The next version included seven columns and represented all the possible gradations between an A grade and a C grade. This is an area that some colleagues may need to tinker with and I note that this rubric was created for use at an elite university, where students were highly motivated, both in terms of GPA as well as in their interest in taking an elective language course. Still, even in different educational environments, I generally ask students to resubmit papers that won't be gradable on this scale; I believe students owe it to themselves to submit work that is at least within the realm of average, and that part of our job as educators is to encourage students to try their best and learn to exhibit some pride in their work.

The implementation of this revised rubric was an improvement though it still had a few issues that made it clunky. For lack of specific adjectives, I had repeated a few descriptions from one column to the next, so my grading of those specific issues might have looked quite arbitrary to students. Within the individual categories, I often hesitated when assigning an A or A- grade, because the student work fit within both descriptions, but I tried to tell myself that I would recalibrate that when coming up with a final grade for the composition. To indicate work that was right on the line in a specific category, I simply circled the line separating the columns for that particular category.

The most recent version of my "composition" rubric is still divided into seven columns (Figure 2) and includes differentiated descriptions for every column. I print out a black-and-white copy of this rubric for each assignment I grade, and as I am evaluating student written work, I underline any and all descriptions that apply. This way each student can see at a glance the strong and weak points of his/her work. By underlining the precise language I painstakingly chose for each column and each category, I am showing students specifically how their work dialogues with my expectations. In most cases, the underlined portion stretches across several columns; sometimes a student is clearly strong in grammatical accuracy but does not show fluidity in writing, other times a student clearly excels in originality and style but has not made an effort to incorporate new and specific vocabulary. Over several semesters I have experimented with adding a quantitative score to each box of the rubric and creating a mathematical "average" for the final composition grade, but most recently I eyeball the various underlined language and determine what column best represents where the majority of the ink lies.[8] Another procedure I've incorporated which has helped streamline the

---

[8] Did I mention that I never grade in red? See: Semke, Harriet D., "Effects of the Red Pen," Foreign Language Annals, 17:3 (May 1984), 195-202.

grading of original compositions and revisions is to assign a letter grade to both. This way, I have a record of both grades and am not left with a gaping hole in my gradebook if a student never turns in a revision, while the student still has an opportunity to improve his/her grade during the revision process.

I use this particular rubric at several different levels of Portuguese instruction and still struggle with several issues. For instance, it is hard to make students understand that my expectations are different at the 100- and 200- levels (as well as at the beginning and the end of the semester) without "dumbing down" the lower-level rubric. Also, I may need to upgrade to a more professional layout design to accommodate all of the text and formatting. I also still struggle somewhat with students who lose the rubric before they turn in a revision, as I don't have an easy way to keep a copy of each rubric for each assignment and thus can't easily eyeball the original version when assigning a final grade. But in general I am infinitely happier with this rubric than with previous versions. I welcome you to try it and to contribute your own improvements to it.

There are several genres of rubrics included in this chapter: composition, oral presentation (Figure 3), oral interview (Figure 4), final project (Figure 5), and participation (Figure 6), as well as a shorter rubric used for an abbreviated in-class presentation (Figure 7). Each represents the categories and assignment details I prioritize in my classroom.[9] Inevitably, though, instructors will need to create rubrics for other kinds of assignments. My advice is to start by defining the top three, four or five results that the teacher wants students to gain from the assignment. Imagine what a "dream" assignment would look like, and an average one. From there you can begin to craft narrative descriptions for each category. After defining very specifically what an A grade for a specific category would be, I work horizontally within each category, defining first an A-, then a B+, etc. I copy and paste the description from one column to the next as I am creating the rubric so I can be sure that the gradation from one level to the next represents a similar difference of quality. At the end of the process, I read through the descriptions again, from C back to A, to make sure that the gradations are smooth and realistic for my students. (Note: sometimes the A descriptions are not realistic! I want to set the bar HIGH for my students, so I push them quite hard. You may want to reward students for trying their best, and may alter the descriptions accordingly.)

I think you'll find that creating rubrics is an intense exercise that helps

---

[9] I've chosen not to include details for every element of these rubrics, but I would like to emphasize what a revolutionary impact including Portuguese-language extracurriculars as a key component in the participation grade has had. I highly recommend obliging students to get involved with their Portuguese outside of class! Those that can't make events because of scheduling conflicts can always explore the internet for interesting opportunities. See the next chapter of this manual for ways to boost your extracurricular offerings and attendance.

you reflect on your priorities for your students. Not only that, the process of creating a rubric can help to further connect the different pieces of your teaching, from planning to implementation to assessment. A well-designed rubric should help communicate your expectations to students and help them to do their best in your course. I encourage you to use the rubrics included here but also to branch out and create your own. As much as standardized tests can't possibly measure everyone's unique learning progress, a standardized rubric can't possibly define every instructor's unique assessment priorities.

Figure 1.

Composições - Rúbrica 1

1-4 = inaceitável; 5-6 = pobre; 7-8 = satisfatório; 9-10 = excelente

MÉRITO GERAL

1 2 3 4 5 6 7 8 9 10	Ideias originais
1 2 3 4 5 6 7 8 9 10	Organização e formato
1 2 3 4 5 6 7 8 9 10	Sofisticação do conteúdo e sintaxe

ESCRITA

1 2 3 4 5 6 7 8 9 10	Ortografia & pontuação
1 2 3 4 5 6 7 8 9 10	Vocabulário apropriado e variado
1 2 3 4 5 6 7 8 9 10	Concordância
1 2 3 4 5 6 7 8 9 10	Conjugação e tempos verbais
1 2 3 4 5 6 7 8 9 10	Outros aspectos de gramática
	Total (de 80)

COMENTÁRIOS E SUGESTÕES:

Composições - Rúbrica 2

1 = inaceitável; 2 = pobre; 3 = satisfatório; 4 = bom; 5 = excelente

MÉRITO GERAL

1 2 3 4 5	Sofisticação do conteúdo e sintaxe
1 2 3 4 5	Sugestões incorporadas

ESCRITA

1 2 3 4 5	Ortografia & pontuação
1 2 3 4 5	Vocabulário apropriado e variado
1 2 3 4 5	Concordância
1 2 3 4 5	Conjugação e tempos verbais
1 2 3 4 5	Outros aspectos de gramática
1 2 3 4 5	Correção Gramatical

/2 = Nota 2nda versão

Nota Original + Nota 2nda versão = **Notal Final**

COMENTÁRIOS E SUGESTÕES:

Figure 2.

COMPOSITION GRADE

	Outstanding (A)	Excellent (A-)	Very Good (B+)	Good (B)	Satisfactory (B-)	Adequate (C+)	Below Average (C)
Content: 20%	Paper approaches assigned topic in a highly *creative* and *original* way and is very well organized (including a sophisticated central argument and substantial supporting evidence). Shows a logical progression of captivating ideas that are well connected. Overall product is exceptionally polished.	Paper approaches assigned topic in a *creative* and *original* way and is well organized (including a clear central argument and substantial supporting evidence). Shows a logical progression of interesting ideas that are well connected. Overall product is fully developed with little room for improvement.	Paper clearly addresses the prompt and is well organized (including a central argument and solid supporting evidence.) Shows a logical progression of ideas that are well connected. Overall product is well developed.	Paper addresses the prompt and is relatively organized (though the argument and/or supporting evidence could be stronger). Shows a progression of ideas that are well connected. Overall product is pretty well developed.	Paper largely addresses the prompt, but includes a somewhat rough argument and little supporting evidence. Shows several interesting ideas related to the argument. Overall product is engaging but could be further developed.	Paper doesn't entirely address the prompt (and includes an inadequate argument and/or insufficient supporting evidence). Shows a few interesting ideas tangentially related to the argument. Overall product could be further developed.	Paper doesn't address the prompt (and has little or no argument or supporting evidence.) Shows few interesting ideas. Overall product needs much improvement.
Style: 20%	Project tone is highly engaging and and language flows beautifully. Student uses highly sophisticated syntax for his/her level (ex. correct prepositional use, compound sentences and embedded clauses) as well as varied sentence length. Student has clearly not translated directly from another language and style is similar to what a native speaker might produce.	Project tone is engaging and language flows very well. Student uses sophisticated syntax for his/her level as well as varied sentence length. Student has not translated directly from another language and style is nearly of a level that a native speaker might produce.	Project tone is generally engaging and language flows quite well. Student uses relatively sophisticated syntax for his/her level. Student probably did not translate directly from another language. Style approaches typical oral production in the target language.	Project tone is mostly engaging. Student uses somewhat sophisticated syntax for his/her level. Student may have translated directly from another language. Style may be inconsistent but generally comprehensible.	Project tone is somewhat engaging. Student uses varying levels of syntax for his/her level. Student has most likely translated directly from another language. Style is largely made up of chunks of commonly used material and has included some incomprehensible elements.	Project tone is not particularly engaging. Student uses a relatively low level of syntax for his/her level. Student has unsuccessfully translated directly from another language. Style may require additional effort for an untrained native and has included many incomprehensible elements.	Project tone does not draw i the reader at all. Student use low level of syntax for his/h level. There is is no discernable style and inaccuracies regularly inhibi sympathetic reader from understanding the text fully.
Grammar & Mechanics: 20%	Writing shows impressive mastery of gender, number and subject/verb agreement in familiar tenses. Student is obviously comfortable using a wide variety of verb tenses/forms/moods. Shows no negative interference from other languages. Has nearly no errors in punctuation, spelling, capitalization and use of accents.	Writing shows excellent agreement of gender, number and subject/verb in familiar tenses. Student is comfortable using a variety of verb tenses/forms/moods. Shows nearly no negative interference from other languages. Has very few isolated errors in punctuation, spelling, capitalization and use of accents.	Writing shows good agreement of gender, number and subject/verb in familiar tenses. Student is comfortable using several verb tenses/forms/moods. Shows little negative interference from other languages. Has few errors in punctuation, spelling, capitalization and use of accents.	Writing shows adequate agreement of gender, number and subject/verb in familiar tenses. Student is comfortable using a few verb tenses/forms/moods. Shows some negative interference from other languages. Has some errors in punctuation, spelling, capitalization and use of accents (though some are systematic).	Writing shows several problems with agreement of gender, number and subject/verb in familiar tenses. Student is comfortable using only a few verb tenses/forms/moods. Shows a lot of negative interference from other languages. Has many errors in punctuation, spelling, capitalization and use of accents (and some are systematic).	Writing shows several systematic problems with agreement of gender, number and subject/verb in familiar tenses. Student uses only a few verb tenses/forms/moods. Shows some systematic negative interference from other languages. Has many errors in punctuation, spelling, capitalization and use of accents (and many are systematic).	Writing shows many systematic problems with agreement of gender, numbe and subject/verb in familiar tenses. Student uses very limited verb tenses/forms/moods. Shows lot of systematic negative interference from other languages. Has many errors in punctuation, spelling, capitalization and use of accents (and almost all are systematic).
Vocab: 20%	Incorporates a rich variety of original (not found in the textbook), specialized and precise vocabulary to express ideas. Vocabulary is incredibly nuanced and appropriate. Incorporates a rich abundance of adjectives and adverbs. Uses no false cognates.	Incorporates a variety of original (not found in the textbook), specialized vocabulary to express ideas. Vocabulary is nuanced and appropriate. Incorporates a variety of adjectives and adverbs. Uses nearly no false cognates.	Incorporates a variety of new vocabulary to express ideas. Vocabulary is appropriate. Incorporates several adjectives and adverbs. Uses very few false cognates.	Incorporates appropriate vocabulary to express ideas. Incorporates some adjectives and adverbs. Uses few false cognates.	Incorporates mostly appropriate vocabulary to express ideas. Uses several false cognates.	Uses somewhat inappropriate vocabulary to express ideas. Uses many false cognates.	Uses a lot of inappropriate vocabulary to express ideas. Uses enough false cognates to obfuscate meaning even with a sympathetic reader.
Revision: 20%	Student has substantially edited original draft, including ample revisions to *content*, not just grammar. Revision shows intense and detailed edits on style, grammar, mechanics and vocabulary. Student discovered some issues on his/her own and contacted instructor with specific questions about unclear comments.	Student has carefully edited original draft, including ample revisions to *content*, not just grammar. Revision shows detailed edits on style, grammar, mechanics and vocabulary. Student discovered some issues on his/her own and corrected them. Student contacted instructor about unclear comments.	Revision shows detailed edits on style, grammar, mechanics and vocabulary.	Revision shows edits on content, style, grammar, mechanics and vocabulary.	Revision shows edits on content, style, grammar, mechanics and vocabulary (though not necessarily improvements).	Revision shows partial edits on content, style, grammar, mechanics and vocabulary (though many not necessarily improvements).	Revision lacks key edits on content, style, grammar, mechanics and vocabulary (and many "corrections" are not necessarily improvements).

Figure 3.

ORAL PRESENTATION GRADE

	Outstanding (A)	Excellent (A-)	Very Good (B+)	Good (B)	Satisfactory (B-)	Adequate (C+)	Below Average (C)
Content: 20%	Presentation has a clear, concise and sophisticated argument about an engaging topic. It is very detailed and comprehensive while fitting perfectly into time limit and is linguistically ideal for its audience.	Presentation has a clear and concise argument about an interesting topic. It is detailed and comprehensive while fitting into time limit and is linguistically appropriate for its audience.	Presentation has a relatively clear and concise argument. It is mostly detailed and comprehensive while nearly fitting into time limit and is mostly linguistically appropriate for its audience.	Presentation has a somewhat clear and concise argument. It could use more detail and/or could be more comprehensive and is sometimes linguistically appropriate for its audience.	Presentation does not have a clear and/or concise argument. It clearly needs to be more detailed and/or more comprehensive (and these categories could be better balanced) and is not always linguistically appropriate for its audience.	Presentation has no argument. It lacks detail and content (and these categories are not entirely balanced) and is often linguistically inappropriate for its audience.	Even the presentation topic (much less the argument) is unclear. It lacks detail and content (and these categories are not at all balanced) and is generally linguistically inappropriate for its audienc
Preparation: 20%	Presentation is very clearly organized and is communicated entirely orally ("no reading allowed."). Accompanying materials (prezi, .ppt, youtube, etc.) are of excellent quality and enhance presentation while not overwhelming the oral component. Visual media include few written words – with no typos. Student has clearly practiced many times.	Presentation is clearly organized and student rarely checks his/her notes for prompts. Accompanying materials (prezi, .ppt, youtube, etc.) are of very good quality and enhance presentation. Visual media include few written words – with very few typos. Student has clearly practiced.	Presentation is well organized and student sometimes checks his/her notes for prompts. Accompanying materials (prezi, .ppt, youtube, etc.) are of good quality. Visual media include some large chunks of text (but with few typos). Student has most likely practiced.	Presentation is relatively well organized and student regularly checks his/her notes for prompts or language. Accompanying materials (prezi, .ppt, youtube, etc.) are of mostly good quality. Visual media include some large chunks of text with several typos. Student has most likely not practiced enough.	Presentation could be better organized and student sometimes reads from his/her notes. Accompanying materials (prezi, ppt, youtube, etc.) are of adequate quality. Visual media include many large chunks of text with many typos. Student has not practiced enough.	Presentation is poorly organized and student mostly reads from his/her notes. Accompanying materials (prezi, ppt, youtube, etc.) are of sub-par quality. Visual media are actively distracting from presentation and/or unrelated to oral content. Student has clearly not practiced enough.	Presentation is completely unorganized and student regularly gets lost and/or tongue-tied. There are no accompanying materials. Student has clearly not practiced at all.
Interaction: 20%	Student appears very comfortable in front of audience; s/he makes seamless transitions, visual contact and appropriate gestures. Student makes a genuine effort to engage other students in question/answer sessions: s/he is able to elegantly answer questions.	Student appears comfortable in front of audience; s/he makes clear transitions, adequate visual contact and appropriate gestures. Student makes an effort to engage other students in question/answer sessions: s/he is able to answer questions..	Student appears mostly comfortable in front of audience; s/he makes mostly clear transitions, some visual contact and some appropriate gestures. Student makes a limited effort to engage other students in question/answer sessions: s/he is often able to answer questions.	Student appears somewhat comfortable in front of audience; s/he makes some clear transitions, and occasionally awkward visual contact and/or gestures. Student makes little effort to engage other students in question/answer sessions; s/he is sometimes able to answer questions.	Student does not appear entirely comfortable in front of audience; s/he makes few clear transitions, little visual contact and few appropriate gestures. Student makes very little effort to engage other students in question/ answer sessions; s/he is occasionally able to answer questions.	Student appears somewhat uncomfortable in front of audience; s/he makes rough transitions, little visual conta and/or few appropriate gestures. Student makes almost no effort to engage other students in question/ answer sessions; s/he is rarely able to adequately answer questions.	Student appears uncomfortable in front of audience; s/he generally mak rough transitions, no visual contact and few appropriate gestures Student makes no effort to engage other students in question/answer sessions; s/he is never able to adequately answer questions.
Grammar: 20%	Shows excellent command of multiple verb tenses and high rate of gender/number agreement. Is able to recognize most errors and correct them immediately.	Shows very good command of multiple verb tenses and high rate of gender/number agreement. Is able to recognize some errors and correct them immediately.	Shows good command of multiple verb tenses and quite high rate of gender/number agreement. Is able to recognize a few errors and correct them immediately.	Shows good command of several verb tenses and good rate of gender/number agreement.	Shows adequate command of two or fewer verb tenses and an adequate rate of gender/number agreement.	Shows limited command of two or fewer verb tenses and an adequate rate of gender/number agreement.	Shows limited command of few verb tenses and a limited rate of gender/number agreement.
Pronunciation & Intonation: 20%	Student has clearly practiced phonomes that have been a challenge throughout the course. S/he has no pronunciations which might impede understanding by a native speaker. Student uses native-like intonations in his/her expression.	Student has practiced some phonomes that have been a challenge throughout the course. S/he has nearly no pronunciations which might impede understanding by a native speaker. Student uses very accurate intonations in his/her expression.	Student has few pronunciations which might impede understanding by a native speaker. Student uses generally accurate intonations in his/her expression.	Student has some pronunciations which might impede understanding by a native speaker. Student often uses accurate intonations in his/her expression.	Student has several pronunciations which might impede understanding by a native speaker. Student only occasionally uses accurate intonations in his/her expression.	Student has many pronunciations which might impede understanding by a native speaker. Student occasaionlly uses accurate intonations in his/her expression.	Student has many pronunciations which might impede understanding by a sympathetic listener. Student rarely uses accurate intonations in his/her expression.

Figure 4.

ORAL INTERVIEW GRADE

	Outstanding (A)	Excellent (A-)	Very Good (B+)	Good (B)	Satisfactory (B-)	Adequate (C+)	Below Average (C)
Vocabulary: 20%	Student has an abundance of rich vocabulary to express meaning without excessive frustration. Student always uses vocabulary correctly and never incorporates English or Spanish words in an attempt to be understood.	Student has more than sufficient vocabulary to express meaning without excessive frustration. Student usually uses vocabulary correctly and generally does not incorporate English or Spanish words in an attempt to be understood.	Student has sufficient vocabulary to express meaning without excessive frustration. Student generally uses vocabulary correctly and rarely incorporates English or Spanish words in an attempt to be understood.	Student usually has sufficient vocabulary to express meaning. Student sometimes uses vocabulary incorrectly and occasionally incorporates English or Spanish words in an attempt to be understood.	Student sometimes has sufficient vocabulary to express meaning. Student often uses vocabulary incorrectly and often incorporates English or Spanish words in an attempt to be understood.	Student often has insufficient vocabulary to express meaning. Student regularly uses vocabulary incorrectly and regularly incorporates English or Spanish words an attempt to be understood.	Student generally has insufficient vocabulary to express meaning. Student has very little control over vocabulary and a large portion of his/her speech is borrowed from English or Spanish in an attempt to be understood.
Preparation: 20%	Student has clearly practiced many times and dominates the necessary vocabulary to express nuanced meanings. Student has obviously thought through potential questions and answers and has planned highly coherent responses that are easily expressed with his/her level of language.	Student has practiced many times and has learned necessary vocabulary to express meanings. Student has thought through potential questions and answers and has planned coherent responses that can be clearly expressed with his/her level of language.	Student has practiced and has learned most necessary vocabulary to express meanings. Student has thought through some potential questions and answers and has planned some coherent responses that can be expressed with his/her level of language.	Student has practiced (though not enough) and has learned some vocabulary necessary to express meanings. Student has given some thought to potential questions and answers and has planned some responses that can be expressed with some difficulty with his/her level of language.	Student has practiced a bit (though certainly not enough) and has learned limited vocabulary necessary to express meanings. Student has given some thought to potential questions but not to answers and has planned only a few partially coherent responses that can be expressed with difficulty with his/her level of language.	Student has not practiced sufficiently and has learned little vocabulary necessary to express meanings. Student has given little thought to potential questions. Somewhat incoherent responses are expressed with difficulty with his/her level of language.	Student has not practiced at all and has not learned adequate vocabulary necessary to express meanings. Student has not thought through potential questions or answers. Responses are mostly incoherent and expressed with great difficulty with his/her level of language.
Interaction: 20%	Student appears very comfortable in front of interviewer; s/he makes seamless transitions, visual contact and appropriate gestures. Student makes a genuine effort to engage interviewer in question/answer sessions: s/he is able to answer questions elegantly and completely as well as create many original questions for the interviewer in order to continue the conversation.	Student appears comfortable in front of interviewer; s/he makes clear transitions and familiar visual contact and gestures. Student makes an effort to engage interviewer in question/answer sessions: s/he is able to answer questions completely as well as create many questions for the interviewer in order to continue the conversation.	Student appears mostly comfortable in front of interviewer; s/he makes mostly clear transitions, and mostly appropriate visual contact and/or gestures. Student makes a limited effort to engage interviewer in question/answer sessions: s/he is able to answer questions (mostly) as well as create questions for the interviewer but occasionally allows conversation to get somewhat stilted.	Student appears somewhat comfortable in front of interviewer; s/he makes some clear transitions, and occasionally awkward visual contact and/or gestures. Student makes little effort to engage interviewer in question/answer sessions: s/he is able to answer questions (sometimes) as well as create some questions for the interviewer but often allows conversation to get stilted.	Student appears somewhat uncomfortable in front of interviewer; s/he makes few clear transitions, visual contact and/or appropriate gestures. Student makes very little effort to engage interviewer in question/answer sessions: s/he is seldom able to answer questions or create sufficient questions for the interviewer to keep conversation from getting stilted.	Student appears uncomfortable in front of interviewer; s/he makes rough transitions, little visual contact and/or few appropriate gestures. Student makes almost no effort to engage interviewer in question/ answer sessions; s/he has difficulty answering questions and/or creating questions for his/her interviewer.	Student appears very uncomfortable in front of interviewer; s/he makes rough transitions, no visual contact and/or few appropriate gestures. Student makes no effort to engage interviewer in question/answer sessions; s/he is not able to answer or create questions.
Grammar: 20%	Shows excellent command of multiple verb tenses and high rate of gender/number agreement. Is able to recognize most errors and correct them immediately.	Shows very good command of multiple verb tenses and high rate of gender/number agreement. Is able to recognize some errors and correct them immediately.	Shows good command of multiple verb tenses and quite high rate of gender/number agreement. Is able to recognize a few errors and correct them immediately.	Shows good command of several verb tenses and good rate of gender/number agreement.	Shows adequate command of two or fewer verb tenses and an adequate rate of gender/number agreement.	Shows limited command of two or fewer verb tenses and an adequate rate of gender/number agreement.	Shows limited command of few verb tenses and a limited rate of gender/number agreement.
Pronunciation & Intonation: 20%	Student has clearly practiced phonomes that have been a challenge throughout the course. S/he has no pronunciations which might impede understanding by a native speaker. Student uses native-like intonations in his/her expression.	Student has practiced some phonomes that have been a challenge throughout the course. S/he has nearly no pronunciations which might impede understanding by a native speaker. Student uses very accurate intonations in his/her expression.	Student has few pronunciations which might impede understanding by a native speaker. Student uses generally accurate intonations in his/her expression.	Student has some pronunciations which might impede understanding by a native speaker. Student often uses accurate intonations in his/her expression.	Student has several pronunciations which might impede understanding by a native speaker. Student sometimes uses accurate intonations in his/her expression.	Student has many pronunciations which might impede understanding by a native speaker. Student only occassionally uses accurate intonations in his/her expression.	Student has many pronunciations which might impede understanding by a native speaker. Student rarely uses accurate intonations in his/her expression.

Figure 5.

	Outstanding (A)	Excellent (A-)	Very Good (B+)	Good (B)	Satisfactory (B-)	Adequate (C+)	Below Average (C)
Preparation: 20% *Research* *Questions* *Practice* *Logistics*	Student has conducted very extensive preliminary research to prepare for the interview. Student has prepared a comprehensive list of questions (including key vocabulary) and detailed related follow-up questions and has put great thought into the structure of the interview. Student has met with a partner to practice the interview with enough time to make extensive edits to first version of interview format. Student team has contacted interviewee in a courteous manner within a comfortable amount of time to plan interview.	Student has conducted extensive preliminary research to prepare for the interview. Student has prepared a list of questions (including key vocabulary) and detailed follow-up questions and has put considerable thought into the structure of the interview. Student has met with a partner to practice the interview and has made appropriate edits to first version of interview format. Student team has contacted interviewee in a courteous manner to plan interview.	Student has conducted quality preliminary research to prepare for the interview. Student has prepared a list of questions and follow-up questions and has put much thought into the structure of the interview. Student has met with a partner to practice the interview but has made few edits to first version of interview format. Student team has contacted interviewee to plan interview.	Student has conducted some preliminary research to prepare for the interview. Student has prepared a list of questions and some follow-up questions and has put some thought into the structure of the interview. Student has met with a partner to practice the interview. Student has contacted interviewee (on his own) in a somewhat courteous manner to plan interview.	Student has conducted limited preliminary research to prepare for the interview. Student has prepared a list of questions and has put some thought into the structure of the interview. Student has met with a partner to practice the interview but provides no proof. Student has contacted interviewee (on his own) in a somewhat abrupt and/or rushed manner to plan interview.	Student should have conducted more preliminary research to prepare for the interview. S/he has prepared a slapdash list of questions. Student has not practiced with his/her partner. Student and/or student team has contacted interviewee in an abrupt and/or rushed manner to plan interview.	Student conducted no preliminary research to prepare for the interview. S/he has not prepared an adequate list of questions. S/he did not contact partner to practice and required assitance from instructor to contact interviewee.
Interaction: 20% *Spontaneity* *Register* *Intercultural competency* *Negotiation of Meaning*	Student appears highly comfortable in front of interviewee; s/he makes very fluid transitions, visual contact and appropriate gestures. Student makes a genuine effort to actively engage interviewer in question/answer sessions. S/he always uses an appropriate register and is easily able to mirror subtle nuances in conversation. Student shows no need for strategies to clarify him/herself and asks detailed follow-up questions in order to fully understand the interviewee.	Student appears comfortable in front of interviewee; s/he makes quite fluid transitions, visual contact and appropriate gestures. Student makes an real effort to engage interviewer in question/answer sessions. S/he usually uses an appropriate register and is able to mirror subtle nuances in conversation. Student successfully uses strategies to clarify him/herself and asks detailed follow-up questions in order to understand the interviewee.	Student appears mostly comfortable in front of interviewee; s/he makes mostly fluid transitions, visual contact and appropriate gestures. Student makes an effort to engage interviewer in question/answer sessions. S/he regularly uses an appropriate register. Student uses largely successful strategies to clarify him/herself and asks follow-up questions in order to understand the interviewee.	Student appears somewhat comfortable in front of interviewee; s/he makes some fluid transitions, visual contact and appropriate gestures. Student makes some effort to engage interviewer in question/answer sessions. S/he uses a mostly appropriate register. Student uses somewhat successful strategies to clarify him/herself and occasionally asks follow-up questions in order to understand the interviewee.	Student appears somewhat uncomfortable in front of interviewee; s/he makes few clear transitions, visual contact and appropriate gestures. Student makes a limited effort to engage interviewer in question/answer sessions. S/he sometimes uses an appropriate register. Student uses somewhat poor strategies to clarify him/herself and rarely asks follow-up questions in order to understand the interviewee.	Student appears uncomfortable in front of interviewee; s/he makes rough transitions, nearly no visual contact and few appropriate gestures. Student makes a very limited effort to engage interviewer in question /answer sessions. S/he generally does not use an appropriate register. Student uses quite poor strategies to clarify him/herself and does not ask follow-up questions in order to understand the interviewee.	Student appears quite uncomfortable in front of interviewee; s/he makes no transitions, no visual contact and few appropriate gestures. Student makes nearly no effort to engage interviewer in question/answer sessions. S/he never uses an appropriate register. Student does not bother to clarify him/herself a does not ask follow-up comprehension questions.
Technical: Speaking 20% *Grammar* *Pronunciation & Intonation* *Syntax*	Shows excellent command of multiple verb tenses/modes and a very high rate of gender/number agreement. Has nearly no errors. His/her pronunciation is impeccable. Sentence structure is almost always syntactically correct; s/he shows serious effort toward producing a variety of complex constructions.	Shows excellent command of several verb tenses and high rate of gender/number agreement. Is able to recognize some errors and correct them immediately. S/he has a nearly native pronunciation. Sentence structure is generally syntactically correct; s/he shows an effort toward producing a variety of complex constructions.	Shows very good command of several verb tenses and quite high rate of gender/number agreement. Is able to recognize a few errors and correct them immediately. Student has no pronunciations which might impede understanding by a native speaker. Sentence structure is mostly syntactically correct; s/he shows some effort toward producing a variety of complex constructions.	Shows good command of several verb tenses and an adequate rate of gender/number agreement. Student has nearly no pronunciations which might impede understanding by a native speaker. Sentence structure is mostly syntactically correct.	Shows good command of two or fewer verb tenses and an adequate rate of gender/number agreement. Student has a few pronunciations which might impede understanding by a native speaker. Sentence structure is somewhat syntactically correct.	Shows adequate command of two or fewer verb tenses and a limited rate of gender/number agreement. Student has several pronunciations which might impede understanding by a native speaker. Sentence structure is somewhat syntactically incorrect.	Shows limited command of two or fewer verb tenses and a quite limited rate of gender/number agreement. Student has many pronunciations which might impede understanding by a native speaker. Sentence structure is often syntactically incorrect.
Technical: Writing 20% *Grammar* *Mechanics* *Syntax* *Vocab*	Writing shows mastery of gender, number and subject/verb agreement in familiar tenses. Student uses a wide variety of verb tenses/forms/moods. Shows nearly no negative interference from other languages. Nearly no errors in punctuation, spelling, capitalization and/or use of accents.	Writing shows excellent agreement of gender, number and subject/verb in familiar tenses. Student uses a variety of verb tenses/forms/moods. Shows very little negative interference from other languages. Very few isolated errors in punctuation, spelling, capitalization and use of accents.	Writing shows good agreement of gender, number and subject/verb in familiar tenses. Student uses several verb tenses/forms/moods. Shows little negative interference from other languages. Few errors in punctuation, spelling, capitalization and use of accents.	Writing shows adequate agreement of gender, number and subject/verb in familiar tenses. Student uses a few verb tenses/forms. Shows some negative interference from other languages. Some errors in punctuation, spelling, capitalization and use of accents (though some are systematic).	Writing shows several problems with agreement of gender, number and subject/verb in familiar tenses. Student uses only a few verb tenses/forms. Shows negative interference from other languages. Several errors in punctuation, spelling, capitalization and use of accents (and many are systematic).	Writing shows many problems with agreement of gender, number and subject/verb in familiar tenses. Student uses very limited verb tenses/forms. Shows many negative interference from other languages. Many errors in punctuation, spelling, capitalization and use of accents (and most are systematic).	Writing is difficult to understand due to problems with agreement of gender, number and subject/verb in familiar tenses. Even verbs in the present tense show regular breakdown. Shows negative interference from Spanish. Many errors in punctuation, spelling, capitalization and use of accents (and almost all are systematic).
Follow-through: 20% *Portfolio* *Reflection* *Gratitude*	Student submitted a complete portfolio on time and entirely in Portuguese. Student reflection details a deep awareness of intercultural difference and details many personal / intellectual epiphanies that resulted from the project in an organized manner. Student submitted a thoughtful and original thank-you note that	Student submitted a complete portfolio on time and entirely in Portuguese (though with some prompting). Student reflection shows a heightened awareness of intercultural difference and details a few personal / intellectual epiphanies that resulted from the project. Student submitted a thoughtful	Student submitted a complete portfolio slightly late and/or with instructor prompting. Student reflection discusses a few personal / intellectual epiphanies that resulted from the project. Student submitted a nice thank-you note.	Student submitted a nearly complete portfolio. Student reflection details the perspective gained from the interview. Student submitted an adequate thank-you note.	Student submitted a nearly complete portfolio slightly late or with instructor prompting. Student reflection connects the interview experience to the student's learning. Student submitted a rushed thank-you note separate from the portfolio and/or after instructor prompting.	Student submitted a nearly complete portfolio late. Student reflection richly details the content of the interview. Student submitted an offensive thank-you note.	Student submitted a partially complete portfolio late. The journalistic essay partially narrates the content of the interview. Student did not submit a thank-you note.

Figure 6.

PARTICIPATION GRADE

	Outstanding (A)	Excellent (A-)	Very Good (B+)	Good (B)	Satisfactory (B-)	Adequate (C+)	Below Average (C)
Attendance: 20%	Never misses class and always arrives on time.	Misses nearly no class and almost always arrives on time. Contacts instructor about - and creates a plan of action to address - any planned or unexpected absences.	Misses very little class and usually arrives on time. Contacts instructor about - and helps to create a plan of action to address - any planned or unexpected absences.	Misses very little class and/or often arrives on time. Contacts instructor about any planned or unexpected absences.	Occasionally misses class and/or sometimes arrives tardy (but without causing a disruption).	Regularly misses class and/or often arrives late (but without causing a disruption).	Often misses class and/or often arrives late.
Preparation: 20%	Is very diligent about assignments and due dates as well as verbal & written instructions. Is always ready to help explain concepts and eager to ask informed questions from assigned pages.	Is usually diligent about assignments and due dates as well as verbal & written instructions. Is usually ready to help explain concepts and usually able to ask informed questions from assigned pages.	Is often diligent about assignments and due dates as well as verbal & written instructions. Is often ready to help explain concepts and often able to ask informed questions from assigned pages.	Is sometimes diligent about assignments and due dates as well as verbal & written instructions. Is sometimes ready to help explain concepts and sometimes able to ask informed questions from assigned pages.	Is sometimes careless about assignments and due dates as well as verbal & written instructions. Is occasionally ready to help explain concepts and occasionally able to ask informed questions from assigned pages.	Is often careless about assignments and due dates as well as verbal & written instructions. Is rarely ready to help explain concepts and rarely able to ask informed questions from assigned pages.	Is usually careless about assignments and due dates as well as verbal & written instructions. Is uncooperative in explaining concepts and asking informed questions from assigned pages.
Contributions: 20%	Enthusiastically and respectfully volunteers engaging comments many times per session. Noticeably improves classroom dynamic with questions/ comments/etc.	Enthusiastically and respectfully volunteers comments many times per session. Often improves classroom dynamic with questions/comments/etc .	Enthusiastically volunteers comments several times per session. Sometimes improves classroom dynamic with questions/ comments/etc.	Volunteers comments several times per session. Sometimes improves classroom dynamic with questions/comments/etc .	Volunteers comments occasionally. Does not significantly improve classroom dynamic with questions/comments/etc.	Must be called upon in order to elicit active participation. Occasionally disrupts classroom dynamic with questions/comments/etc.	Must be called upon in order to elicit ambivalent participation. Regularly disrupts classroom dynamic with questions/comments/etc .
Attitude: 20%	Arrives on time, with a positive attitude and enthusiastic to learn. Is actively, respectfully and positively engaged with classroom. Is not distracted by unrelated work, media, or chit-chat.	Arrives mostly on time, with a positive attitude and ready to learn. Is usually actively, respectfully and positively engaged with classroom. Is rarely distracted by unrelated work, media, or chit-chat.	Arrives mostly on time. Is usually engaged with classroom, though sometimes too ill / tired to do so actively. Is usually not distracted by unrelated work, media, or chit-chat.	Arrives mostly on time. Is often engaged with classroom, though often too ill / tired to engage actively. Is sometimes distracted by unrelated work, media, or chit-chat.	Occasionally arrives late. Is usually interested, though regularly too ill / tired to engage actively. Is often distracted by unrelated work, media, or chit-chat.	Regularly arrives late. Shows an ambivalent attitude and is not always enthusiastic to learn. Is regularly distracted by unrelated work, media, or chit-chat.	Always arrives late. Shows a negative attitude and is rarely enthusiastic to learn. Is generally not positivesly engaged with classroom. Is too distracted by unrelated work, media or chit-chat to perform at an acceptable level.
Immersion: 20%	Speaks only in target language with peers during groupwork. Makes an outstanding effort to engage in target language outside of classroom (bate-papos, lectures, office hours, teletandem, target-language events, online resources, etc.)	Usually speaks only in target language with peers during groupwork. Makes a real effort to engage in target language outside of classroom (bate-papos, , lectures, teletandem, target-language events, online resources, etc.).	Mostly speaks only in target language with peers during groupwork. Makes an effort to engage in target language outside of classroom (bate-papos, lectures, teletandem, target-language events, online resources, etc.).	Sometimes has to be reminded to speak only in target language with peers during groupwork. Makes a limited effort to engage in target language outside of classroom (bate-papos, lectures, teletandem, target-language events, online resources, etc.).	Often has to be reminded to speak only in target language with peers during groupwork. Makes very little effort to engage in target language outside of classroom (bate-papos, lectures, teletandem, target-language events, online resources, etc.).	Regularly speaks only in English with peers during groupwork. Makes almost no effort to engage in target language outside of classroom (bate-papos, lectures, teletandem, target-language events, online resources, etc.).	Makes no effort to speak in target language with peers during groupwork. Makes no effort to engage in target language outside of classroom (bate-papos, lectures teletandem, target-language events, online resources, etc.).

Figure 7[10]

	Preparation	Content	Interaction	Visual Aid	Grammar
A	Extensive research and detail on a fascinating topic	Outstandingly professional and/or creative presentation; extremely well-organized	Delivered in a stunning and poised manner	Superior	Almost no grammatical errors
A-	Excellent research and detail on a captivating topic	Highly polished and/or creative presentation with excellent structure and organization	Delivered in an impressive and confident manner	Excellent	Only a few minor grammatical errors
B+	Very good research and detail on an very interesting topic	Sophisticated presentation with commendable structure and organization	Delivered in an effective and composed manner	Very good	Some minor grammatical errors
B	Good research and detail on a noteworthy topic	Effective presentation with successful structure and organization	Delivered in a suitable yet reticent manner	Good	Infrequent major and some minor grammatical errors
B-	Satisfactory research and detail on a trivial topic	Sufficient presentation with passable structure and organization	Delivered in a satisfactory and uncertain manner	Adequate	Some major and many minor grammatical errors
C+	Inadequate research and detail on an irrelevant topic	Disappointing presentation with inadequate structure and organization	Delivered in a stunning and insecure manner	Disappointing	Regular major and minor errors that affect communication

[10] Special thanks to Amy George-Hirons, Director of the Spanish Language Program at Tulane University, for sharing her rubric for in-class essays. I have adapted it slightly for use in my own classroom.

Figure 8

…ncias de raça.

A- A

COMPOSITION GRADE

	Outstanding (A)	Excellent (A-)	Very Good (B+)	Good (B)	Satisfactory (B-)	Adequate (C+)	Below Average (C)
Content: 20%	Paper approaches assigned topic in a highly *creative* and *original* way and is very well organized (including a sophisticated central argument and substantial supporting evidence). Shows a logical progression of captivating ideas that are well connected. Overall product is exceptionally polished.	Paper approaches assigned topic in a *creative* and *original* way and is well organized (including a clear central argument and substantial supporting evidence). Shows a logical progression of interesting ideas that are well connected. Overall product is fully developed with little room for improvement.	Paper clearly addresses the prompt and is well organized (including a central argument and solid supporting evidence.) Shows a logical progression of ideas that are well connected. Overall product is well developed.	Paper addresses the prompt and is relatively organized (though the argument and/or supporting evidence could be stronger). Shows a progression of ideas that are well connected. Overall product is pretty well developed.	Paper largely addresses the prompt, but includes a somewhat rough argument and little supporting evidence. Shows several interesting ideas related to the argument. Overall product is engaging but could be further developed.	Paper doesn't entirely address the prompt (and includes an inadequate argument and/or insufficient supporting evidence). Shows a few interesting ideas tangentially related to the argument. Overall product could be further developed.	Paper doesn't address the prompt (and has little or no argument or supporting evidence.) Shows few interesting ideas. Overall product needs much improvement.
Style: 20%	Project tone is highly engaging and and language flows beautifully. Student uses highly sophisticated syntax for his/her level (ex. correct prepositional use, compound sentences and embedded clauses) as well as varied sentence length. Student has clearly not translated directly from another language and style is similar to what a native speaker might produce.	Project tone is engaging and language flows very well. Student uses sophisticated syntax for his/her level as well as varied sentence length. Student has not translated directly from another language and style is nearly of a level that a native speaker might produce.	Project tone is generally engaging and language flows quite well. Student uses relatively sophisticated syntax for his/her level. Student probably did not translate directly from another language. Style approaches typical oral production in the target language.	Project tone is mostly engaging. Student uses somewhat sophisticated syntax for his/her level. Student may have translated directly from another language. Style may be inconsistent but generally comprehensible.	Project tone is somewhat engaging. Student uses varying levels of syntax for his/her level. Student has most likely translated directly from another language. Style is largely made up of chunks of commonly used material and has included some incomprehensible elements.	Project tone is not particularly engaging. Student uses a relatively low level of syntax for his/her level. Student has unsuccessfully translated directly from another language. Style may require additional effort for an untrained native and has included many incomprehensible elements.	Project tone does not draw i[n] the reader at all. Student use[s] low level of syntax for his/h[er] level. There is is no discernable style and inaccuracies regularly inhib[it] sympathetic reader from understanding the text fully.
Grammar & Mechanics: 20%	Writing shows impressive mastery of gender, number and subject/verb agreement in familiar tenses. Student is obviously comfortable using a wide variety of verb tenses/forms/moods. Shows no negative interference from other languages. Has nearly no errors in punctuation, spelling, capitalization and use of accents.	Writing shows excellent agreement of gender, number and subject/verb in familiar tenses. Student is comfortable using a variety of verb tenses/forms/moods. Shows nearly no negative interference from other languages. Has very few isolated errors in punctuation, spelling, capitalization and use of accents.	Writing shows good agreement of gender, number and subject/verb in familiar tenses. Student is comfortable using several verb tenses/forms/moods. Shows little negative interference from other languages. Has few errors in punctuation, spelling, capitalization and use of accents. cuidado: ser/estar	Writing shows adequate agreement of gender, number and subject/verb in familiar tenses. Student is comfortable using a few verb tenses/forms/moods. Shows some negative interference from other languages. Has some errors in punctuation, spelling, capitalization and use of accents (though some are systematic).	Writing shows several problems with agreement of gender, number and subject/verb in familiar tenses. Student is comfortable using only a few verb tenses/forms/moods. Shows a lot of negative interference from other languages. Has many errors in punctuation, spelling, capitalization and use of accents (and some are systematic).	Writing shows several systematic problems with agreement of gender, number and subject/verb in familiar tenses. Student uses only a few verb tenses/forms/moods. Shows some systematic negative interference from other languages. Has many errors in punctuation, spelling, capitalization and use of accents (and many are systematic).	Writing shows many systematic problems with agreement of gender, numb[er] and subject/verb in familiar tenses. Student uses very limited verb tenses/forms/moods. Shows lot of systematic negative interference from other languages. Has many errors in punctuation, spelling, capitalization and use of accents (and almost all are systematic).
Vocab: 20%	Incorporates a rich variety of original (not found in the textbook), specialized and precise vocabulary to express ideas. Vocabulary is incredibly nuanced and appropriate. Incorporates a rich abundance of adjectives and adverbs. Uses no false cognates.	Incorporates a variety of original (not found in the textbook), specialized vocabulary to express ideas. Vocabulary is nuanced and appropriate. Incorporates a variety of adjectives and adverbs. Uses nearly no false cognates. urbanização, modernização, neoliberais	Incorporates a variety of new vocabulary to express ideas. Vocabulary is appropriate. Incorporates several adjectives and adverbs. Uses very few false cognates.	Incorporates appropriate vocabulary to express ideas. Incorporates some adjectives and adverbs. Uses few false cognates.	Incorporates mostly appropriate vocabulary to express ideas. Uses several false cognates.	Uses somewhat inappropriate vocabulary to express ideas. Uses many false cognates.	Uses a lot of inappropriate vocabulary to express ideas. Uses enough false cognates to obfuscate meaning even with a sympathetic reader.
Revision: 20%	Student has substantially edited original draft, including ample revisions to *content*, not just grammar. Revision shows intense and detailed edits on style, grammar, mechanics and vocabulary. Student discovered some issues on his/her own and contacted instructor with specific questions about unclear comments.	Student has carefully edited original draft, including ample revisions to *content*, not just grammar. Revision shows detailed edits on style, grammar, mechanics and vocabulary. Student discovered some issues on his/her own and corrected them. Student contacted instructor about unclear comments.	Revision shows detailed edits on style, grammar, mechanics and vocabulary.	Revision shows edits on content, style, grammar, mechanics and vocabulary.	Revision shows edits on content, style, grammar, mechanics and vocabulary (though not necessarily improvements).	Revision shows partial edits on content, style, grammar, mechanics and vocabulary (though many not necessarily improvements).	Revision lacks key edits on content, style, grammar, mechanics and vocabulary (and many "corrections" are not necessarily improvements).

2.5 CREATIVE CURRICULA: CRAFTING 'COMMUNITIES' INSIDE AND OUTSIDE THE CLASSROOM

Megwen May Loveless
Tulane University

ACTFL's World-Readiness Standards for Learning Languages, or "the 5 C's," as they have come to be known, include communication, cultures, connections, comparisons and communities. The 5 C's are meant to dialogue with one another, but the reality is that certain "C's can be more difficult than others to incorporate into different teaching environments. This chapter focuses on various strategies for incorporating "communities" into the language classroom. According to ACTFL, the "communities" category recommends that students participate in multilingual communities at home and in the world, both within and beyond the school setting, and that they learn the lifelong skill of using language as a tool to enrich their lives by building and maintaining relationships.

As is clear from its prominence in the ACTFL framework, exposing our language students to the larger language community is an essential part of learning, one that will deeply enhance our students' linguistic and cultural proficiency. Yet most language classrooms continue to limit student exposure to "communities" to films or YouTube videos, because providing access to a constantly changing language community can seem overly daunting. This chapter attempts to introduce a few strategies to incorporate "communities" into regular classroom practice. Inevitably, every locale, every institution, every instructor and every student contribute a myriad of differences that ultimately create a vastly diverse context for each classroom, so in this chapter I detail a series of diverse initiatives. Each can enhance units already built into the local curricula or can become modules around which new curricula are structured. I highly encourage instructors to be creative in adapting these suggestions and to try different iterations over time to see what is the best fit for their classrooms. For ease, I will feature several different kinds of community interactions; each might be more or less practical for different readers depending on their geographical, curricular or financial possibilities. I have tried to provide a wide array of programs and, again, urge instructors to adapt these models where and when necessary.

Teletandem: Conversational Partner Program

Teletandem is an amazing resource developed by João Telles at the Universidade Estadual de São Paulo.[11] It is becoming increasingly well-

[11] Contact: http://www.teletandembrasil.org/home.asp

known and popular at a variety of institutions across the world. It is essentially a pen-pal program that utilizes twenty-first century technology to create real-time conversational interactions between two partners. Generally, each partner is learning a language in which his/her partner has native fluency. The most typical interaction is a weekly or twice-weekly 50-60 minute conversation on a Skype-like interface, in which 20-25 minutes are dedicated to language #1, 20-25 minutes to language #2, and 5-10 minutes are dedicated to a "recap" session on either side, where each local project leader facilitates a conversation about linguistic or socio-cultural issues that came up during the session.

Part of what makes these partnerships successful is that each partner pair develops a relationship with each over the entire course of the semester, cultivating an environment of intimacy and trust. One recent student said: "It's really a bonding experience in the way that we help each other, and I really feel that I have developed a friend." Conversations are not scripted, though students are encouraged to bring questions each week to help direct the dialogue. Some project leaders are open to providing mini-content (for example, a short video clip) that might steer students toward practicing specialized vocabulary, but in general students discover common interests and allow the discussion to build quite organically. As they chat, students often pull up numerous web resources, including dictionaries and YouTube, and share material via Facebook and email. They take notes on new vocabulary and chuckle at new words or concepts. Students enjoy learning in an informal way, much as we learn in our native languages. Another student noted, "Being able to see improvement week-to-week and incorporate new vocabulary has been confidence-boosting and helpful. It's been a special part of the course thus far." Students agree at the start of the semester on the best way to help each other linguistically, and most often correct each other during the course of the conversation. Because these conversations mimic how language is learned in the real world, students are able to apply what they learn in the classroom in a more natural environment than instructors can generally offer, leading to exciting epiphanies. One enthusiastic participant noted at the end of a 12-week Teletandem pilot project: "One thing that surprised me was how at times I find that I know more Portuguese than I thought I did."

Teletandem: What You Need to Know

The most practical setting in which to participate is a computer lab that has stations set up at computers with headphones, cameras and the necessary software already installed.[12] In the case of an institution without a computer

---

[12] In the Fall of 2015 some Teletandem programs experimented with a new platform, "Zoom," which improved interactions as well as international online discussions with

lab or language lab, the instructor should request a large room (or several rooms in close proximity) with relatively dead acoustics that has/have a good wifi connection. Students could bring their own laptops and/or smart phones or tablets and headphones. There is potential for students to call from remote locales (their dorm rooms or homes, for instance), but I have found that remote calls can complicate the interactions because there is no one else nearby to facilitate troubleshooting in the event of technology complications or absentee partners.[13]

Because Teletandem relies on participating students on either end, it can be challenging to sync schedules perfectly; often semesters do not coincide. There is a not insignificant risk of strikes in Brazilian public universities and there are often problems matching class times or days between universities, especially when staggered day-light savings schedules can mean three-hour time differences over the course of one semester. There may be delays in establishing meeting times because North American universities do not have enough registration information to set up interactions until after the new semester has begun (meaning less time to generate a group of partners in Brazil) and semesters may not sync up perfectly, leaving students on either end waiting for several weeks for the interactions to begin. In my experience, however, the doctoral students who generally work with student groups at UNESP are well oriented on how to maneuver successfully around scheduling complications. Sometimes interactions can be scheduled for the full 12-15 weeks of the semester and other times they will be limited to 8-10 weeks. Interactions tend to be more successful when scheduled MTWTh after UNESP's morning classes are completed. (I don't include specific times here because issues of time zone will impact institutions across the United States differently.) To address these logistical challenges, the Teletandem team does an excellent job managing scheduling fluctuations internally; they generally keep their students on a flexible schedule to accommodate US partner schedules, which makes the scheduling process much more streamlined on the US end.)

Instructors of Portuguese are highly encouraged to send as much information as they have about upcoming semester needs (course times and days as well as a projected number of students) as soon as they have information, and the Teletandem program will work to plan accordingly. Generally, there is a period of some fluctuation at the beginning of the semester as enrollment on both sides settles, and then Teletandem asks participating instructors to update a spreadsheet with information, including student names, ages, gender and contact information.

---

participating faculty. Previously they have used their own software as well as Skype, but Zoom offers several advantages for research and collaboration.

[13] Students may also become complacent and not complete each full session. Zoom may be able to help with this issue, another reason for its adoption.

Native Tutorial: Learning in Context

Most instructors know at least a small handful of native speakers of their target language that live in the vicinity, and this community project could be limited to a one-off event or to a year-long series. Consider inviting someone from the community to do a presentation and/or share a skill with your students. Native speakers of a language are generally thrilled to get to know students and speak to them in their native tongue. This type of activity also makes them the resident expert, which can be an interesting role; oftentimes recent immigrants don't realize how much they have to offer in a language-learning context. Like so many other activities that are organized around the theme of "community," an event like this also touches on all of the other "5 C's," and as such can lead to enhanced language learning at any level. Presentations or workshops don't have to be at all academic in tone or content; watching a Portuguese baker make pastries or a Brazilian percussionist show some basic rhythms on a *pandeiro* can be just as intellectually stimulating as accompanying a consulate official to a diplomatic event or listening to a famous director speak about his recent documentary. Students will come away from the event with an enriched understanding of cultural differences and similarities, with a heightened appreciation for their individual competencies and challenges in the target language, with a better grasp of one or more sociocultural phenomena and with an increased ability to make intercultural comparisons.

Native tutorial: What You Need to Know

Keep in mind that tutorials will have an enhanced impact if students are allowed to actively participate. For example, instead of simply having an artist show his/her work, consider offering a workshop where the artist shows his/her techniques to the students and then has them create their own artwork, or in addition to having a group of dancers perform a folkloric piece, have them teach students the basic steps. Your institution might have strict regulations about student travel outside of campus grounds. You may need to present a detailed itinerary and/or signed waivers, and you should research any other rules your administration requires. (Sometimes you must chaperone back to campus after the event, for example.)

Be clear that speaker remuneration may be difficult, particularly if your institution does not have many funding opportunities or if the volunteer cannot provide official US documents. (For institutional funding opportunities, see below.) Some institutions will allow you to offer an honorarium or a small gift. Another way to show you value the volunteer's time and contribution might be to offer payment in kind, or an exchange. Perhaps you or your students could provide a translation or some information that would be helpful to the volunteer, or perhaps your event will create a commodity that you could then donate to the volunteer. As an example, for a cooking demonstration, students accompanied the volunteer to a Portuguese grocery store, assisted in buying all the necessary ingredients, and helped to cook a traditional meal. All remaining food and ingredients (a value of perhaps $50, down from the original grocery bill of $100) were given to the volunteer.

Local Interest Groups: Creating a Language Community in Your Backyard

Exposure to native speakers of the target language can provide invaluable cultural and linguistic content and opportunities for communication and comparison, but even in today's globalized context, not all places are teeming with obvious international prospects. Instructors in certain geographical areas may need to get creative about forming a local language community. Some studies[14] show that interactions with a native and/or advanced speaker are more beneficial for language learners, but keep in mind that *any* contact hours with *any* level of speaker will ultimately benefit your students. Not only can creating a local group of non-native speakers improve individual language proficiency among participants, but it also will help to build a local community of language learners. This can in turn help to create positive buzz about your program and positive word of mouth – the most precious of promotional materials.

Local interest groups: What You Need to Know

You probably already have several potential members to your group, because you have a classroom full of students who are motivated to learn the language. Tweak your syllabus and participation rubric slightly,[15] and students will be even more keen to get credit for outside-of-class activities. To find additional members, introduce yourself to anyone who you hear speaking near campus in the target language, and ask for their emails. Put your students in charge of recruiting additional members; they are likely to know other students who may already speak the language (and you will be amazed how many turn into linguistic bloodhounds if you offer extra credit!). Ask your friends and/or colleagues to make a commitment to attend just one event per semester. You may also be able to tap into local communities who speak the target language by posting advertisements, either on a traditional bulletin board or in internet-based community site like *meetup.com*.

Choose a reliable way to reach group members. You may prefer an email-based list-serv or a social media site like Facebook. Both have advantages as well as drawbacks; you may decide to do both. If you keep both active, be

---

[14] See, for example: Pica, Teresa, Felicia Lincoln-Porter, Diana Paninos and Julian Linnell. "Language Learners' Interaction: How Does It Address the Input, Outut and Feedback Needs of L2 Learners?" Tesol Quarterly, Vol. 30, Issue 1 (59-84), Spring 1996.

[15] See figure 1 for a sample participation rubric.

careful about cross-posting too enthusiastically; you want to reach your audience regularly enough that they know about your events but not so much that they feel overburdened and lose interest.Your institution likely has a protocol for creating list-servs; alternately you can look for a free list-serv service online.[16]

Keep your events simple and oriented toward maximizing communication in the target language. You could start by initiating a coffee klatch hour in a local café (extra points if you can manage enough funding to bring a culturally unique dessert to your meetings!). Or perhaps a meet-up at a local affordable restaurant with flexible seating. You may have better luck in an outdoor park near cafés or shops so that participants can purchase a snack or beverage if they want but are not forced to spend any money in order to attend your event. It should go without saying that if you find out about an already established local meetup (perhaps through *meetup.com*) in your target language, you can build upon it by bringing your own group members. Another way to piggy-back on already organized events and to grow your membership would be to meet at a local capoeira, dance, or *baile folklórico* lesson.

Once you have a regularly occurring event, gauge interest in group members and in new students for additional activities. Find out what kinds of interests might draw out different potential members: a group that gets together once a week to watch athletic games or soap operas on satellite television, to help one another in an informal tutoring co-op, to view new film releases in the target language, to practice a team sport or *capoeira* or a culturally unique form of dance, to listen to and/or learn to play new music, to play board games in the target language[17] or to start a cooking club. The more variety you are open to, the more chance you have of finding a good fit with your current active members, and of finding a partner to help you coordinate events.

Enlist help from enthusiastic students, particularly ones who have recently returned from study abroad programs, because they are often extra motivated to practice their recently acquired language. As a faculty member, you can both plan your own events and/or sponsor events organized by students (student-planned and promoted events often have far better attendance than faculty-oriented programs). The key is to start small and build consistently; do not start four recurring language club activities at the same time!

---

[16] A few possibilities: groups.google.com; groupspaces.com; lsoft.com

[17] Loveless, Megwen. "I'd Like To Buy a Vowel: Using Games To Build Linguistic Competence." Presentation at American Association of Teachers of Spanish and Portuguese (AATSP) conference. Denver, CO: July 2015.

Native Interviews: Student-led Inquiry

Inspired by the "Backward" course design framework laid out by Grant Wiggins,[18] this genre of community-based project requires students to plan and execute an in-person interview with an individual of native fluency in the target language. Too often, instructors tend to organize their curricula based on the structure of their chosen textbook, forgetting that part of our responsibility as educators is to determine long-term goals for language learning. When considering the course content that I expect our students to remember *years* after completing the course, I've realized the importance of arranging syllabi to reflect not just linguistic content but an entire intellectual/emotional framework geared toward understanding language in context.

When reflecting upon the competencies that I want my students to demonstrate in their first semesters of a new language, I realized that carrying out an interview with a native speaker is a much better gauge of a student's progress than a traditional exam. In the process of completing an interview project, the student must conduct preliminary research in the target language, establish register-specific contact in the target language, complete a series of real-world tangible tasks in the target language, demonstrate strategic competence and ability to make him/herself understood as well as to understand in the target language, follow up and express gratitude in the target language and reflect upon his/her expectations and reactions in the target language.

By asking students to engage in this type of project, then, I am asking them to use the linguistic tools I have shared with them over the course of the semester(s) and to further develop other invaluable life skills like overcoming fear and shyness, showing respect, learning how to ask follow-up questions and to lead conversation in a particular direction, finding ways to circumvent their linguistic inadequacies, acting gracious and expressing thanks, and ultimately believing in their own linguistic abilities. In my experience, nearly every student begins this project terrified of not understanding their interviewee or committing an awkward gaffe, but generally each student emerges with an increased confidence in his/her ability to get by in a foreign place in the target language.

A similar model developed by Cristiane Soares[19] included regular class visits to a single family over a semester-long intermediate language course on

---

[18] Wiggins, Grant and Jay McTighe. Understanding by Design. Alexandria, Virginia: Association for Supervision and Curriculum Development, 2005.

[19] Soares, Cristiane. "A comunidade brasileira nos Estados Unidos como base do currículo de PLE: Os 5 Cs aplicados ao ensino de português como língua estrangeira." Portuguese Language Journal, 8, Fall 2014.

immigration.[20] Students prepared questions each visit from their readings on the immigrant experience. Because they met several times over several months, both the students and the interviewees built up a strong connection, arguably a valuable improvement on the one-off project described above. The two families that worked with her were given small honorariums for their participation in the project.

Another alternative for areas without a large sample of native speakers would be to conduct interviews over the phone or via video conference call. There are clear disadvantages to this model, but I believe it would still bring enhanced learning to our students. Before assuming that your community has no native speakers of the target language, do some sleuthing! Often you only need to meet one person in order to create a network of ten participants in an interactive initiative like this. I have successfully created this program through a network of neighbors, through co-workers at a Portuguese-language daycare, through undergraduate and graduate study abroad students and through foreign-born faculty members and visiting scholars.

Native interviews: What you Need to Know

The logistics for this type of project can be crippling, particularly if your class size is daunting and if you live in an area with few native speakers. The outcome, however, far outweighs the logistical challenge! Early on in the semester, you should contact potential interviewees and tell them about the project. In your outreach, stress the learning potential for your students, the informal nature of the interviews, and the relatively small and flexible time commitment. In my experience, I've found email communication to be the most practical, but social etiquette might require you to visit candidates in person.

Determine if students can carry out interviews on their own (this will depend on how far away the interview site is; you may want to suggest a public space that is convenient for both parties) and if so, consider putting them entirely in charge of all subsequent communication. That provides extra opportunities for your students to practice register-specific communication (written greetings in the formal register, for example) and fewer logistics for you to handle personally. You can free yourself somewhat to assist students who are having difficulty getting in touch with their interviewees or who cannot find a time or place to meet. Students may like to work in teams to alleviate the stress of having to communicate in the target language with a stranger. In this case, students can work together to come up with interview questions and/or take turns asking questions. Pairing two students with each interviewee also decreases the number of native speakers you require for your

[20] Groups of three and four students spent the first six weeks of the semester visiting two respective families.

project

Make sure that you clearly communicate your expectations for the project. Students should know if they are on a fact-finding mission or if you are more interested in how the experience has impacted them personally and/or intellectually. You should also provide a detailed rubric so students understand how they are being assessed. Consider whether they will receive a grade depending on the "quality" of their work, or simply be given points upon completion of the project, for example. If you want to stress register or linguistic accuracy, consider having students record sections of the interview.[21]

Request that students save all communications, as well as preparatory documents (sample interview questions and/or other evidence of practice interview session with a peer, for example), to include in a portfolio. The portfolio can also include a final reflection paper about how the experience shaped the language learner's understanding of language in context as well as a personalized thank-you note for the interviewee. Have several back-ups available in case one or more of the interviewees are not able to complete the project with your students. If at all possible, try not to ask an interviewee to commit to more than one twenty-minute interview per calendar year, and consider asking students for a second copy of their final reflection, as interviewees may really appreciate reading the profound impact they have had on your students.

Service Learning: Gaining Knowledge by Providing Support

One of the new buzz-words around college campuses is "service learning," though to be fair, it is not a new concept. Half a century ago, educators like Paulo Freire led the call to engage in "participatory research," in which community members would engage in research alongside scholars with the goal of understanding social problems and creating solutions *for the people, by the people.* There has been extensive research over the past hundred years of the benefits of service learning, but only in recent years has it truly taken off as a supplement and/or component to second language acquisition.[22] By interacting on a recurrent basis in an intimate setting with native speakers, language students can greatly enhance both their proficiency in the target language and their command of cultural knowledge and perspectives.

Though there are many potential models, most service learning courses

---

[21] You may need to assure interviewees that this recording is for educational purposes only and will not be seen by any other parties. Students should comply with any refusal to be filmed and you may need to adjust your assessment accordingly. See figure 2 for a native interview sample rubric.

[22] See Wendy Caldwell. "Taking Spanish Outside the Box: a Model for Integrating Service Learning into Foreign Language Study." Foreign Language Annals, Vol. 40, N. 3 (2007), 463-71.

include a set number of contact hours per semester with one or more local organizations that can facilitate student attention to the needs of the local population. The "on the ground" experiences augment readings that students prepare and often underscore the main foci of the course. In its most recent iteration, service learning has often been referred to as *community-based learning*, and this approach highlights situational knowledge and aims to show students that one can learn more *from* a community through engaged service than one can learn *about* a community through other forms of research. In community-based research, the community helps the researcher to formulate hypotheses and research questions, and the researcher contributes resources (sometimes in the form of institutional access, sometimes in the form of a number of interested students who can carry out surveys or interviews). This new model helps to assuage many of the problematic issues related to power that emerged from prior attempts to engage students in service learning projects.[23]

An early pioneer in the realm of service learning in Portuguese was Clémence Jouët-Pastré, who organized the "Portuguese in the Community" course at Harvard University in 2004.[24] One of the interesting features of this course was its focus on Portuguese-speaking immigrants as "invisible;" its incorporation of a semester-long volunteering position for each student radically transformed how students intellectually and emotionally processed the invisibility hypothesis. In its first iteration, students dedicated four hours a week to their choice of one of eight community organizations or agencies. Volunteering responsibilities included assistance with citizenship classes, human-rights workshops, after-school programs, publicity materials, immigrant legal document processing and medical and legal translations.

By no means does your project need to incorporate eight community organizations in order to be successful, however! The key to building a successful service learning course is to find a local group that is open to collaboration and to remain flexible as both you and the group come to an understanding of what might be helpful for both sides. You may both have to compromise on some of your goals, and you may need to change strategy in the middle of the semester to address unexpected issues that emerge. It's important to see these growing pains as progress, and to include your students in the learning process.

Service Learning: What you Need to Know

Certain contexts may not lend themselves to this type of program development, because embarking on a volunteering program in the target

---

[23] See: Strand, Kerry J. "Community-Based Research as Pedagogy." Michigan Journal of Community Service Learning, Vol. 7, Issue 1, 2000 (85-96).

[24] Joüet-Pastré, Clémence and Leticia Braga. "Community-Based Learning: A Window into the Portuguese-Speaking Communities of New England." Hispania, Vol. 88, No. 4 (Dec., 2005), 863-72.

language requires a relatively large and well-organized sample of community members. For this reason, and because of the tremendous effort involved in managing individual student volunteering tasks, few programs of this type exist outside of summer study abroad programs. Still, this route offers a particularly rich experience through which language students can both improve their speaking and writing skills and better come to understand and address contemporary social, economic and political issues in the target language.

This type of project requires a local population of native speakers of the target language that is both sizeable and organized enough to allow for the development of a project. It requires a lot of preparatory work up to a year before the student semester actually commences: the instructor must meet with local leaders to get a sense of what small-scale problems could be addressed in a relatively short amount of time, with relatively small sums of money and by students who are not technically trained nor necessarily fluent in the target language.

Instructors should begin contacting potential partner organizations well before the start of the semester, and build up a strong rapport with organization leaders. The better the instructor's communication with local leaders, the closer the students' projects will come to addressing community concerns.

Try to establish a set of specific projects that could be mutually beneficial for students, instructors, community leaders and community members. Though it is tempting to overestimate your students' ability to contribute, focus on small interventions that fill a niche need for the organization. Are they in need of personnel for special events? Promotional materials? Other resources? Perhaps your students could staff a particular event or series of events, or distribute information, or create flyers or other media. Perhaps your students could complete a survey of local needs, or act as liaisons between different organizations, or design a website. Perhaps your students could translate documents, or accompany elderly or young community members on a field trip, or help to organize a key resource. Think in particular about the skill sets that your students bring to the table: they may have more access to and knowledge about technological innovations, or statistical sampling methods, or academic journals than the organization with which you are partnering.

Depending on the number of enrolled students and the number of partner organizations as well as course goals and needs of all participants, the instructor will need to decide how to pair students with organizations as well as how to facilitate scheduling. You will want to prepare students for the extra time commitment before registration by noting the volunteering component in the course description. I have had mixed success with scheduling field trips that include all enrolled students at one time; instructors who create a flexible module that can incorporate separate "waves" of student visits may be more successful. Other program directors have suggested including a schedule of visits in the course description or as a mandatory laboratory component, so students can plan accordingly before the start of the semester (though potential conflicts might also be a disincentive for enrolling in the course, potentially causing low matriculation levels).

Many institutions have a center or department that specializes in civil service and/or outreach to the community.[25] These are great resources for assistance creating a course goal and/or project(s) as well as for finding funding for incidental costs like transportation, supplies, team-building, meals or other incidentals. A center within your institution may also help you advocate for creating a new course, or help you convince administration to further develop an existing course toward a community-oriented focus. Other professional organizations that may be able to provide some mentorship include the SIG (Special Interest Group) of ACTFL (the American Council on the Teaching of Foreign Languages), and Imagining America,[26] a consortium of activists working to affect change in public and academic realms.

In terms of curricular development, most programs create service-learning courses or course components at the intermediate level, where students are already relatively confident in the target language. At the intermediate level, students can generally communicate spontaneously with relative ease to partners in the target language, and subsequent interactions enhance what a student is already able to do (as opposed to completely overwhelming the student, which is likely at lower levels of proficiency). For assessment, instructors generally rely on student journals over the course of the semester, which can be worth anywhere from 10-25% of the semester grade and are generally graded only for content (though problematic grammar and/or spelling may be marked). Depending on the nature of the service component, instructors may choose to develop a more detailed rubric[27] that evaluates individual tasks more judiciously.

When preparing a service learning course from the ground up, I encourage instructors to prepare as extensively as possible and to plan for last-minute surprises and to remain open to modifying even carefully constructed modules. Perhaps most important of all is to keep expectations reasonable. In your role as instructor, you may have to reiterate this point

[25] Keywords to search for local centers: community-based research, community-based learning, service learning, civic engagement, public service, community counseling & engagement, community family and engagement, center for service, learning in action, center for social justice & action.

[26] http://imaginingamerica.org/

[27] See figure 3 for a non-traditional service learning sample rubric.

several times to student participants and/or community members or leaders. I am not convinced that anyone has yet discovered a "perfect" model for bridging the classroom and the community, and everyone should expect a few difficulties when organizing a service learning project for the first time.

Funding: What You Need to Know

Not all of the activities detailed here necessarily require external funding; some, like Teletandem, may be entirely free of cost if your institution is well outfitted with an appropriate space for the interactions. However, you may find that some funding may make your event or series much more successful. For example, even a small amount of funding may allow you to bring culturally-specific treats, which draw more students, which draws more attention, which helps to spread positive word of mouth about your initiative(s). Depending on the infrastructure of your institution, you may also be in need of serious funding in order to make your initiative happen.

Though every institution has different financial ins and outs, I would like to make some very basic recommendations here. To begin with, each instructor must do creative detective work into local sources of funding. Investigate funding possibilities in your own department for student initiatives, program development, professional development and for recruiting majors and minors. Sometimes there is more funding available for these types of programs for students (as opposed to faculty, for whom funding is often research-related) and you may need to enlist the assistance of some enthusiastic undergraduates to help you sleuth out funding. Contact undergraduate programming centers to see if they can help underwrite any of your activities. Since the focus of your initiative is (in broad strokes) bridging academics with the community, some residence halls and student club/government associations may be able to contribute. Consider specialized centers throughout your institution: humanities programs, language development programs, area studies programs, arts programs, alumni programs, or technology, recreational or education centers.

If your event or series is related in some way to their mission, they may be happy to contribute a small amount in return for a mention on your department website or in your printed program. Become an expert at making inter-disciplinary connections and showing potential funding departments how your event is just as much in their interest as in yours. If you are able to secure funding for one event, ask a student participant to write a thank-you note explaining what a positive impact it had on his/her learning. This kind of small gesture can make for a strengthened relationship with the donor and can lead to more financial opportunities. Find out what kind of internal grants your institution offers, and meet with committee members to find out what specific qualities they are looking for in proposals. If you invest the time and effort, you can uncover funding even in bleak financial times.

What are You Waiting For?

Globalization and internationalization are, in many ways, the driving force behind contemporary initiatives in higher education, and we as language educators should be at the forefront of this rapidly expanding sphere. The linguistic and socio-cultural tools that we teach in our classrooms are the very matrix through which future generations will communicate with colleagues, friends and family, as our world becomes more globalized. Our job is to build not only linguistic competence in our students, but to familiarize them with the communities in which they may utilize their language skills in the future. Let us lead the way toward a new model in which members of our community share a role as mentors to our students and where the walls of the traditional classroom collapse in order to integrate an educational space of truly global scale.

Figure 1:

PARTICIPATION GRADE

	Outstanding (A)	Excellent (A-)	Very Good (B+)	Good (B)	Satisfactory (B-)	Adequate (C+)	Below Average (C)
Attendance: 20%	Never misses class and always arrives on time.	Misses nearly no class and almost always arrives on time. Contacts instructor about - and creates a plan of action to address - any planned or unexpected absences.	Misses very little class and usually arrives on time. Contacts instructor about - and helps to create a plan of action to address - any planned or unexpected absences.	Misses very little class and/or often arrives on time. Contacts instructor about any planned or unexpected absences.	Occasionally misses class and/or sometimes arrives tardy (but without causing a disruption).	Regularly misses class and/or often arrives late (but without causing a disruption).	Often misses class and/or often arrives late.
Preparation: 20%	Is very diligent about assignments and due dates as well as verbal & written instructions. Is always ready to help explain concepts and eager to ask informed questions from assigned pages.	Is usually diligent about assignments and due dates as well as verbal & written instructions. Is usually ready to help explain concepts and usually able to ask informed questions from assigned pages.	Is often diligent about assignments and due dates as well as verbal & written instructions. Is often ready to help explain concepts and often able to ask informed questions from assigned pages.	Is sometimes diligent about assignments and due dates as well as verbal & written instructions. Is sometimes ready to help explain concepts and sometimes able to ask informed questions from assigned pages.	Is sometimes careless about assignments and due dates as well as verbal & written instructions. Is occasionally ready to help explain concepts and occasionally able to ask informed questions from assigned pages.	Is often careless about assignments and due dates as well as verbal & written instructions. Is rarely ready to help explain concepts and rarely able to ask informed questions from assigned pages.	Is usually careless about assignments and due dates as well as verbal & written instructions. Is uncooperative in explaining concepts and asking informed questions from assigned pages.
Contributions: 20%	Enthusiastically and respectfully volunteers engaging comments many times per session. Noticeably improves classroom dynamic with questions/ comments/etc.	Enthusiastically and respectfully volunteers comments many times per session. Often improves classroom dynamic with questions/comments/etc.	Enthusiastically volunteers comments several times per session. Sometimes improves classroom dynamic with questions/ comments/etc.	Volunteers comments several times per session. Sometimes improves classroom dynamic with questions/comments/etc.	Volunteers comments occasionally. Does not significantly improve classroom dynamic with questions/comments/etc.	Must be called upon in order to elicit active participation. Occasionally disrupts classroom dynamic with questions/comments/etc.	Must be called upon in order to elicit ambivalent participation. Regularly disrupts classroom dynamic with questions/comments/etc.
Attitude: 20%	Arrives on time, with a positive attitude and enthusiastic to learn. Is actively, respectfully and positively engaged with classroom. Is not distracted by unrelated work, media, or chit-chat.	Arrives mostly on time, with a positive attitude and ready to learn. Is usually actively, respectfully and positively engaged with classroom. Is rarely distracted by unrelated work, media, or chit-chat.	Arrives mostly on time. Is usually engaged with classroom, though sometimes too ill / tired to do so actively. Is usually not distracted by unrelated work, media, or chit-chat.	Arrives mostly on time. Is often engaged with classroom, though often too ill / tired to engage actively. Is sometimes distracted by unrelated work, media, or chit-chat.	Occasionally arrives late. Is usually interested, though regularly too ill / tired to engage actively. Is often distracted by unrelated work, media, or chit-chat.	Regularly arrives late. Shows an ambivalent attitude and is not always enthusiastic to learn. Is regularly distracted by unrelated work, media, or chit-chat.	Always arrives late. Shows a negative attitude and is rarely enthusiastic to learn. Is generally not positivesly engaged with classroom. Is too distracted by unrelated work, media or chit-chat to perform at an acceptable level.
Immersion: 20%	Speaks only in target language with peers during groupwork. Makes an outstanding effort to engage in target language outside of classroom (bate-papos, lectures, office hours, teletandem, target-language events, online resources, etc.)	Usually speaks only in target language with peers during groupwork. Makes a real effort to engage in target language outside of classroom (bate-papos, , lectures, teletandem, target-language events, online resources, etc.).	Mostly speaks only in target language with peers during groupwork. Makes an effort to engage in target language outside of classroom (bate-papos, lectures, teletandem, target-language events, online resources, etc.).	Sometimes has to be reminded to speak only in target language with peers during groupwork. Makes a limited effort to engage in target language outside of classroom (bate-papos, lectures, teletandem, target-language events, online resources, etc.).	Often has to be reminded to speak only in target language with peers during groupwork. Makes very little effort to engage in target language outside of classroom (bate-papos, lectures, teletandem, target-language events, online resources, etc.).	Regularly speaks only in English with peers during groupwork. Makes almost no effort to engage in target language outside of classroom (bate-papos, lectures, teletandem, target-language events, online resources, etc.).	Makes no effort to speak in target language with peers during groupwork. Makes no effort to engage in target language outside of classroom (bate-papos, lectures teletandem, target-language events, online resources, etc.).

Figure 2:

	Outstanding (A)	Excellent (A-)	Very Good (B+)	Good (B)	Satisfactory (B-)	Adequate (C+)	Below Average (C)
Preparation: 20% *Research* *Questions* *Practice* *Logistics*	Student has conducted very extensive preliminary research to prepare for the interview. Student has prepared a comprehensive list of questions (including key vocabulary) and detailed related follow-up questions and has put great thought into the structure of the interview. Student has met with a partner to practice the interview with enough time to make extensive edits to first version of interview format. Student team has contacted interviewee in a courteous manner within a comfortable amount of time to plan interview.	Student has conducted extensive preliminary research to prepare for the interview. Student has prepared a list of questions (including key vocabulary) and detailed follow-up questions and has put considerable thought into the structure of the interview. Student has met with a partner to practice the interview and has made appropriate edits to first version of interview format. Student team has contacted interviewee in a courteous manner to plan interview.	Student has conducted quality preliminary research to prepare for the interview. Student has prepared a list of questions and follow-up questions and has put much thought into the structure of the interview. Student has met with a partner to practice the interview but has made few edits to first version of interview format. Student team has contacted interviewee to plan interview.	Student has conducted some preliminary research to prepare for the interview. Student has prepared a list of questions and some follow-up questions and has put some thought into the structure of the interview. Student has met with a partner to practice the interview. Student has contacted interviewee (on his own) in a somewhat courteous manner to plan interview.	Student has conducted limited preliminary research to prepare for the interview. Student has prepared a list of questions and has put some thought into the structure of the interview. Student has met with a partner to practice the interview but provides no proof. Student has contacted interviewee (on his own) in a somewhat abrupt and/or rushed manner to plan interview.	Student should have conducted more preliminary research to prepare for the interview. S/he has prepared a slapdash list of questions. Student has not practiced with his/her partner. Student and/or student team has contacted interviewee in an abrupt and/or rushed manner to plan interview.	Student conducted no preliminary research to prepare for the interview. S/he has not prepared an adequate list of questions. S/he did not contact partner to practice and required assitance from instructor to contact interviewee.
Interaction: 20% *Spontaneity* *Register* *Intercultural competency* *Negotiation of Meaning*	Student appears highly comfortable in front of interviewee; s/he makes very fluid transitions, visual contact and appropriate gestures. Student makes a genuine effort to actively engage interviewer in question/answer sessions. S/he always uses an appropriate register and is easily able to mirror subtle nuances in conversation. Student shows no need for strategies to clarify him/herself and asks detailed follow-up questions in order to fully understand the interviewee.	Student appears comfortable in front of interviewee; s/he makes quite fluid transitions, visual contact and appropriate gestures. Student makes an real effort to engage interviewer in question/answer sessions. S/he usually uses an appropriate register and is able to mirror subtle nuances in conversation. Student successfully uses strategies to clarify him/herself and asks detailed follow-up questions in order to understand the interviewee.	Student appears mostly comfortable in front of interviewee; s/he makes mostly fluid transitions, visual contact and appropriate gestures. Student makes an effort to engage interviewer in question/answer sessions. S/he regularly uses an appropriate register. Student uses largely successful strategies to clarify him/herself and asks follow-up questions in order to understand the interviewee.	Student appears somewhat comfortable in front of interviewee; s/he makes some fluid transitions, visual contact and appropriate gestures. Student makes some effort to engage interviewer in question/answer sessions. S/he uses a mostly appropriate register. Student uses somewhat successful strategies to clarify him/herself and occasionally asks follow-up questions in order to understand the interviewee.	Student appears somewhat uncomfortable in front of interviewee; s/he makes few clear transitions, visual contact and appropriate gestures. Student makes a limited effort to engage interviewer in question/answer sessions. S/he sometimes uses an appropriate register. Student uses somewhat poor strategies to clarify him/herself and rarely asks follow-up questions in order to understand the interviewee.	Student appears uncomfortable in front of interviewee; s/he makes rough transitions, nearly no visual contact and few appropriate gestures. Student makes a very limited effort to engage interviewer in question /answer sessions. S/he generally does not use an appropriate register. Student uses quite poor strategies to clarify him/herself and does not ask follow-up questions in order to understand the interviewee.	Student appears quite uncomfortable in front of interviewee; s/he makes no transitions, no visual contact and few appropriate gestures. Student makes nearly no effort to engage interviewer in question/answer sessions. S/he never uses an appropriate register. Student does not bother to clarify him/herself a does not ask follow-up comprehension questions.
Technical: Speaking 20% *Grammar* *Pronunciation & Intonation* *Syntax*	Shows excellent command of multiple verb tenses/modes and a very high rate of gender/number agreement. Has nearly no errors. His/her pronunciation is impeccable. Sentence structure is almost always syntactically correct; s/he shows serious effort toward producing a variety of complex constructions.	Shows excellent command of several verb tenses and high rate of gender/number agreement. Is able to recognize some errors and correct them immediately. S/he has a nearly native pronunciation. Sentence structure is generally syntactically correct; s/he shows an effort toward producing a variety of complex constructions.	Shows very good command of several verb tenses and quite high rate of gender/number agreement. Is able to recognize a few errors and correct them immediately. Student has no pronunciations which might impede understanding by a native speaker. Sentence structure is mostly syntactically correct; s/he shows some effort toward producing a variety of complex constructions.	Shows good command of several verb tenses and an adequate rate of gender/number agreement. Student has nearly no pronunciations which might impede understanding by a native speaker. Sentence structure is mostly syntactically correct.	Shows good command of two or fewer verb tenses and an adequate rate of gender/number agreement. Student has a few pronunciations which might impede understanding by a native speaker. Sentence structure is somewhat syntactically correct.	Shows adequate command of two or fewer verb tenses and a limited rate of gender/number agreement. Student has several pronunciations which might impede understanding by a native speaker. Sentence structure is somewhat syntactically incorrect.	Shows limited command of two or fewer verb tenses and a quite limited rate of gender/number agreement. Student has many pronunciations which might impede understanding by a native speaker. Sentence structure is often syntactically incorrect.
Technical: Writing 20% *Grammar* *Mechanics* *Syntax* *Vocab*	Writing shows mastery of gender, number and subject/verb agreement in familiar tenses. Student uses a wide variety of verb tenses/forms/moods. Shows nearly no negative interference from other languages. Nearly no errors in punctuation, spelling, capitalization and/or use of accents.	Writing shows excellent agreement of gender, number and subject/verb in familiar tenses. Student uses a variety of verb tenses/forms/moods. Shows very little negative interference from other languages. Very few isolated errors in punctuation, spelling, capitalization and use of accents.	Writing shows good agreement of gender, number and subject/verb in familiar tenses. Student uses several verb tenses/forms/moods. Shows little negative interference from other languages. Few errors in punctuation, spelling, capitalization and use of accents.	Writing shows adequate agreement of gender, number and subject/verb in familiar tenses. Student uses a few verb tenses/forms. Shows some negative interference from other languages. Some errors in punctuation, spelling, capitalization and use of accents (though some are systematic).	Writing shows several problems with agreement of gender, number and subject/verb in familiar tenses. Student uses only a few verb tenses/forms. Shows negative interference from other languages. Several errors in punctuation, spelling, capitalization and use of accents (and many are systematic).	Writing shows many problems with agreement of gender, number and subject/verb in familiar tenses. Student uses very limited verb tenses/forms. Shows many negative interference from other languages. Many errors in punctuation, spelling, capitalization and use of accents (and most are systematic).	Writing is difficult to understand due to problems with agreement of gender, number and subject/verb in familiar tenses. Even verbs in the present tense show regular breakdown. Shows negative interference from Spanish. Many errors in punctuation, spelling, capitalization and use of accents (and almost all are systematic).
Follow-through: 20% *Portfolio* *Reflection* *Gratitude*	Student submitted a complete portfolio on time and entirely in Portuguese. Student reflection details a deep awareness of intercultural difference and details many personal / intellectual epiphanies that resulted from the project in an organized manner. Student submitted a thoughtful and original thank-you note that	Student submitted a complete portfolio on time and entirely in Portuguese (though with some prompting). Student reflection shows a heightened awareness of intercultural difference and details a few personal / intellectual epiphanies that resulted from the project. Student submitted a thoughtful	Student submitted a complete portfolio slightly late and/or with instructor prompting. Student reflection discusses a few personal / intellectual epiphanies that resulted from the project. Student submitted a nice thank-you note.	Student submitted a nearly complete portfolio. Student reflection details the perspective gained from the interview. Student submitted an adequate thank-you note.	Student submitted a nearly complete portfolio slightly late or with instructor prompting. Student reflection connects the interview experience to the student's learning. Student submitted a rushed thank-you note separate from the portfolio and/or after instructor prompting	Student submitted a nearly complete portfolio late. Student reflection richly details the content of the interview. Student submitted an offensive thank-you note.	Student submitted a partially complete portfolio late. The journalistic essay partially narrates the content of the interview. Student did not submit a thank-you note.

Figure 3:

	Outstanding (A)	Excellent (A-)	Very Good (B+)	Good (B)	Satisfactory (B-)	Adequate (C+)	Below Average (C)
Content: final project	Content is sophisticated, providing key topic information as well as deep interpretation. Content is ideally matched for the needs of the partner institution. Multi-authored piece flows beautifully, with no detectable style differences between sections. Overall product is one that could easily be used in a wide variety of professional settings.	Content is complex and provides insight into topic. Content is well-matched for the needs of the partner institution. Multi-authored piece flows well, with barely any detectable style differences between sections. Overall product is one that could easily be used in several professional settings.	Content is stimulating and provides raw information as well as basic analysis of subject matter. Content addresses most of of the needs of the partner institution. Multi-authored piece flows reasonably well, though there are some detectable style differences between sections. Overall product is one that could be used in at least one professional setting.	Content is interesting and gives a general idea of topic. Content addresses some of of the needs of the partner institution. Multi-authored piece could flow better; there are detectable style differences between sections. Overall product is one that could be used (with minor changes) in at least one professional setting.	Content has interesting components but includes only a rough idea of topic. Content could better address the needs of the partner institution. Piece is obviously written by multiple writers. Multi-authored piece flows reasonably well, though there are some detectable style differences between sections. Overall product is one that could be used (with some significant changes) in at least one professional setting.	Content shows few interesting components only tangentially related to the argument. Content does not adequately address the needs of the partner institution. Style differences between sections somewhat obscure overall content. Overall product would be more appropriate for an informal context than a professional setting.	Shows few interesting and / or applicable ideas. Content is severely inadequate for the needs of the partner institution. Style differences between sections almost entirely overwhelm / obscure overall content. Overall product should probably not be shared.
Content: individual research	Content represents a superior understanding of topic gleaned from extensive research of primary and secondary sources. Content explores many hypotheses not apparent in easily accessible background information. Data is clearly organized and synthesized into a narrative that can be easily applied to group project.	Content represents an excellent understanding gleaned from intensive research of a variety of sources. Content presents some hypotheses not apparent in easily accessible background information. Data is organized and synthesized into a narrative that can be applied to group project.	Content represents an admirable amount of knowledge gleaned from rigorous research of many sources. Content presents some ideas not apparent in easily accessible background information. Data is somewhat organized and synthesized into a narrative that (with minor changes) can be applied to group project.	Content represents a large amount of knowledge gleaned from thorough research of a few sources. Content presents some information not apparent in easily accessible background information. Data is roughly organized and (with some interpretation) can be applied to group project.	Content represents a reasonable amount of knowledge gleaned from somewhat haphazard research of a few sources. Some of the content is easily accessible from basic background information. Data is messy, though project attempts to apply it to group project.	Content could include more knowledge gleaned from more rigorous research of more sources. Most of the content is easily accessible from basic background information. Data is indecipherable and not clearly applied to group project.	Content includes inadequate knowledge gleaned from inadequate research of one or fewer sources. All of the content is gleaned entirely from easily accessible public sources (and therefore does not provide an extra service to partner organizaton). Data is indecipherable and takes away from the group project.
Content: individual creative contributions	Student makes a concerted effort to improve overall creative product conceptually, thematically, visually, etc. while assuring artistic/thematic integration of diverse content. Student has eagerly dedicated extensive time and resources to assure an incredibly dynamic, accurate, and cohesive portrayal of data. Contribution shows a genuine effort to explore potential of multi-media platform(s).	Student makes an effort to improve overall creative product conceptually, thematically, visually, etc. while encouraging artistic/thematic integration of diverse content. Student has readily dedicated much time and resources to assure a dynamic, accurate, and cohesive portrayal of data. Contribution shows an effort to explore potential of multi-media platform(s).	Student makes some effort to improve overall creative product while allowing artistic/thematic integration of diverse content. Student has willingly dedicated time and resources in the hopes of creating a dynamic, accurate, and cohesive portrayal of data. Contribution shows some effort to explore potential of multi-media platform(s).	Student makes a limited effort to improve overall creative product. Student has dedicated minimal time and / or resources in the hopes of creating a somewhat dynamic, accurate, and cohesive portrayal of data. Contribution shows a nominal effort to explore potential of multi-media platform(s).	Student could make a much more concerted effort to improve overall creative product. Student could have dedicated more time and / or resources toward creating an effective portrayal of data. Contribution shows a lack of effort in exploring potential of multi-media platform(s).	Student makes no effort whatsoever to improve overall creative product. Student did not dedicate adequate time and / or resources toward creating a sufficient portrayal of data. Contribution shows a severe lack of effort in exploring potential of multi-media platform(s).	Student impinges group effort to improve overall product. Student detracted from the time and / or resources that other students could dedicate toward creating what was ultimately a sub-par portrayal of data. Student impaired group from exploring potential of multi-media platform(s).

Collaboration	Student has earnestly participated in all elements of the project, including brainstorming, planning, organizing, delegating, follow-through, verification of completion and assessment. Student has enthusiastically contributed outstanding content on par with that of his/her peers as well as constructive opinions and suggestions regularly throughout the process. Student could be always counted on to complete his/her portion of work on time and to the very best of his/her ability.	Student has actively participated in almost all elements of the project, such as brainstorming, planning, organizing, delegating, follow-through, verification of completion and assessment. Student has cooperatively contributed excellent content basically on par with that of his/her peers as well as practical opinions and suggestions at several points during the process. Student could usually be counted on to complete his/her portion of work on time and to the best of his/her ability.	Student has participated in most elements of the project, such as brainstorming, planning, organizing, delegating, follow-through, verification of completion and assessment. Student has contributed quality content almost on par with that of his/her peers as well as some opinions and suggestions at some points during the process. Student could often be counted on to complete his/her portion of work on time. Student made a genuine effort.	Student has participated in many elements of the project, such as brainstorming, planning, organizing, delegating, follow-through, verification of completion and assessment. Student has contributed content somewhat below par with that of his/her peers as well as opinions and suggestions at least a few times during the process. Student could sometimes be counted on to complete his/her portion of work on time. Student made a good effort.	Student could have participated in more elements of the project, such as brainstorming, planning, organizing, delegating, follow-through, verification of completion and assessment. Student could have contributed more content of better quality as well as opinions and suggestions during the process. Only rarely could student be counted on to complete his/her portion of work on time. Work was of varying degrees of readiness.	Student barely participated elements of the project such as brainstorming, planning, organizing, delegating, follow-through, verification of completion and assessment. Student barely contributed content (of dubious quality) and barely contributed opinions and suggestions during the process. Student could not be counted on to complete his/her portion of work on time. Work was quite inconsistent.	Student disrupted several elements of the project, including brainstorming, planning, organizing, delegating, follow-through, verification of completion and / or assessment. Student disrupted the building of content and revision process. Student left his/her group inadequately prepared because of inability to complete his/her portion of work on time. Work was not acceptable for inclusion in project.
Evaluation: peer							
Evaluation: service organization partner							
Evaluation: self							

2.6 LANGUAGE LEARNING IN A DIGITAL WORLD

Orlando R. Kelm
University of Texas at Austin

Language learning is messy, despite the fact that our pedagogy traditionally strives to clean up the mess. Portuguese is no exception. We try to clean up the messiness by controlling and structuring our courses. For example, in grammar classes, teachers generally present gender and agreement before learning the subjunctive because, somehow, that is seen as an appropriate build-up. If we were to be brutally honest with ourselves, however, much of this control is motivated more by our need to manage students and classes than by our belief in what is helpful for language learning. A language supervisor at a large university once told me, "Our methodology may not be the best way to learn a language, but it's an effective way to teach the language to 5,000 students." A large part of our methodology is centered on convenience and practicality.

Currently, we have a new challenge: Our traditional methodology is confronting the reality of the digital age. Instant access to information, video, audio, chats, conversations with people from anywhere at any time, communication, and information flows all potentially change our approach to education and learning. It is partly for this reason that we sometimes look at technology and social media as hindrances to our language learning pedagogy. Why? Because all of our efforts to make language learning less messy seem to crumble as technology exposes learners to hundreds—no, thousands—of new ways to communicate with others and access information. The result is that we sometimes feel like we are losing control of the classroom, the students, and the learning environment. Given this situation, there is push-back. Some instructors forbid students to open their laptops in class, others do not allow mobile devices at school, and others still discourage learners from accessing online resources because, after all, who knows what kind of incorrect and incomplete information is out there? And this is true without even fanning the flames that suggest that technology will someday replace teachers.

There are additional challenges as well. Even if we want to incorporate more technology and social media into our language learning, these are moving targets. Every day, there are new options, sites, applications, and programs. How do educators make a decision about how to incorporate technology and social media into foreign language learning while faced with the real issues of cost, quality, scalability, copyrights, time commitments, accuracy, and age appropriateness? It becomes overwhelming. Let's be honest; school or university professionals are going to make a broad decision to use a specific content management system, and we will go with it. Department heads are going to make a broad decision to use a specific textbook, which comes with ancillary online materials, and we will go with it.

Still, even if we go with it, inevitably, there are students, often the self-motivated and independent ones, who approach language learning differently. These learners find ways to read news updates and articles from anywhere in the world. They use translation technologies to enhance their understanding. They find ways to talk in real time with native speakers who are thousands of miles away. They download music, talks, lectures, grammar exercises, podcast lessons, movies, and videos.

With all of this in mind, the objective of this chapter is to provide some ideas about how to use technology and social media to enhance the learning of Portuguese. For learners of Portuguese, labeled with the famous acronym LCTL (Less Commonly Taught Language), this is especially important because there are fewer published materials for language learning.

The premise and starting point for this essay is the following: Look at how technology is used in society in general, and build on that for pedagogical purposes. If people use a program or application for communication purposes, how can we modify that for language teaching? If people share information with others in a certain way, how can we adjust that for language learning purposes? If, in everyday life, we access information in certain ways, how can we replicate a part of that in teaching and education? In other words, we must observe what happens in real life and figure out a way to tweak that when learning a foreign language.

Background Stories to Set the Stage

Let's begin with two brief examples that illustrate how technology and social media have changed the way we interact with students and how students learn foreign languages. Recently, I introduced our Portuguese language students to HelloTalk (hellotalk.com), a free app that allows learners to use their mobile devices to chat, record, correct, and edit language with native speakers. During class one day, I told students that almost every Brazilian will have heard of the poem, *Canção do exílio* by Gonçalves Dias. At that very instant, a student named Kris pulled out his mobile phone and asked his Brazilian contacts on HelloTalk if they had ever heard of the poem. It was not even 2 minutes later when Kris raised his hand to let me know that he had just asked a few Brazilians and, indeed, they had all heard of the poem, but none of them really knew it. It was an amazing, and slightly intimidating, experience. First, it was impressive to see how quickly students were able to confirm what I was simultaneously discussing in class. Second, the experience served as a catalyst for new ideas about how I could integrate classroom activities and immediate Brazilian input.

Also, in another recent course, there was a miscommunication with the university bookstore, and the textbook did not arrive at the bookshelves on time. Serendipitously, there was an electronic version of the textbook. However, when we tried to access the textbook through our university library, it was not available for our students. As the instructor, I went to the library to see if there was any way to obtain access to the electronic version. The official answer from the library staff was, "*No.*" However, some students clicked on one or two new search options and found that the electronic version was indeed available and, legitimately so, through a different portal. Not even the staff member at the library was aware of the other option. Had it not been for the savvy searching of the students, we would have been without the textbook at the beginning of our semester. Again, it was an amazing experience. Students were able to use technology to keep our class progressing, even when the library and the teacher did not know what to do.

What Is Out There and How We Can Use It

This section features some of the tools of the trade, such as programs, applications, and websites, that can be used to enhance language learning and foreign language teaching. Please notice the use of the word *enhance.* If a person asks, "What should I do to learn Portuguese?" the answer is never found in just one practice. There is no single best and only way to learn a language. There is not just one textbook or one podcast lesson that miraculously covers all aspects of language learning at all levels of proficiency. The same is true with everything presented here. Some resources work well to organize time, others work well for students at beginning levels, some work well to improve reading ability, and others work better to improve oral fluency. The point is, there are hundreds of practices we can implement to improve our language learning, but each is valid within its area. It is unfair to criticize, for example, an audio recording because it does not help a learner to correctly spell difficult words. Almost everything featured here works as an ancillary, but nothing covers all aspects of language learning.

Tools to Organize Materials and Sort Presentations

One of the challenges that we face as teachers is the wide assortment of tools from which we can draw, often in class. Sometimes, we move back and forth between text, photos, video, audio, PDF files, URL links, textbooks, handouts, and any other variety of items. It is easy to get lost. What follows are descriptions of four tools that assist in organizing our materials and our presentations.

Padlet.com. Padlet.com is an online wall, similar to a bulletin board, where individuals or groups can post content such as images, videos, text, documents, PDF files, and URL links. It is easy to customize the wall, control who has access, and moderate student interactions. The basic version is free, and the learning curve is probably less than 30 minutes. It is a powerful tool for posting notes, creating portfolios, and adding ancillary materials. It is also effective as a tool for students to build their own walls, where they also include their notes, portfolios, and the results of their own search and research.

Blendspace.com If you have ever had the frustrating experience where a lesson plan or presentation is difficult because you find yourself bouncing in and out of multiple digital resourses, Blendspace will make your life much easier. Blendspace is a platform where users can gather, sort, annotate, and share almost any digital resource. Blendspace makes it easy to draw anything from google searches, flickr, educreations, upload any media, copy from Dropbox, or add from Gdrive. It simply allows you to sort and organize by a simple click and drag. The learning curve is again something that will take you less than 30 minutes to learn.

Recommendation for implementation: Blendspace works well for presentations. In the same way that a person may present electronic slides, think of Blendspace as a presentation tool where you can mix and match multiple digital resources.

Wikispaces.com Wikispaces, or about any other wiki format works well when you want to create something, especially text related, that results in a finished product. That is to say, if the contents continually change over time, I recommend that a blog format will serve better. However, if the objective is to build something (either individually or as a group) that will then serve as a final product, a wiki works well. Of course it may be that your school or university is using a content management system (like BlackBoard or Canvas) that allows you to create wikis, but for educational purposes, Wikispaces is among the easiest to use, the most flexible in development and presentation, and the most compatible with other online tools. The learning curve takes a little longer, but once you have the concept of the wiki, it is easy to build and modify.

Recommendation for implementation: In Wikispaces it is easy to create charts and tables. If you (or your students) want to create grammar review lessons, for example, Wikispaces is a good place to keep them.

Getkahoot.com and socrative.com There are many online resources to create polls (e.g., poll everywhere, survey monkey, etc.), but Getkahoot and Socrative are the best for classroom integration. What makes them unique is that the poll questions and multiple-choice answers are shown on a central screen. The poll takers (i.e., the students) then use any online device (laptop, tablet, phone) to link to the poll and choose their answers. This creates a group activity where everyone needs to interact with the questions on the central screen and then use their clicker individually.

Recommendation for implementation: Use Getkahoot or Socrative as a way to introduce a topic, to get initial opinions about topics, or to serve as a teaser to generate initial interest. They also work well to create questions for practice tests, which can be reviewed together as a class. You will get instant feedback on how well the students have captured a given topic.

YouTube Channel You may not think of YouTube as a tool to organize materials, but when a person creates a YouTube channel, that person can then develop playlists of videos. This is a powerful way to sort and organize videos that you refer to often. For example, suppose that you want students to view videos related to Brazilian history, music, movies, politics and art. You could create a playlist for each topic. Then, when students go to your YouTube channel, all of the videos are already sorted by topic in the playlists.

Also, if you want students to record their own videos, those videos can be uploaded to your YouTube channel. To do so, click on the YouTube account settings and choose "Overview." Listed in the overview is an address for mobile uploads. Anybody who attaches a video to a message sent to that address will then have access to that video on the YouTube channel. This feature makes it possible to allow students to post to your YouTube channel, without having to share the password of the channel with others.

Finally, another advantage of YouTube channels is that the Video Manager has a powerful editing feature. This allows users, for example, to enhance any video with additional annotations and subtitles. There are both Brazilian and Continental varieties of Portuguese, and both are surprisingly accurate at speech recognition. Alternatively, if you already have a textual transcription of a video, it is easy to insert that into the video, and with slight modifications in timing, you end up with easy-to-make subtitles. The manager even supports multiple tracks, to add subtitles in multiple languages.

Recommendation for implementation: As the instructor, as you find videos to sort in your playlist, notice that you will never have to list the URLs in a separate place. All of your sorted videos automatically appear by category on your YouTube channel.

Facebook Groups and Twitter Feeds It almost goes without saying that both Facebook and Twitter serve as excellent resources for organization. Once a group is created, users can join and share text, photos, links and video.

Recommendation for implementation: Facebook groups include an "upload file" feature where you can provide group members with Word documents, spreadsheets, electronic slide presentations and PDF files.

Tools to Enhance Individual Language Practice

In the past couple of years there has been an explosion of online options for language learners, both free and by subscription. Of course they are not all created equal, but do not simply ignore them as an ineffective waste of time. Furthermore, your students know about them, often use them, and will want your opinions about them.

Memrise.com Memrise is a wonderful application to assist in vocabulary memorization. The program uses an algorithm to recycle vocabulary review. Words that the user already knows are reviewed less frequently and words that the user gets wrong are reviewed more frequently. There are options for multiple languages, including lots of Portuguese language options too.

Mangolanguages.com Mango Language walks students through specific language learning lessons, including Portuguese. Especially interesting is the use of color on the screen (laptop, tablet, or phone). For example, when syntax between English and Portuguese differ, Mango makes it easy to see how the parts fit together. Mango does a nice job of recycling phrases and vocabulary from one lesson to another. Mango also has a video feature, built as a capstone at the end of lessons.

Chat With Native Speakers This is another area that has exploded with new options: Hello-Hello.com, Duolingo.com, Busuu.com, Livemocha.com, FluentU.com, LingQ.com, HelloTalk.com, OpenLanguage.com, etc. Each of these is similar in that users can chat with other native speakers, who can then assist with advice and practice. And each also differs a bit in the actual lesson structure and focus. In most cases, the benefit is found more in the interaction with people and less in the actual lessons. LingQ is unique in its approach to vocabulary and the way words are stored in the memory bank. FluentU is unique in the integration of video and subtitles, which allows for a personalized database of vocabulary words. HelloTalk, one of my personal favorites, has an innovative speech to text feature and a correction feature that is very effective. In the case of HelloTalk, there are many Brazilians in the system, so anyone who wants to practice Portuguese will have lots of options. OpenLanguage.com is where we make our audio *Língua da Gente* podcast series available as premium content (more about the podcasts below). Their mobile app allows for extended practice, repetition, recordings, and interaction.

Recommendation for implementation: Each of these provides learners with an opportunity to connect with real people. The key to all of them is to allow learners the freedom to discuss the topics that they want to discuss, with whomever they want. If we impose stringent controls, we lose any sense of real communication. Allow real communication to be real.

Tools to Enhance Classroom Activities

There are a number of digital tools that were not created specifically for foreign language purposes, yet work well in the foreign language arena. Often these tools become excellent resources in the classroom. Let's look at few examples.

Aurasma.com Aurasma is a digital tool to create virtual reality. In simple terms, users create a "trigger image" that works with an "overlay" to create an "aura." Suppose, for example that as your students walk into a classroom, there is a photo on the wall of Neymar playing soccer. As students hover their tablet or phone over the picture of Neymar, suddenly a video clip begins of Neymar's most spectacular goals. Or, suppose that the students hover their mobile device over the word "árvore" that is written on a table in the classroom. Suddenly a video clip about trees of Brazil appears on their screen. In other words, a trigger image causes something to happen, which can be a link to a website, a movie, an image, or a host of other things. And it might also be that the students are the ones who recorded the original video clip, which in turn they save as an aura. Subsequently, as others hover over the trigger image, they then view the student video. There are incredible possibilities for language learning in the application of virtual reality, and Aurasma is one of the easiest applications to get started.

Vyclone.com Vyclone is a social video platform that allows users to co-create a video from multiple angles. Imagine, for example, that five of your students are simultaneously video-recording an event. Later, the students combine the video into one clip, alternating views from each of the five cameras that originally made the recording. If you ever ask students to make video recordings to practice Portuguese, Vyclone will give you a whole new dimension to enhance the experience.

List.ly Despite the weird URL, list.ly offers a way to make online lists, which are then sorted and ranked by users. Suppose, for example, that you are going to travel with a group of fifteen students to Salvador. In preparation for the trip you post twenty photos of different locations in town. The fifteen students then view the list and rank the places they most want to see. As each student ranks the list, little by little you will see the group preference. A teacher can also make lists of sentences with grammar features, or vocabulary features, and again the students will rank all of the entries. List.ly is free to use and the learning curve is short.

Coogle.it If you are looking for a digital tool to assist in brain storming, coogle.it will provide you with easy access, group participation, slick sharing capabilities, and a fast learning curve. Imagine a site where ideas can be shared by simply adding another branch to a tree. I have seen students use coogle.it to practice verb conjugations, post pictures from a trip, sort vocabulary by topics, and outline ideas for class presentations. Coogle.it is the ideal example of a digital tool that was not created with foreign language in mind, but at the same time can be adapted to language learning situations.

Recommendation for implementation: Our education system imposes grading, and necessarily so. However, in the case of language practice with innovative technologies, if we are too strict in our discrete point grading, we diminish learner's ability to experiment with language learning. Allow for practice without constant discrete-point grading.

Open Access Portuguese Language Resources at the University of Texas

Among the National Foreign Language Resource Centers that are funded by the U.S. Department of Education, The University of Texas at Austin is home to The Center for Open Educational Resources and Language Learning (COERLL). The mission of COERLL is to disseminate Open Educational Resources that enhance the learning of foreign languages to the Internet public. These materials are also available with permission to re-mix, improve, and redistribute under the Creative Commons license. There are currently a number of Portuguese language materials that are available at COERLL. All of the Portuguese language materials can be viewed at the Brazilpod homepage: http://coerll.utexas.edu/brazilpod/. Of course, there are many other locations that have digital tools for Portuguese, but as a one-stop shopping site, Brazilpod offers many options.

Portuguese Communication Exercises A compilation of nearly 350 brief video clips of native speakers of Portuguese from various locations throughout Brazil (and some Portugal) who talk about 80 different topics. There is a complete Portuguese transcription and an English translation that accompanies each video clip. The clips are not scripted. Some individuals talk fast, some slow, some are interesting, some are not. It is an excellent resource to hear how native Portuguese speakers really talk. The topics are roughly divided by the level of the difficulty of the task. Beginning level topics include making introductions and describing what you like to do. Intermediate topics include sentence-level communication about favorite foods, buying items and going to the store. Advanced topics include paragraph-level stories about airplane rides and auto accidents. The superior topics include hypothetical ideas about how life would be different without electricity.

ClicaBrasil ClicaBrasil is a series of lessons for intermediate-level students of Portuguese, where you will find topics that highlight aspects of Brazilian culture. The materials include videos of Brazilians from all walks of life talking about their lives, their country, and their numerous activities. All of the lessons integrate reading, writing, listening comprehension, grammar, vocabulary, oral communication, and cultural activities, using the videos and PDF files as a point of departure.

Tá Falado The 46 audio podcast lessons cover pronunciation and grammar issues of Portuguese, specifically designed to help those who already speak Spanish. The lessons are built around dialogs performed by Brazilians that are then repeated in Spanish, providing a direct comparison of the two languages. All lessons include downloadable PDF files with the transcripts and notes, mp3 audio files, and blog discussions. Additionally, all of the dialogs present cultural scenarios that illustrate differences between North American and Brazilian culture.

Conversa Brasileira Imagine video scenarios where people are interacting with each other. There are dialogs, questions, turn taking exchanges, clarifications, false starts, hugs, laughter, asides, just everything that makes up real conversation. *Conversa Brasileira* is a compilation of such scenarios, but enhanced by transcriptions, translations, and content analysis. Think of it like a sportscaster's analysis of a game or the director's commentary that accompanies movies. The roleplay scenarios provide learners with a view of everyday exchanges, but also a way to analyze its parts. *Conversa Brasileira* also includes a print on demand textbook that is available via lulu.com.

Língua da Gente This is the newest and ongoing audio podcast series that currently has over 100 lessons, and new ones are introduced each week. The focus is to provide language that people actually use in everyday speech and it does this by presenting brief, slice-of-life dialogs, which focus on some daily situation, scenario or task that we encounter every day. In addition to the free podcast lessons, COERLL has partnered with OpenLanguage.com, by subscription, to provide a full range of complete online and via tablet language services. Users who subscribe to the full-featured version of Língua da Gente at OpenLanguage receive additional benefits (e.g. lesson exercises, including matching, reordering, dictation, and multiple choice).

Recommendation for implementation: Create a task-based curriculum, where you ask students to perform a given task orally. In preparation for that task, many of the videos, clips, example, and lessons from BrazilPod serve as a model.

Final Observations

Since the objective of this manual is to provide practical information for teachers of Portuguese, our recommendation is that we maximize the opportunities to implement innovative use of technology into our language learning. Partly because Portuguese is a Less Commonly Taught Language, the people who do want to learn Portuguese usually have a high motivation to do so. They want to learn, and they want the extra practice. This is precisely why we can take advantage of what technology and social media have to offer. There really is no reason to restrict usage of technology, but rather use it to encourage extra practice and increased interaction. Over time, of course, the specific examples that we have shown in this manual will be dated. However, the concept behind them will always be valid. Instructors should look to see how technology and social media are used in everyday life, and implement a slice of that into our foreign language teaching.

Finally, if the items in this chapter make you feel nervous because you are not technologically savvy, we suggest that you start by looking at the Portuguese language materials that are provided by COERLL. These are all open access, free to use, and come without password restrictions. They can be used to enhance any class or any personal learning. Use all of them or use portions, it is up to you and the learners. Second, refer students to any of the tools that were listed to enhance individual learning (e.g., Memrise, Mango Languages, and the various chatting programs). These do not require classroom coordination or specific monitoring from teachers. In many ways, all you have to do is make students aware of them and refer these items to them.

Third, some of the items that we mentioned do imply a brief learning curve, usually less than 1 hour each: (Padlet, Blendspace, Getkahoot, Coogle.it, List.ly). All of these programs also have online tutorials from their homepages, and that is a good place to start. And finally, save for last those programs that do require a more involved learning curve: Wikispaces, YouTube Channels, Aurasma, and Vyclone. Whatever you do, always come back to the premise that we should incorporate into our teaching those same communication tools that are used in our everyday life.

PART 3

ADDRESSING THE NEEDS OF SPECIFIC LEARNERS

3.1 HERITAGE LEARNERS

Gláucia Silva
University of Massachusetts Dartmouth
Ivian Destro Boruchowski
Florida International University

A heritage language (HL) can be described as a non-dominant language that is used in immigrant communities. Here, we follow Valdés's (2001) definition of heritage language learners (HLLs): individuals who were raised in an environment where a minority language was spoken, and who speak or at least understand that language, and are bilinguals to some degree. Since they have been exposed to the HL from a very young age but have often been schooled only (or mainly) in the majority language, HLLs may already understand the HL in its informal spoken register, but may not know how to read and/or write it. In spite of the wide variation in HL proficiency, HLLs tend to be more comfortable with their listening skills than speaking (though many do speak their HL). They also tend to feel more at ease with informal rather than with formal registers. Although there may be HLLs who are somewhat proficient HL readers, most find it difficult to write in the heritage language (Carreira & Kagan, 2011). Furthermore, HLLs may or may not be familiar with pragmatic constraints in their heritage language (Santos & Silva, 2008).

Given this brief (and admittedly broad) description of HLLs, it seems clear that their learning needs tend towards formal registers and written language. While HLLs may not describe much difficulty with listening skills (Santos & Silva, 2015), foreign language learners (FLLs), in contrast, tend to struggle to comprehend spoken registers, especially in the beginning of their studies. On the other hand, FLLs may feel more comfortable than HLLs with certain practices in the foreign language classroom. For example, common approaches to grammar involve listing rules and naming structures such as verb forms. Since HLLs already tend to produce several of those structures, memorizing rules or naming the structures may be of little help to them (Parodi, 2008; Schwarzer & Petrón, 2005).

It is true that HLLs of Portuguese may display some similarities with FLLs in regards to language use, such as failing to distinguish between indicative and subjunctive moods (Amaral, Cunha & Silva, 2011). However, despite possible similarities with FLLs, HLLs exhibit specific needs and would profit from teaching approaches geared toward those needs. In what follows, we discuss the teaching of Portuguese to teenage/adult HLLs, including classroom practices, materials, assessment, and program development. We also discuss what instructors can do when HLLs and FLLs have to share the same classroom. Furthermore, we offer considerations on teaching Portuguese to young heritage learners, also including practices, materials, assessment, and program development. Although at times this chapter makes specific reference to the United States context, it is our hope that most of it may be of use in other contexts as well.

Before we move on, however, a few words about dialectal differences. As we know, Brazilian and European Portuguese can differ quite a bit. Even varieties of these two major dialects can present several differences among them, not to mention varieties of Portuguese used in Africa (but note that the varieties used in Africa tend to follow the European standard, and are thus included in it whenever we mention standard language). If an instructor is a speaker of a variety that differs from the one used by several (or most) of the HLLs in the class (e.g., a Brazilian instructor from Bahia teaching HLLs of European Portuguese as it is spoken in São Miguel, in the Azores), the instructor needs to be quite familiar with the other standard and, preferably, also somewhat familiar with the particular variety that is used by the learners. Given the many points where Brazilian and European Portuguese diverge (referring only to the two main standards), it is essential that instructors be able to guide HLLs in the standard closest to the variety that is familiar to them. On the other hand, instructors need to acknowledge when they are not familiar with something (such as a word used in a given variety) and show their appreciation for the opportunity to learn more about her/his students' Portuguese. After all, the classroom is but a space to exchange experiences and sometimes the roles of learner and instructor can certainly become blurred.

Teenagers and Adult HLLs

Heritage learners of Portuguese in high school (teenagers) and in college/university (young adults) may or may not have had some formal schooling in the language. If they did, they have most likely attended a community-based school (in afterschool or Saturday programs). For many of these learners, however, the first contact with academic Portuguese is in high school or in college. Even those who did attend community-based schools may need quite a bit of practice in skills such as reading and writing, or using formal spoken language and some grammatical structures. In what follows, we provide a few suggestions related to working with HLLs in high school or in college. We discuss classroom approaches and possibilities regarding each linguistic ability, as well as potential ways of using Portuguese beyond the classroom and students' immediate families.

In the Classroom

As has been emphasized in this chapter, HLLs tend to understand spoken Portuguese. Therefore, the first recommendation is an obvious one: the instructor needs to use Portuguese, preferably from the very first day of class, when s/he will set the tone for the course. It is important to note, however, that code switching (i.e., going back and forth between Portuguese and English, often within the same sentence) is a common practice among HLLs and does not need to be abolished in the classroom (Carvalho, 2012). Such a ban would imply that the instructor does not value the learners' contributions and their previous knowledge, and thus may lead to lack of motivation to remain in the course.

Valuing what HLLs bring to the table, so to speak, is essential (Harklau, 2009; Parodi, 2008; Villa, 1997; among others). Most of these learners understand spoken language and many can speak Portuguese. They may speak a version of the language that has features that are not present in standard varieties, but that does not mean that their Portuguese is "wrong." It is essential to make it clear to HLLs that they do speak Portuguese, even if they are not yet familiar with standard Portuguese. Many heritage learners of Portuguese firmly believe that they speak "bad" or "wrong" Portuguese. That notion needs to be dispelled from the beginning. Teaching heritage learners, we should aim for bidialectalism (ie, learners would be familiar both with their dialect and with the standard dialect), as defended by Valdés (2001) and others. The starting point for that work is what learners already know.

Heritage language learners are bilinguals who have learned Portuguese in contact with a dominant language. Therefore, their variety of Portuguese is expected to contain features that evidence this contact, and nothing could be more natural. Clearly, our goal as instructors is to help learners develop their language skills so that they will move beyond informal registers and will be able to utilize Portuguese in any situation, from the dinner table to the workplace. Once again, valuing their contribution is fundamental. We also need to keep in mind that learners tend to be more motivated to participate in class if their contributions are valued. The opposite is also true: as has been previously argued (Harklau, 2009; Parodi, 2008), HLLs become demotivated when their contributions are deemed invaluable.

To help learners develop their skills, we can provide opportunities for metalinguistic analyses. Unlike younger learners, teenagers and adults are capable of comparing, contrasting and generally analyzing linguistic structures. Therefore, instructors may lead learners in activities that compare the type of Portuguese used in their communities to standard (Brazilian or European) Portuguese. To give a concrete example, an activity may request that learners match words that are only used in contact with the dominant language (e.g., "printar" for *imprimir* or "bega" for *saco, bolsa,* when in contact with English) and their equivalent in standard Portuguese. As a follow-up, learners may attempt to construct situations in which each version of a given word would be expected (keeping in mind that there are in fact situations in which a speaker is expected to use words and/or structures that are not necessarily considered standard).

As learners with metalinguistic abilities, teenagers and adults may also be invited to analyze their own linguistic production. Identifying and correcting their own mistakes (such as problems with spelling or use of a certain structure) helps learners retrieve structures that they have seen before.

Given that HLLs comprise a heterogeneous group in terms of language abilities, instructors may want to develop a few differentiated activities that would allow for learners at various stages to achieve a certain goal. Differentiated instruction is particularly useful for groups with different proficiency levels, as tends to be the case in groups of HLLs (Carreira, 2007). Suppose, for example, that a learning goal for a certain lesson is to interpret a written text on markets in the Portuguese-speaking world. Suppose also that some learners are more fluent readers in Portuguese than others. The class can then be divided into groups that will accomplish different tasks based on the same text. For example, one group can read the text and summarize it in English, another can identify the main ideas in Portuguese, and another can compare, in Portuguese, the information with their own shopping/market experiences (where they live or other places). As for how the groups are separated, there are different options. Students can be grouped by level of proficiency or not. In mixed groups, more fluent readers would help less fluent ones; in same-level groups, the activity is assigned according to level of proficiency. Either way, the different activities would all help students interpret the text. Therefore, it is easy to see that differentiated instruction can be quite useful in the Portuguese Heritage Language classroom.

Turning to each of the language skills, below we discuss them and provide suggestions that, we hope, may be useful for the classroom. Naturally, classroom activities should promote communication among learners and the purposeful use of language, thereby allowing learners to develop their skills.

Speaking

As mentioned above, many HLLs arrive at their high school or college/university Portuguese class already speaking at least some Portuguese. Since, most often, there has been no formal schooling in Portuguese, HLLs' speaking abilities tend to be limited to informal/familial language. One of the goals of the HL Portuguese classroom is to develop learners' already existing speaking abilities, so that these will include registers other than informal spoken language (which, we must reinforce, is a wonderful starting point that needs to be valued by instructors, who must acknowledge learners' contributions).

In order to practice different registers (e.g., familial, academic) and vocabulary, learners may be invited to analyze different situations shown in videos. Then, they may be invited to note what characterizes a certain situation (e.g., what makes it formal or informal), from gestures to linguistic forms. Finally, learners would develop situations in which they would create and act out scenarios in which different registers are used. Classmates and instructor would provide feedback on these role play activities, pointing out which linguistic forms were appropriate for the situation, which were not, and if other forms could or should have been used.

Besides developing a variety of linguistic registers in interactive mode, HLLs would also profit from practicing the presentational mode of speaking, which is characterized by its one-way direction. HLLs tend to use language that is both informal and characteristic of interactive mode even in classroom presentations. Having HLLs attend not only to linguistic features of different registers but also to different speaking modes would help develop learners' abilities, expanding their speaking skills.

Listening

Heritage learners of Portuguese tend to be able to understand spoken language in informal, interactive situations. However, even if they can understand dialogues in a soap opera, many may have difficulties understanding a newscast, for example. This type of difficulty may be caused by several factors, including unfamiliarity with a given context, with certain vocabulary, with a certain dialect, with the type of register, etc. In order to help HLLs develop their listening skills, we can discuss and invite learners to practice different listening strategies.

Listening strategies are often categorized into top-down and bottom-up strategies. Top-down strategies are deployed when the learner uses background knowledge (situation, topic, what came before and after) to understand what is heard. These strategies include listening for the gist, predicting, guessing, and summarizing. In the classroom, we can use activities that encourage learners to predict the content of a passage by looking at pictures (in the case of a newscast, for example). Learners can also activate their background knowledge of the topic (for example, from a headline or a title) to predict content. In this type of listening, it is important not to focus on unknown words, but rather to use background knowledge to try to guess the meaning of words that learners encounter for the first time, if those words are essential to the content at hand. Classroom activities that involve top-down strategies may include putting a sequence of events in order or inferring relationships between people in a conversation.

When a listener uses bottom-up strategies, s/he relies on language itself (sounds, words, grammar) to create meaning. Listening for specific details, for example, is a bottom-up strategy. A possible classroom activity is to ask learners to fill out a form based on a narrative or a dialogue.

As might be expected, successful listeners use both types of strategies (Goh, 2005). In the case of HLLs, it is important to provide them with opportunities to listen to types of text with which they may not be very familiar, so they may be able to develop their listening skills. For high school and college-level students, it is important to be able to understand language that is used in a variety of situations, including the workplace, since many HLLs of Portuguese plan to use the language in their careers (Gontijo, 2010). It is also important to expose learners to different varieties of Portuguese. As the official language in nine countries on four continents, Portuguese is a truly global language, with different accents, vocabulary and even grammatical structures. Learners need to be familiar with several varieties of Portuguese in order to be able to communicate successfully with speakers from different parts of the globe.

Reading

Like other heritage learners, HLLs of Portuguese display a wide range of reading abilities. As teenagers and adults, most are capable of reading strings of words (though cognates may sound very close to the dominant language when read out loud). Without prior schooling in Portuguese and with possibly limited exposure to printed texts in the language, many HLLs find that reading is a challenge. To help students overcome this challenge, it is essential to take some important steps.

Reading skills do not necessarily transfer from the dominant to the heritage language (Wang & Green, 2001; Valdés, 2001). Therefore, it is important to address reading strategies (e.g., predicting, skimming and scanning, guessing, paraphrasing). Here, the work may start in (and about) the dominant language: what are the strategies that HLLs utilize to read in their dominant language? Once the successful strategies are established, we can try to determine what strategies, if any, learners use to tackle texts in Portuguese. Being aware of the strategies they use may help learners start changing unsuccessful habits. Naturally, the instructor should model strategies for reading different texts and for different purposes, helping students practice these various strategies.

Motivation is a key factor in developing reading abilities. Therefore, to motivate students to read (both in and out of the classroom), it is important to present them with texts that may interest them. Motivation to read a certain text may be intrinsic (the person enjoys that type of text) or extrinsic (the person needs to read a type of text in order to learn or accomplish something). So, if a student enjoys a certain type of text in his/her dominant language (e.g., mystery novels), we can make that type of text available in Portuguese. If learners are enrolled in the course to understand their family's culture more deeply, instructors can bring texts that speak to that aspect (children's literature, short stories and short texts about cultural features, such as folklore, can be valuable resources in that domain). Of course, in this particular case, the kind of text will depend on the learners' ancestry: if learners descend from speakers of European Portuguese, the first texts should be in that variety and reflect that culture. The same is true for Brazilian Portuguese and African Portuguese: the first texts presented to students would reflect aspects of the learners' family culture. Keeping students motivated is key in promoting literacy in Portuguese. After reading a number of texts about their family's culture, students may be invited to learn about other Portuguese-speaking cultures: folklore, for example, would be a wonderful window into other cultures that can be further explored by teenagers and young adults.

Writing

It has been attested that HLLs believe that their listening and speaking skills are far superior to their reading and (especially) writing skills (Carreira & Kagan, 2011; Shinbo, 2004; Xiao, 2006). Practitioners in different languages highlight the importance of teaching and practicing writing skills in the heritage language classroom. Several authors (e.g., Colombi, 1997, 2003; Solé, 1981) have mentioned that HLLs tend to write the way they speak since they have often not been exposed to written Portuguese in any systematic or lengthy manner before enrolling in the Portuguese language course, HLLs are not necessarily familiar with the differences between spoken and written registers of the language. Furthermore, not all learners transfer their writing abilities in the dominant language to Portuguese. From spelling errors to inadequate expression, HLLs tend to exhibit problems with writing, which they consider to be a very difficult skill (Silva, 2011).

To help HLLs develop their writing skills in Portuguese, we can start by presenting different types of written texts so that learners can identify the features that characterize these texts. One possible starting point is to have learners compare texts on the same topic that are written on social media (closer to the spoken modality) and in newspapers. They would then point out what these texts have in common and where they differ. After analyzing several excerpts from newspapers and magazines, a possible long-term writing activity that may involve the whole classroom would be to produce a class newspaper—say, "O Jornal da Turma"—with news about their school and about them (who traveled where, who is working where, etc.). The "Jornal" might exist in physical form or online.

Naturally, newspapers and magazines would not be the only written forms to be analyzed and practiced. Other texts should be introduced, and students should be invited to analyze and compare them, as well as with the spoken register. The intention here is to help learners identify features that they should try to reproduce, such as lack of unnecessary repetition, appropriate use of modifiers, appropriate punctuation, etc.

As many have said, "writing is rewriting." This may be even truer for teenagers and adult HLLs, who may be used to writing in their dominant language but are only now learning how to write in Portuguese. Writing can start with brainstorming and other activities that will help learners "jump start" their texts. After starting their texts in the classroom, learners can either continue writing in the classroom or finish their texts at home, depending on the text and on what the class has been working on. It is important to call students' attention to the first sentence in this paragraph, reminding them about the process of writing and the several stages involved in it. Once learners have a first draft, the class can proceed to a peer-editing phase in which students read their classmates' texts and offer suggestions. After these suggestions are incorporated, learners can then submit their texts to the instructor, who will make further suggestions. How revisions will be submitted will depend on the assignment and/or on what is stated in the course syllabus.

We have suggested above that teenagers and adults be invited to analyze their own linguistic production. Error analysis exercises are perhaps easiest to prepare if they are based on written production, since instructors can easily compile examples from students' texts (note that we are not suggesting that exercises cannot be prepared on the basis of oral production—they can and they should). Of course, these exercises are normally restricted to the sentence level, but they can be very helpful in calling learners' attention to certain structures. These exercises can also be used to bring to the fore any cross-linguistic influence that appears in writing, helping learners notice where and why their production differs from the target.

While dialectal differences may be more evident in spoken language, they also exist in written language. Instructors of Portuguese as a Heritage Language need to be sensitive to these differences and not penalize students for using a standard that may not be the one that the instructor is familiar with. While the "Acordo Ortográfico" has sought to minimize spelling differences between Brazilian and European Portuguese, those differences have not been completely eliminated. Furthermore, other differences will always remain, since the "Acordo" refers only to spelling. We have suggested here that the variety of Portuguese used by heritage learners must be valued. This includes the standard that they prefer to follow. Of course instructors are not expected to be fluent in more than one variety of Portuguese, but they are expected to be familiar with the Brazilian and the European standards of the language. And because no one is an encyclopedia, instructors should look up information about the other standard when in doubt (colleagues and acquaintances who are speakers of other varieties are wonderful resources).

Grammar

Grammar permeates every aspect of linguistic production. While the foreign language teaching pendulum has swung from teaching only grammar to teaching no grammar, nowadays we seem to find ourselves in the middle, with some explicit grammar instruction in the foreign language classroom, and some practice embedded in other abilities. However, here we address the heritage language classroom, and it is perhaps in relation to grammar instruction that heritage and foreign language instruction differ the most.

As Schwarzer and Petrón (2005) and Parodi (2008) have argued, HLLs find little use in traditional FL grammar instruction. Heritage learners of Portuguese already use correctly several of the grammar forms emphasized in foreign language classes (think, for example, about the difference between *ser* and *estar*, which poses problems for FLLs but rarely for HLLs). Naming and providing rules for those forms already used by learners seems to be of little value in their linguistic development. Furthermore, it is important to take into consideration the knowledge that HLLs already have and dedicate more time to the grammatical forms that they may not have mastered yet.

We have suggested above that teenagers and adult HLLs analyze and compare linguistic production. We would like to suggest that linguistic analyses be extended to grammar instruction: instead of having learners read about rules and memorize names of grammar forms, learners can be invited to compare structures in order to reach conclusions about what forms to use in which situations. To give a concrete example, take the future subjunctive, a form that is often not part of HLLs' production (with the possible exception of some set phrases, such as "se Deus quiser"). Learners may be invited to compare habitual and future conditions, as "Quando eu *vou* ao Brasil/a Portugal/a Angola, converso com os meus parentes" and "Quando eu *for* ao Brasil/a Portugal/a Angola, vou conversar com os meus parentes". After deciding which sentences express habit and which sentences express future action, learners are invited to find what forms are related to which meaning. Then, learners can practice the new form (the future subjunctive) in oral and written exercises, including, possibly, a text in which they discuss future conditions (e.g., in the context of a future project, a political campaign, life in the next century, or the results of future actions).

The type of grammar practice suggested above obviates the need for naming structures while providing learners with opportunities for practice. Given that HLLs have learned Portuguese in a naturalistic environment, the emphasis should be on linguistic development, not on rote memorization of grammar forms and rules. Learners need to know when to use a certain form, not what it is called. Keeping in mind that maintaining motivation is key in HLLs' development, and that grammar instruction can be quite dry, it is our job to include grammar in a stimulating manner that helps learners to incorporate the new forms into their linguistic production.

Having provided suggestions for classroom practice related to each linguistic skill, we now turn to materials and assessment before addressing activities outside of the classroom. In the 21st century, modes of communication abound and learners should be encouraged to use them in order to advance their abilities.

Materials

To the best of our knowledge, there are no materials designed specifically for heritage learners of Portuguese. At the high school and college levels, we use and adapt materials that are originally designed for teaching and learning Portuguese as a foreign language. Needless to say, we also create materials, from lists comparing standard to local Portuguese to guides for viewing newscasts.

In adapting or creating materials for HLLs, we need to take into consideration what learners already know and, consequently, what our goals are for a particular lesson and for the course as a whole. For example, one learning objective for a course for heritage learners of Portuguese might be "to use formal and informal language in appropriate contexts." During the course, there will be opportunities for learners to practice both types of registers. However, language textbooks rarely address differences in register beyond greetings. Therefore, the instructor may develop materials to accompany some of the activities that address this learning objective. Such materials may include situations that learners classify into categories; expressions to be matched to situations; and prompts for the development of situations to be enacted by students.

Assessment

For teenagers and young adults, assessment in heritage language may be associated with placement or with classroom learning. First, we discuss placement of Portuguese HLLs; then we move to assessment of performance in Portuguese language classes.

Placement of HLLs can be done in different ways, from self-assessment to placement tests combined with interviews. Since most high schools and colleges/universities (at least in North America) do not yet have separate tracks for heritage learners of Portuguese, HLLs are often placed in other tracks (accelerated courses, courses for Spanish speakers)—or, depending on the program, directly into advanced composition or literature courses. For programs that do not offer separate tracks for HLLs of Portuguese, it is important to assess learners' abilities beyond reading and writing, which may be the only skills tested in general placement tests. While HLLs tend to need quite a bit of practice in those two skills, placing them in a traditional first or second semester class may prove to be counterproductive. On the other hand, placing every HLL directly in composition or literature courses may also result in frustrations. Unfortunately, we cannot offer a simple solution to the placement conundrum. Heritage learners comprise a heterogeneous group, and placing them in language classes may well require interviews that would allow instructors and/or program directors to decide which of the courses they offer may best help advance a learner's linguistic abilities.

For programs that do have a separate track for HLLs of Portuguese, the task may be a bit easier, especially if more than one level is offered each term. In those programs, a written placement test with short essay questions about how the student learned Portuguese may be sufficient to place the student correctly. However, placement of heritage learners of Portuguese would ideally also involve an oral interview, which would help determine more precisely which course is the best fit for the learner.

In relation to classroom learning, it goes without saying that students can only be tested in what they have practiced. As we have seen above, heritage learners need to practice different spoken registers besides reading and writing. Therefore, assessment of classroom learning should include the functions practiced in class, evaluating how well and how accurately learners carry them out. Presentations can also be used to evaluate speaking: HLLs would have to demonstrate ability to go beyond the informal register used in interactions with friends and family, and use language in presentational mode. While discrete items can be used to evaluate specific grammar points, avoid using grammatical nomenclature to refer to a given structure: HLLs may know how to use a structure, but not necessarily what it is called. Providing one or two examples in these cases would help learners understand what is being asked. Reading and (short) writing test items should follow formats utilized in class. Writing that involves more than a very short paragraph should be evaluated in stages, giving learners the opportunity to turn in several drafts, as described above.

Beyond the Classroom: the Portuguese-speaking World

As the official language of nine countries on four continents (and of the region of Macau in China), Portuguese is a truly global language. Being able to interact in Portuguese opens doors to different countries and cultures, giving those who are comfortable with the language a true advantage over others who are not familiar with it. Naturally, Portuguese has many different varieties, and familiarity with one dialect does not necessarily guarantee ease of communication with speakers of another dialect. Therefore, it is important to provide learners—and perhaps especially heritage learners—with opportunities to listen to and interact with speakers of as many varieties as possible.

Familiarizing students with various dialects of Portuguese can start in the classroom. Learners can work on videos from different regions and interact with guest speakers who use a variety that differs from the one that learners are used to. In order to learn about the many regions in the Portuguese-speaking world, students have only to access the Internet and find publications from different countries. As mentioned above, however, learners are motivated to read texts on topics of their interest. Therefore, it is important to encourage them by pointing them in the right direction, as it were, and inviting them to learn more about their interest as it relates to other cultures in the Portuguese-speaking world.

In order to become even more comfortable with several dialects of Portuguese, learners can be encouraged to interact with people from various regions as well. Even in locales not particularly known for large concentrations of Portuguese-speaking immigrants, it may be possible to find speakers of many varieties: for example, there may be speakers of different Portuguese dialects studying at the same university (reaching out to the Admissions office and/or the Graduate Studies office may be helpful). Nowadays, however, connections do not need to be made in person: in our virtual world, social media can be a very useful tool. Suppose the preferred variety in the class is a given dialect of European Portuguese. The class can connect with students in Brazil and use Portuguese to exchange thoughts about habits and customs, thus not only familiarizing themselves with a different dialect, but also learning about another Portuguese-speaking culture. (To connect specifically with Brazilian college students, the project Teletandem may be very helpful.) Of course, we would not want our students to befriend anybody that uses Facebook in any given country. The instructor should act as facilitator in this process, possibly using her/his own contacts to reach social media users who would be willing to exchange experiences with her/his students.

Besides connecting with the larger Portuguese-speaking world, teenagers and adults can also connect with their own community, if they live near a significant Portuguese-speaking population. Service-learning opportunities can be created to encourage learners to serve their community while using their Portuguese language skills. This type of opportunity allows for linguistic development and civic engagement, and may also serve as a springboard for future employment.

Mixed Classrooms

This text has addressed Portuguese for heritage learners, highlighting their needs and suggesting activities and materials that might be developed for this cohort. However, in many, perhaps most cases (especially at the college/university level), heritage learners are enrolled in Portuguese courses for foreign language learners (in the case of colleges/universities in the United States, sometimes these courses are designed specifically for speakers of Spanish). Given this reality, instructors need to create opportunities for both types of learners to develop their Portuguese language skills.

Roca (1997) mentions the high expectations that are placed on heritage learners. Since these students can typically understand spoken language and can often already communicate in Portuguese, instructors might expect that these learners will also write well, read perfectly and know the difference between the present indicative and the present subjunctive. It is very important to keep those expectations in check: even if they can already speak informal Portuguese, HLLs do have a lot to learn, and some of that can be learned with their classmates who have not been exposed to Portuguese before.

When grouping students in mixed classrooms to carry out a given activity, it is important to keep in mind who is going to benefit from the activity. Research has shown that HLLs and FLLs can work together and profit from the activity, as long as each group can help the other. For example, if a mixed group works on an activity that involves vocabulary related to the house, FLLs can profit from interacting with HLLs, but HLLs will learn little in the exchange. If, however, the groups work on a collaborative writing task, HLLs can benefit from FLLs' knowledge of spelling and accentuation, while FLLs can learn from HLLs' intuitions regarding use of Portuguese.

Above we have suggested that students may benefit from (at least some) differentiated instruction. In mixed classes, differentiation may be an option as well. We acknowledge that differentiating each class and each activity would be too time-consuming, and few instructors would be able to dedicate that much time and energy to preparing each lesson. However, in mixed classes, some activities may be differentiated so that both FLLs and HLLs may benefit from them. Take, for example, an activity involving house vocabulary. The activity may be differentiated so that both HLLs and FLLs may profit from it, working separately. Below we detail how such an activity may be carried out.

Sample Activities

Activity 1. House Vocabulary

Find a picture of a room that is crowded with furniture and objects in general. Groups will work with this picture.

HLLs: Writing activity. Students will work in pairs, playing the role of decorators. They have been hired to decorate the room. They will write an email to their client explaining what they will do: the pieces of furniture they will keep, the pieces they will not keep, what they will buy and where the pieces will be situated in the room.

FLLs: Speaking activity. Students will work in pairs. They will rearrange the furniture and the objects in the room, deciding on what they will keep and what they will get rid of. They must also agree on where to place the remaining pieces. To make sure they agree, they can sketch the new room based on the picture they were given.

As we can see, both HLLs and FLLs practice the same vocabulary. However, since HLLs may already be familiar with those words, they have the chance to practice them in writing, a skill which is often considered more difficult by these learners than speaking or listening. For FLLs, the new vocabulary can be practiced in a speaking activity that will help them use the vocabulary in context.

As we mentioned above, not all activities would be differentiated, even in a mixed classroom. Furthermore, HLLs and FLLs can and should work together in several activities throughout the term. To provide an example of how a mixed group can work together, let's take a writing activity, as the one detailed below.

Activity 2. Responding to a "Want Ad"

Provide students with a text that contains an advertisement for a job. Before having students read the text, be sure to carry out a brief pre-reading discussion or activity. Also provide them with salutations and other "formulas" that may be used in formal letters in Portuguese.

In groups of three, students read the ad and determine what position is being advertised. First, they write a list of qualifications that a desirable candidate must possess. Then, they will compose a letter to respond to the ad, using some of the phrases for formal letters provided by the instructor.

In Activity 2, FLLs and HLLs can work together. It is possible (though by no means certain) that HLLs may understand the ad more quickly than FLLs. If that is the case, the HLL(s) in the group must be sure to aid the FLL(s). Both types of learners would then compose the list of qualifications (they may all write lists or they may elect one person to write a common list). Next, one person puts the letter onto paper (or screen), using the formal phrases provided. It is important to direct students to check on each other's work: while one student may be the scribe, the other two must still make sure that the scribe is using correct spelling and grammar (and FLLs may well help HLLs, whose writing skills often are not on par with their speaking skills). Students should also be instructed to use their textbook to check spelling and grammar (although FLLs may resort to the textbook a little more than HLLs, neither group seems to use this precious resource often enough).

At the college/university level, Portuguese language classes may have both HLLs and FLLs. We hope that this section has shown that these groups of learners can work together as well as separately to achieve the same lesson objectives. Of course, each class is different and the instructor has to decide what type of approach might work best depending on the activity and its goal. Next, we discuss how a program for heritage learners might be developed at the college/university level.

Program Development in Colleges and Universities

In most colleges and universities in North America, the number of heritage learners of Portuguese still does not warrant a separate track. However, as children of more recent immigrants reach colleges and universities, this picture may change. We offer a few suggestions regarding the creation of a separate track for heritage learners as well as directing students to that track.

First of all, it is necessary to make a case for the heritage Portuguese track. In most colleges and universities, creation of new courses is tied to projected enrollment. It is important to make sure that the new courses will have the number of students necessary to make them viable.

In some cases, heritage learners enroll (or are enrolled if they are freshmen) in regular first semester Portuguese language courses, even if that level is not appropriate for them. Several actions can be taken to try to remedy this situation. Instructors and/or program directors can reach out to Academic Advising (or equivalent office) and work with them in placing freshmen. Instructors and/or program directors can also send emails to students enrolled in first semester Portuguese before classes start, alerting them to the existence of the heritage language track. Assuming heritage learners still end up in other tracks, instructors and/or directors may visit each first semester class during their first meeting to let students know about the heritage Portuguese courses. Since not every student starts fulfilling the foreign language requirement as soon as s/he enters college (in institutions that have the requirement), academic advisors should be reminded of the heritage Portuguese option every advising season (an email to advisors and/or information sent via campus mail should suffice). These measures should ensure that the new track has the required enrollment, even if some heritage learners stay in the traditional language track.

The heritage language track may have a better chance of attracting enrollment if it offers students some advantage over the regular track (besides being specifically designed for them). Given that heritage learners often already understand (much of) spoken Portuguese and can speak at least some informal language, one possible way of attracting students is to make the heritage language track shorter than the regular Portuguese language track. That way, students can save some time and money fulfilling their requirement—and, by taking a course that is designed for them, some heritage learners will likely decide to major or minor in Portuguese, thus helping to boost other important numbers.

In relation to content, a heritage Portuguese track needs to include topics that help HLLs develop both their linguistic and their cultural awareness. As mentioned above, one topic of discussion can be comparisons between standard Portuguese and the variety learners are familiar with—i.e., discussions and practice of different linguistic registers and when/where each is used. Other topics may include native and heritage language, language and identity, code switching, immigration, linguistic prejudice, the importance of Portuguese and of the dominant language (which will include discussions about language used locally and globally), etc. Some of these topics yield productive conversations among learners with little preparation needed. For others, some reading prior to class may help jump start the discussion and/or introduce different points of view. While these exchanges would ideally happen in Portuguese in order to promote linguistic development, sometimes learners feel more comfortable discussing some of these issues in the dominant language. What language is used might be less important than getting learners to share their views (one possibility is for the instructor to use Portuguese consistently but give learners the option to use Portuguese or the dominant language, or to code switch).

The topics suggested above can be woven into topics normally found in textbooks for Portuguese as a foreign language. For example, language and identity can be tied to a conversation about identity in college/university, which in turn would fit into a unit on "a universidade." Immigration can be discussed in relation to food (immigrants and their meals), health and medicine (health care for immigrants), etc. Different registers can be included in a unit on family, which would allow for discussions on language used with family and friends, and in other contexts.

As we can see, the main barrier for developing a heritage Portuguese language track at the university level may be guaranteeing enrollment. Once that is done, discussing topics that are important for HLLs while also practicing the necessary linguistic skills will certainly make for very interesting classes, both for students and instructors.

So far, we have considered HLLs as teenage or adult learners and how their needs may be addressed. We turn next to children learning a heritage language and discuss their specific needs. Those considerations are followed by a discussion on developing heritage language programs for young HLLs.

Young Heritage Language Learners: Specific Needs and Learning Expectations

The U.S. educational system has a growing population of bilingual children. The first language used by a child may not be his or her dominant language later on, and that first language may become the child's heritage language. As an example, a child may have been born in a country where Portuguese has the status of a majority language, and may have immigrated at an early age to another country that uses a different dominant language. In this case, Portuguese will be considered the child's HL (as in the case of a child who is born to a Lusophone immigrant family who maintains the use of Portuguese at home).

Within a family, siblings can develop different range of abilities in a HL. Consequently, Young Heritage Language Learners (YHLLs) can have different profiles and experiences, even within the same family.

Typically an YHLL's knowledge extends to spoken language that includes vocabulary and grammar constructions related to the language register and variety that the family uses at home in their everyday life. YHLLs also develop some familiarity with sociocultural knowledge related to specific areas such as pragmatics of the language, traditions, sports, and food. However, Lynch (2003) and Valdés (1995), among others, observed that heritage learners can show different ranges of language competence, from having only receptive skills to being a fairly balanced bilingual, and these differences tend to start from a young age. Consequently, teachers should not mistakenly assume that all HLLs, including YHLLs, have the same history and language knowledge.

To maintain and develop a HL for YHLLs is first a family choice, meaning that it is the caretakers who usually decide if they will interact in the HL with their children at home. This decision is usually influenced by a family's beliefs and attitudes about their own identity. When minority-language families decide to make efforts to preserve and develop their HL and culture at home, they need to establish a family language policy, which is planning the language use at home among their members (King & Mackey, 2010). Couples need to negotiate between them in order to make sure that children will have enough language exposure and use.

Minority-language families may adopt strategies to guarantee exposure and establish a consistent pattern of language use. Grosjean (2010) observed that a common strategy is the "home outside the home" or "minority language at home", when parents choose to use the family language at home and the majority language outside home settings. Another common strategy is the "one-person-one-language" approach, when each adult family member speaks only his or her language to the children (in the case of different first languages). These strategies are usually successful with young children. However, some caregivers struggle to keep the selected strategy consistently after the child enters school.

Families need to keep monitoring the linguistic environment to ensure that their children have a real need for HL use and that they are receiving enough and high quality of language exposure. Grosjean (2010) also postulated that it is essential that exposure come from human interaction (speaking to, playing with, or reading and retelling) because children are pragmatic and they will only use the HL if there is a purpose for it. Passive activities such as watching DVDs or TV can be a complementary source, but not the main one.

Given the struggle to maintain the HL at home after a child starts school, as well as difficulties to provide real interaction in the HL with peers,

Boruchowski (2014) has shown that parents need constant encouragement and support from teachers in order to continue using the HL at home. Therefore, it is important to keep in mind that, when working with YHLLs, professionals should also support parents so that they can understand best practices when raising bilingual children.

In the Classroom

YHLLs acquire the HL and develop some language abilities at home. However, usually when children enter mainstream school their use and knowledge of the majority language increase and develop much more than their HL. Furthermore, it is important to be aware that when YHLLs enter school, they can experience explicit or implicit negative attitudes towards their home language. Regarding minority students in the United States, Nieto (2002) observed a predominant ideology of "either/or" belonging has been observed. This ideology implicitly says that to participate in American society, heritage learners, including YHLLs, must abandon their family culture, identity and language.

If there are hurdles to maintaining a child's HL speaking abilities, these obstacles may be even more difficult to overcome in relation to achieving biliteracy. Families deciding to make efforts to maintain and develop their children's HL usually have two main educational options to develop biliteracy: (1) bilingual education offered in mainstream schools or (2) HL community-based schools. Researching bilingualism, linguists have confirmed that proficiency in the first language is a predictor of how well one acquires the second language (Baker, 2001). The number of years of instruction in the child's first language is a key predictor of how quickly the child will advance academically in school in her second language (Gathercole, 2007; Gathercole & Thomas, 2009; Paradis, 2010). Consequently, teaching YHLLs to read and write in their heritage language will promote their reading abilities in the majority language as well. However, in American schools, the predominant mentality is to see these students as "at risk" for English language development, directing them to transitional special programs designed to only master English.

In the American school system, HL students are currently classified as English Language Learners (ELLs) and are placed in classes where they are to receive assistance with the English language. This label makes invisible the linguistic resource of those who speak languages other than English when entering the mainstream school system (Caldas, 2013). Moreover, schools do not typically accommodate the need of YHLLs to develop full biliteracy. When mainstream schools offer languages other than English, these HL students are usually enrolled in foreign language (FL) courses, which do not address their specific needs. It is important that universities and professional development programs approach this issue when preparing teachers to value children's HL skills.

In the U.S., there are few options of high schools offering Portuguese, and fewer schools offering this language at the elementary level. Additionally, there are no data of how many of these courses address YHLLs' specific needs, if they do so. Teachers and families should work together and share the responsibility for advocating for a curriculum that embraces and nurtures HL maintenance and development. As Boruchowski (2014) indicated, Portuguese as HL programs should aim to:

1. Develop linguistic and cultural belonging in the HL in order to help YHLLs to develop a strong connection with the extended family, and create the possibility for learners to develop identity discourses of belonging in the HL and culture.
2. Maintain and develop students speaking, listening, reading, and writing abilities. The goal is not only to strengthen family connections, but also to offer the opportunity for learners to participate in different modalities of communication in different situations of everyday life. The development of reading skills can be understood as a door to access unlimited cultural knowledge in the HL.
3. Enhance children's pride in speaking a language other than English. Creating interaction among peers in the HL can soften the idea of being different from other children at the mainstream school, and soften as well the implicit negative attitude towards a heritage identity.
4. Help parents to be aware of the family's crucial role raising a bilingual child. When working with YHLLs, it is important to support parents so they can understand their role and the best practices of raising bilingual children.
5. Design courses that are focused on teaching and experiencing language and culture as inseparable, i.e., not focusing on language only. For YHLLs, it is recommended that instructors explore deeper cultural knowledge, focus on macro-approach language teaching, and design activities with purposeful and real social interaction.
6. HL programs also need to embrace their learners multiculturalism and hybrid identities, consequently should focus on developing plurilingualism and pluricultural competences.

In the absence of Portuguese in the school curriculum, many families opt for community-based schools to help maintain and develop their children's linguistic abilities. In mainstream schools or in HL community-based schools, it is important that teachers value and embrace concepts such as additive bilingualism, biliteracy, biculturalism, bidialectalism, multiculturalism, plurilingualism and pluricultural competence. Additive bilingualism occurs when a language is learned without replacing another one. When a student develops reading and writing skills in both languages it is called biliteracy, which sometimes does not come along with biculturalism. The latter is the ability to understand and participate in various degrees in the culture and society of the languages learned. Another important concept that teachers need to embrace and value is bidialectalism (Silva, 2010): teachers need to recognize the language register that the student brings and not dismiss or correct the student's family language; rather, other varieties of the language will be incorporated, thus leading learners to fluency in more than one variety (also called dialect).

For HL students, language is not only an ability to be developed for communication purposes; it also carries an identity relationship to their family and culture. Consequently, teachers working with YHLLs need to value multiculturalism, which assumes that students can belong to multiple cultures and create multiple identity discourses for themselves. Teachers also need to embrace a curriculum that develops plurilingualism and pluricultural competence, which looks not only to develop YHLLs' communicative competences, but also to value their ability of being social actors in different languages and cultures that can relate with each other (Coste, Moore & Zarate, 2009).

Researchers (Parodi, 2008; Valdés, 1995) have observed that heritage learners' literacy is considered a key issue in HL education. HL curriculum for young learners should be designed to expand the functional domain of the family language register to include the oral and written standard registers of the target language. Register is understood as a particular use of the language in a particular social setting that varies from more formal to more informal purposes. In HL courses for young learners, literacy must be related to social practices and cultures, and children need to be active participants in their own language and literacy development.

In the classroom, Kagan and Dillon (2002) recommend a macro-approach for HL teaching. This approach works with age appropriate texts and academically challenging assignments because usually these students already come with a high degree of acquired internal grammar. So a macro-approach works with grammar and lexicon through discourse-level and genre-based activities, which means offering large amount of texts and proposing complex tasks from the beginning, instead of focusing on teaching isolated grammar structures case by case.

One example of a recommended activity for YHLLs was designed as a partnership between two teachers from different HL community-based schools that teach Brazilian Portuguese, one in Japan and another in Chicago. The teachers paired their students in order to have them exchange letters. The purpose of this project was to develop children's literacy skills in a real and meaningful social interaction. Through this project, students wrote about their routine, their HL use and cultural identity, and also exchanged art projects. The successes of these activities were related to creating a meaningful and contextualized interaction between peers based on a writing genre (letters). Through the text editing process, learners started to become aware of the differences between language use in speaking and writing contexts. They also became more aware of some grammar structures.

As instructional strategies, it is recommended that teachers use authentic and age appropriate texts, build upon students' abilities acquired at home and work to expand their communicative and cultural skills, proposing activities that have meaningful and real social interaction purposes. A common challenge for teachers is to address different needs in the same class. One language class may have FL learners and HLLs, as well as HLLs with different linguistic abilities. Differentiated instruction has been shown to be a useful tool to design lessons for students with different needs, because it provides specific activities to address the needs of each student, or of a group of students (Carreira, 2007). In order to use this strategy, teachers first need to assess what learners already know in order to design differentiation. Teachers can differentiate content, process, pacing, and material by interest, readiness, and learning profile.

Besides these recommendations, the American Council on the Teaching of Foreign Languages (ACTFL) has recently released the "World-Readiness Standards for Learning Languages" which included the participation of the American Association of Teachers of Spanish and Portuguese (AATSP) that can guide teachers in developing their curriculum. In the Resources section, at the end of this text, you can find the website address to purchase these standards.

Materials

Commonly, teachers equate materials with textbooks. However, it is important to understand that teachers need to build their own curricula based on their students' needs. When preparing class activities, teachers usually design their own materials, selecting, adapting, and preparing activities to address their students' profile. Lessons, units, and courses should be designed from the learning expectations, and not derived from methods, books, and activities. Consequently, it is important that teachers use textbooks as a support material and not as the curriculum or the main resource for the class. Accordingly, textbooks can help with activities and as an extra resource.

For YHLLs of Portuguese, there are few resources available. For families with a Portuguese background, an option is the *Salpicos* series, developed by the Instituto Camões. The book presents Geography and History from Portugal based on characters that represent the daily life of a family. For Brazilian families there are options with different approaches. The series *Ciranda Cirandinha, vamos todos aprender a ler e escrever*, by Felicia Jennings-

Winterle, focuses on vocabulary building and early literacy development based on letter and syllabic awareness. The books were designed for young children between 4-6 years old. An option for older children (7-11 years old) of Brazilian background is *Vamos Falar Português!* by Sussana Florissi and Anna Claudia Ramos. Based on the legendary characters from "Turma da Mônica", by Mauricio de Sousa, this book presents some regions and sights from Brazil, such as museums and stadiums. Its exercises focus on grammar, mainly on verb conjugation, gender, and plural. Another option is the *Turminha Animada de Lucy e Tuca*, by Arlete Falkowski.

Despite the availability of some materials, further discussion related to curriculum goals, content selection, and instructional strategies for YHLLs is needed. Even if a textbook or series is adopted, teachers should be authors of their own courses based on their students' specific needs. It is also possible to use QuaREPE as a reference. The QuaREPE (Quadro de Referência para o Ensino de Português no Estrangeiro), developed in Portugal, is a document that discusses parameters for teaching Portuguese for foreign, second, and heritage learners (see Resources section at the end of this text). The document suggests competences and themes that teachers can work on with their learners. It also presents a model for developing lessons and materials.

Assessment

To the best of our knowledge, there are no assessment tools or guidelines discussed in the U.S. for YHLLs of Portuguese. The existing research on HL placement and assessment is limited and related to students at the university level. At this point, instructors at this level assess their students' abilities based on ACTFL proficiency guidelines and can evaluate their performances using two tests: NEWL (National Examinations in World Languages), which is equivalent to an AP test; and AAPPL (ACTFL Assessment of Performance Toward Proficiency in Languages). In the resources section of this chapter you can find websites for these exams.

In regards to students' linguistic development, it is important that teachers establish curriculum goals specific for their HLLs. It has already been pointed out that HLLs usually have strong listening and speaking skills in interpersonal mode. Based on research discussing assessment in Spanish as a heritage language (Beaudrie, 2012; MacGregor-Mendoza, 2012) we recommend that teachers analyze the real abilities that students bring in at the beginning of a course by checking their history of HL use, such as setting, whether they have had any schooling in the HL and, if so, for how long. With this information, teachers can set specific curriculum goals that will drive the assessment process.

A continuous assessment process is also recommended in order to check students' understanding of cultural knowledge, as well as their linguistic performance. We suggest the use of formative assessment, including checks for understanding (such as oral questions, observations, dialogues), and performance tasks and projects. It is important to understand that assessment can vary in terms of scope (from simple to complex), time frame (from short- to long-term), setting (from decontextualized to authentic contexts), and structure (from highly directive to unstructured). The QuaREPE document offers a brief discussion about assessing students' development.

Beyond the Classroom: Involving Family and Community

Acquisition of Portuguese by YHLLs directly relies on interactions with the family and the community. In this context, aspects impacting early bilingual language acquisition are the different language combination in the family (both parents speak the language, only one parent, or a grandparent) and quantity, consistency, and contexts of language exposure and use, such as conversation, reading books, and community relationship. It is well documented (Gathercole, 2002; Rivera-Mills, 2012; You & Liu, 2011) that maintenance and development of a HL is related to efforts by the family and participation in a large-scale community at various levels, which contributes to learning and using different language domains and registers, as well as experiencing some aspects of the cultural dimension. Researchers understand that the value that families and communities place on the HL plays a crucial role in HL acquisition by young learners.

When the family decides to make an effort to preserve and develop their children's HL and culture, it is important to address bilingualism as a family identity component. Boruchowski (2014), You and Liu (2011), as well as Lico (2011) observed that bringing YHLLs to participate in a HL community-based school strengthens parents' own relationship with their primary language. Stakeholders have reported that bringing children to HL classes has some effects on family attitudes, such as making parents recover their own ethnic cultural identity. Such an effort is usually appreciated and valued by the extended family, and the children become more confident about the bilingual family choice. All these aspects lead to positive results that help to enhance children's bilingualism. For more information about how families can help develop their heritage language look for the link to the book "Como manter e desenvolver o português como língua de herança: sugestões para quem mora fora do Brasil" in the resources section.

Portuguese speaker communities have intensified their efforts to maintain and develop children's language abilities. In the last decade, Brazilian community leaders and parents have been organizing community-based schools. Some examples include ABRACE, in the Washington, DC area; the *Movimento Educacionista* and its several branches in Massachusetts; *ProGente* in Framingham, MA; *Centro Educacional da Herança Brasileira* (CEHB) in Woburn, MA; *Fundação Vamos Falar Português*, in the Miami, FL area; *Aqui se Fala Português*, in Chicago, IL. Community leaders have also been making efforts to implement Portuguese in public schools such as Ada Merrritt, FL, and Downtown Doral Charter Elementary School, FL; at this point, there are also Portuguese schools in Utah, Massachusetts, and Rhode Island. In the end of this chapter, as a resource, there is a link to a manual explaining the steps to start a Portuguese program in a school.

Program Development for Young Heritage Language Learners

Mainstream Schools for Portuguese YHLLs

Thomas and Collier (2002) observed that the optimal program for long-term academic success of language minority students is the two-way bilingual education, also known as dual language bilingual programs. These programs are believed to be the most effective course to achieve biliteracy and higher academic skills in both languages taught. Despite the recent growing number of K-12 schools offering bilingual programs, Portuguese YHLLs' needs regarding development of bilingualism and biliteracy have not yet been addressed because of the small number of bilingual dual language schools currently offering Portuguese from kindergarten in the U.S. In dual language programs students develop literacy and content areas in both languages taught. The advantage of dual language programs is related to having high quality of input exposure and output demand for a long period of time per day. This type of program invites children to use the language for diverse contents and domains such as math, science, literature, discussing social problems, etc. Usually, they use the partner language for at least half of the instructional period. At mainstream schools there are also transitional bilingual education programs that offer Portuguese as language of instruction for a period, usually 3 years, until the students have learned English enough to make the transition to English-only classes.

As observed before, there are increasing options to develop Portuguese. Programs are mainly located at university level, however, and are not available in large numbers. Although a few programs for YHHLs of Portuguese have been created in mainstream schools in the U.S., they are not enough to serve the whole community. Consequently, it is recommended that families of YHLLs actively organize efforts to demand dual language bilingual programs at mainstream schools, which can address their children's biliteracy needs. At the end of this chapter, in the Resources section, you can find a link to a document elaborated by the "Portuguese-American Citizen Project", organized to guide parents and community leaders on how to work to implement a Portuguese program at a school. Setting up a program demands a lot of efforts from the community. Usually, community leaders form a committee that will assess the community's expectations in order to show to the public school administration the need for a biliteracy program. The committee will also need to organize petitions and establish relationships among community members, the school administration, and the school that will adopt the program.

Portuguese Language Community-based Schools for YHLLs

HL community-based schools are organizations controlled by parents, teachers, and community leaders that aim to maintain and develop children's HL and culture. Joshua Fishman (2001) mentioned different types of community-based schools in the U.S.: weekday afternoon schools, weekend schools, schools offering summer programs, evening classes, and special classes in community centers. Students at these schools vary in age, background, and interest. The staff may consist of administrators, teachers, interns, parents, and other community members who are paid or work on a voluntary basis.

HL community-based schools face many challenges (Douglas, 2008; Duff, 2008). Usually personnel implementing these programs do not have a professional background in education; they inconsistently discuss a pedagogical project that could guide them to prepare teacher instruction, material and curriculum development; they have difficulties in accommodating students into multi-level classes; they also commonly experience insufficient funding, and are also challenged in raising public awareness.

Despite their many challenges, HL community-based schools offer an important support for YHLLs' language maintenance. These schools act as major agents to prevent "language shift" and promote language maintenance, as well as to help students form a sense of cultural ethnic identity (You & Liu, 2011). Language shift usually happens when YHLLs, who are fluent in the HL as a consequence of major exposure at home, start mainstream schooling. Soon, their dominant language changes to the language mostly used outside the home. As a consequence, usually the child starts to refuse to use the HL at home. Researchers have observed that participation in a HL community-based school helps YHLLs to maintain their family language. Boruchowski (2014) observed that, from the stakeholders' perspective, usually HL community-based schools aim to accomplish four goals:

1. To develop linguistic and cultural belonging in an HL
2. To maintain and develop students' HL abilities
3. To enhance children's pride in speaking a language other than English at home
4. To make parents aware of the family's crucial role in raising a bilingual child.

Usually, HL community-based schools are created because parents are concerned with their children's language maintenance and development. Commonly, they start as informal meetings such as play dates or story telling hours in an attempt to make children use the HL and meet with peers, and then they become quite structured. These schools usually understand that the family holds the main responsibility for keeping and developing the children's bilingualism. These schools also often understand the need to support parents in the challenges they face raising bilingual children.

We have discussed recommendations for courses for YHLLs (see 4.1 above). HL community-based schools should discuss these parameters as well. In these programs, usually teachers work with topics focused on cultural aspects related to Luso-Brazilian family life, typical foods, folklore, geographical and cultural regional differences, popular holidays and festivals (Almeida Filho, 2008; Boruchowski, 2014). However, it is important to understand that cultural knowledge is not limited to these topics, but also related to ways of speaking and doing things, discussing student identity and the socio-historical trajectory of the learner's family, participating and experiencing community events, and understanding the diverse culture of the Portuguese-speaking world.

Final Remarks

In this text we have highlighted the fact that heritage language learners, whether children, teenagers or adults, do not comprise a homogeneous group. Although HLLs of Portuguese may be enrolled in the same class, they likely have different linguistic skills. Nevertheless, they are also likely to understand already some informal spoken Portuguese and have some pragmalinguistic knowledge in their HL. However, we must reinforce that this by no means signifies that HLLs do not need to practice, for example, speaking or sociopragmatic skills. Keep in mind that these learners are most likely familiar only with an informal language repertoire in their HL and need to practice structures, vocabulary and skills beyond what they may already know. Furthermore, attention must be paid to the cultural and linguistic diversity of the Portuguese-speaking world in courses at all levels. In terms of what HLLs bring to the classroom, instructors need to keep in mind the specific needs of HLLs, especially in mixed classrooms (with both HLLs and FLLs): although HLLs may already understand some Portuguese, that does not mean that their production is flawless or that they can't learn with their peers who were not exposed to Portuguese in the home. Remember that FLLs and HLLs have different needs, but they also go about learning Portuguese in different ways, and therefore can complement each other's strengths when working together.

References

Almeida Filho, J. P. (2008). *Tornar-se professor de língua(s) na estrangeiridade domada*. São Paulo: Pontes.

Amaral, L., Cunha, F. & Silva, G. (2011). The acquisition of a semantic contrast in subordinate clauses by heritage speakers of Portuguese.

Paper presented at the American Association for Applied Linguistics (AAAL) conference, Chicago, March 26-29.

Baker, C. (2001). Foundations of bilingual education and bilingualism (5th.ed.). Clevedon, England: Multilingual Matters.

Beaudrie, S. M. (2012). Introduction: Development in Spanish heritage language assessment. *Heritage Language Journal*, 9(1). i-xi.

Boruchowski, I. D. (2014) Curriculum development in a heritage language community-based school: A Qualitative inquiry regarding a Brazilian-Portuguese program in South Florida.. FIU Electronic Theses and Dissertations. Paper 1588. Retrieved from http://digitalcommons.fiu.edu/etd/1588

Caldas, S. J. (2013). Assessment of academic performance: The impact of no child left behind policies on bilingual education--A ten-year retrospective. In V. C. M. Gathercole (Ed.), *Issues in the assessment of bilinguals* (pp. 205-231). Clevedon, UK: Multilingual Matters.

Carreira, M. (2007). Teaching Spanish in the US: Beyond the one-size-fits-all paradigm. In K. Potowski & R. Cameron (Eds.), *Spanish in contact: Policy, social and linguistic inquiries* (pp. 61-80). Amsterdam & Philadelphia: John Benjamins

Carreira, M. & Kagan, O. (2011). The results of the National Heritage Language Survey: Implications for teaching, curriculum design, and professional development. *Foreign Language Annals, 44 (1)*, 40-64.

Carvalho, A. (2012). Code-switching: From theoretical to pedagogical considerations. In S. Beaudrie & M. Fairclough (Eds.), *Spanish as a heritage language in the United States: State of the field (pp. 139-160). Washington, DC: Georgetown University Press.*

Colombi, M. C. (1997). Perfil del discurso escrito en textos de hispanohablantes: Teoría y práctica. In M. C. Colombi & F. X. Alarcón (Eds.), *La enseñanza del español a hispanohablantes* (pp. 175-189). Boston & New York: Houghton Mifflin.

Colombi, M. C. (2003). Un enfoque funcional para la enseñanza del ensayo expositivo. In M. C. Colombi & A. Roca (Eds.), *Mi lengua: Spanish as a heritage language in the United States* (pp. 51-77). Washington, DC: Georgetown University Press.

Coste, D., Moore, D. & Zarate, G. (2009). Plurilingual and pluricultural competence: Studies toward a Common European Framework of Reference for language teaching. Strasbourg: Language Policy Division. Retrieved from www.coe.int/lang.

Douglas, M. O. (2008). Curriculum design for young learners of Japanese as a heritage language. In K. Kondo-Brown & J. D. Brown. (Eds.), *Teaching Chinese, Japanese, and Korean heritage language students* (pp. 237-298). New York: Lawrence Erlbaum Associates.

Duff, P. (2008). Heritage language education in Canada. In D. Brinton, O.

Kagan & S. Bauckus (Eds.), *Heritage language: A new field emerging* (pp. 71-90). New York: Taylor & Francis.

Fishman, J. (2001). 300-plus years of heritage language education in the United States. In J. K. Peyton, D. A. Ranard, & S. McGinnis (Eds.), *Heritage languages in America: Preserving a national resource* (pp. 81-89). DC: Center for Applied Linguistics & Delta Systems.

Gathercole, V. C. (2002). Monolingual and bilingual acquisition: Learning different treatments of that-trace phenomena in English and Spanish. In D. K. Oller & R. E. Eilers (Eds.), *Language and literacy in bilingual children* (pp.1-32) Clevedon, UK: Multilingual Matters.

Gathercole, V. C. (2007). Miami and North Wales, so far and yet so near: A constructivist account of morphosyntatic development in bilingual children. *The International Journal of Bilingual Education and Bilingualism, 10*(3), 1-24.

Gathercole, V. C., & Thomas, E. M. (2009). Bilingual first-language development: Dominant language takeover, threatened minority language take-up. *Bilingualism: Language and cognition, 12*(2), 213-237.

Goh, C. C. M. (2005). Second language listening expertise. In K. Johnson (Ed.), *Expertise in second language learning and teaching* (pp. 64-84). Basingstoke, UK: Palgrave Macmillan.

Gontijo, V. (2010). *The role of attitudes, motivation and heritage in learning Portuguese (Unpublished M.A. thesis).* University of Massachusetts Dartmouth, Dartmouth, MA.

Grosjean, F. (2010). *Bilingual: Life and reality*. Cambridge: Harvard University Press.

Harklau, L. (2009). Heritage speakers experiences in new Latino diaspora Spanish classrooms. *Critical Inquiry in Language Studies, 6*, 211-242.

Kagan, O. & Dillon, K. (2012). Heritage languages and L2 learning. In S. Gass & A. Mackey (Eds.), *The Routledge handbook of second language acquisition* (pp. 491-505). London: Routledge

King, K., & Mackey, A. (2010). *The bilingual edge: Why, when, and how to teach your child a second language*. New York: HarperCollins.

Lico, A. L. (2011). Ensino do português como língua de herança: Prática e fundamentos. *Revista Siple, 2(1).* Retrieved from http://www.siple.org.br/

Lynch, A. (2003). Toward a theory of heritage language acquisition. In A. Roca & M.C. Colombi (Eds.), *Mi lengua: Spanish as a heritage language in the United States* (pp. 25- 50). Washington, DC: Georgetown University Press.

MacGregor-Mendoza, P. (2012). Spanish as a heritage language assessment: successes, failures, lessons learned. *Heritage Language Journal*, 9(1), 1-26.

Nieto, S. (2002). *Language, culture, and teaching: Critical perspectives for a new century.*

Mahwah, NJ: Lawrence Erlbaum Association.

Paradis, J. (2010). Bilingual children's acquisition of English verb-morphology: Effects of language exposure, structure complexity, and task type. *Language Learning, 60*(3), 651-680.

Parodi, C. (2008). Stigmatized Spanish inside the classroom and out: A model of language teaching to heritage speakers. In D. M. Brinton, O. Kagan, & S. Bauckus (Eds.), *Heritage language education: A new field emerging* (pp. 199-214). New York & London: Routledge.

Rivera-Mills, S. (2012). Spanish heritge language maintenance: Its legacy and its future. In S. M. Beaudrie & M. Fairclough (Eds.), *Spanish as a heritage language in the United States: The state of the field* (pp. 21-42). Washington, DC: Georgetown University Press.

Roca, A. (1997). La realidad en el aula: logros y expectativas en la enseñanza del español para estudiantes bilingües. In M. C. Colombi & F. X. Alarcón (Eds.), *La enseñanza del español a hispanohablantes* (pp. 55-64). Boston & New York: Houghton Mifflin.

Santos, D., & Silva, G. (2008). Making suggestions in the workplace: Insights from learner and native speaker discourses. *Hispania, 91*, 651-664.

Santos, D., & Silva, G. (2015). Exploring Portuguese heritage and non-heritage learners' perceptions of and performance in listening. *The Canadian Journal of Applied Linguistics, 18(1)*, 63-86.

Schwarzer, D., & Petrón, M. (2005). Heritage language instruction at the college level: Reality and possibilities. *Foreign Language Annals, 38(4)*, 568-578.

Silva, G.V. (2010). On starting a course sequence for heritage learners of Portuguese. *Portuguese Language Journal, 4*, Fall. Retrieved from http://www.ensinoportugues.org/archives/

Silva, G.V. (2011). Textbook activities among heritage and non-heritage learners of Portuguese. *Hispania, 94*(4), 734-750.

Shinbo, Y. (2004). *Challenges, needs, and contributions of heritage language students in foreign language classrooms.* (Unpublished M.A. thesis). The University of British Columbia, Vancouver. Retrieved from https://circle.ubc.ca/bitstream/handle/2429/15703/ubc_2004-0626.pdf

Solé, Y. (1981). Consideraciones pedagógicas en la enseñanza del español a estudiantes bilingües. In G. Valdés, A. Lozano & R. García-Moya (Eds.), *Teaching Spanish to the Spanish bilingual: Issues, aims and methods* (pp. 21-29). New York: Teachers College Press.

Thomas, W. P., & Collier, V. P. (1997). *School effectiveness for language minority students.* Washington, DC: National Clearinghouse for Bilingual Education.

Valdés, G. (1995). The teaching of minority languages as academic subjects: Pedagogical and theoretical challenges. *The Modern Language Journal,*

79(3), 299-328.

Valdés, G. (2001). Heritage language students: Profiles and possibilities. In J. Peyton, D. Ranard, & S. McGinnis (Eds.), *Heritage languages in America: Preserving a national resource* (pp. 37-77). McHenry, IL: Delta Systems e Center for Applied Linguistics.

Villa, D. (1997). Theory, design, and content for a "grammar" class for native speakers of Spanish. In M.C. Colombi & F. Alarcón (Eds.), *La enseñanza del español a hispanohablantes: Praxis y teoría* (pp. 93-102). Boston: Houghton Mifflin.

Wang, S. & Green, N. (2001). Heritage language students in the K-12 education system. In J. Peyton, D. Ranard, & S. McGinnis (Eds.), *Heritage languages in America: Preserving a national resource* (pp. 167-196). McHenry, IL: Delta Systems e Center for Applied Linguistics.

Xiao, Y. (2006). Heritage learners in the Chinese language classroom: Home background. *Heritage Language Journal, 4*(1), 47-56.

You, B., & Liu, N. (2011). Stakeholders views on the roles, challenges, and future prospects of Korean and Chinese heritage language-community schools in the Phoenix Metropolitan Area: A comparative study. *Heritage Language Journal, 8*(3), 67-92.

Resources

This section lists some of the resources available (besides those included in the References section) for those who wish to learn more about HL teaching and learning, and about Portuguese as a heritage language. Note, however, that this list is not exhaustive.

Websites

Center for Applied Linguistics
Heritage Language Briefs
http://www.cal.org/resource-center/resource-archive/heritage-briefs
http://www.cal.org/resource-center/resource-archive/heritage-languages-schools-briefs
Heritage Language Programs Database
http://webapp.cal.org/Heritage/

National Heritage Language Resource Center
http://nhlrc.ucla.edu/nhlrc

National Capital Language Resource Center
http://www.nclrc.org/about_teaching/heritage_learners.html
http://www.nclrc.org/essentials/listening/stratlisten.htm

Online journals

Heritage Language Journal
http://www.heritagelanguages.org/

Portuguese Language Journal (see especially Volume 5)
http://www.ensinoportugues.org/

Books

Beaudrie, S. M. & Fairclough, M. (Eds.) (2012). *Spanish as a heritage language in the United States: The state of the field.* Washington, DC: Georgetown University Press.

Brinton, D. M., Kagan, O., & Bauckus, S. (Eds.) (2008). *Heritage language education: A new field emerging.* New York & London: Routledge.

Jennings-Winterle, F., & Lima-Hernandes, M. C. (2015). *Português como língua de herança: A filosofia do começo, meio e fim*. New York: Brasil em Mente.

Peyton, J. K., Ranard, D. A., & McGinnis, S. (Eds.) (2001). *Heritage languages in America: Preserving a national resource.* McHenry, IL: Center for Applied Linguistics and Delta Systems.

Roca, A., & Colombi, M. C. (Eds.) (2003). *Mi lengua: Spanish as a heritage language in the Unnited States*. Washington, DC: Georgetown University Press.

Trifonas, P. P., & Aravossitas, T. (Eds.) (2014). *Rethinking heritage language education.* Cambridge, UK: Cambridge University Press.

Valdés, G., Lozano, A. & García-Moya, R. (Eds.) (1981). *Teaching Spanish to the Hispanic bilingual: Issues, aims, and methods.* New York: Teachers College Press.

Wiley, T., Peyton, J. K., Christian, D., Moore, S. C. K., & Liu, N. (Eds.) (2014). *Handbook of heritage, community, and Native American languages in the United States: Research, policy, and educational practice.* New York, NY and Abingdon, UK: Routledge and Center for Applied Linguistics.

Articles

Bowles, M., Adams, R., & Toth, P. (2014). A comparison of L2-L2 and L2-heritage learner interactions in Spanish language classrooms. *The Modern Language Journal, 98(3)*, 497-517.

Correa, M. (2011). Advocating for critical pedagogical approaches to teaching Spanish as a heritage language: Some considerations. *Foreign Language Annals, 44(2)*, 308-320.

Edstrom, A. (2006). Oral narratives in the language classroom: A bridge between non-native, heritage, and native-speaking learners. *Hispania, 89(2)*, 336-346.

Edstrom, A. (2007). The mixing of non-native, heritage, and native speakers in upper-level Spanish courses: A sampling of student opinion. *Hispania, 90(4)*, 755-768.

Kondo-Brown, K. (2005). Differences in language skills: Heritage language learner subgroups and foreign language learners. *The Modern Language Journal, 89(4)*, 563-581.

Leeman, J., Rabin, L., & Román-Mendoza, E. (2011). Identity and activism in heritage language education. *The Modern Language Journal, 95(4)*, 481-495.

Potowski, K., Jegerski, J., & Morgan-Short, K. (2009). The effects of instruction on linguistic development in Spanish heritage language speakers. *Language Learning, 59*, 537-579.

Silva, G. V. (2008). Heritage language learning and the Portuguese subjunctive. *Portuguese Language Journal, 3*, Fall 2008. http://www.ensinoportugues.org/archives/

Sohn, S.-O., & Shin, S.-K. (2007). True beginners, false beginners, and fake beginners: Placement strategies for Korean heritage speakers. *Foreign Language Annals, 42(3)*, 483-504.

Valdés, G., Fishman, A., Chávez, R., & Pérez, W. (2008). Maintaining Spanish in the United States: Steps toward the effective practice of heritage language re-acquisition/development. *Hispania, 91(1)*, 4-24.

Xie, Y. (2014). L2 self of beginning-level heritage and nonheritage postsecondary learners of Chinese. *Foreign Language Annals, 47(1)*, 189-203.

Theses about Portuguese as a Heritage Language

Boruchowski, I. D. (2014). Curriculum development in a heritage language community-based school: A qualitative inquiry regarding a Brazilian Portuguese program in South Florida. Florida International University. http://digitalcommons.fiu.edu/cgi/viewcontent.cgi?article=2734&context=etd&sei-redir=1&referer=http%3A%2F%2Fwww.google.com%2Fsearch%3Fclient%3Dsafari%26rls%3Den%26q%3Divian%2Bboruchowski%26ie%3DUTF-8%26oe%3DUTF-8#search=%22ivian%20boruchowski%22

Da Silva, A. V. (2014). Maintaining Brazilian Portuguese as a heritage language in a bilingual French-English environment. Concordia University, Canada. http://spectrum.library.concordia.ca/978513/1/DaSilva_MSc_S2014.pdf

Mota, C. (1997). The maintenance of Portuguese as a heritage language in Winnipeg. University of Manitoba, Canada. http://www.collectionscanada.gc.ca/obj/s4/f2/dsk2/tape15/PQDD_0002/MQ32197.pdf

Other resources

QuaREPE (Quadro de Referência para o Ensino de Português no Estrangeiro)
http://d3f5055r2rwsy1.cloudfront.net/images/stories/EPE_incricoes_2011_2012/quarepe/manual_quarepe_orientador_versao_final_janeiro_2012.pdf

https://cepealemanha.files.wordpress.com/2010/12/manual_quarepe_orientador.pdf

Differentiated Instruction
https://www.youtube.com/watch?v=LGYa6ZacUTM (Getting started on differentiated instruction, by Carol Ann Tomlinson)
http://www.glencoe.com/sec/teachingtoday/subject/di_meeting.phtml (an explanation of differentiated instruction)
https://www.fbcinc.com/e/learn/e/russian2011/presentations/Tues_Khalil_1_Chevalier_O'Neil.pdf (differentiating for FLLs and HLLs)

Starting Portuguese in your school: A manual for community leadership
http://www.portugueseamerican.org/StartingPortugueseinYour%20School04_15_12.pdf

2014 ACTFL World-Readiness Standards for Learning Languages
http://www.actfl.org/publications/all/world-readiness-standards-learning-languages

3.2 TEACHING PORTUGUESE TO SPANISH SPEAKERS

Blair Bateman
Brigham Young University

Although Spanish speakers have long shown an interest in learning Portuguese due to the similarity between the two languages, enrollment by Spanish speakers in Portuguese courses in the U.S. has increased significantly in recent years (Milleret, 2012). At many universities in the United States, Spanish speakers now constitute a majority in beginning-level and even upper-division Portuguese courses. At my own university, approximately 70% of students enrolled in first- and second-year Portuguese courses are Spanish speakers.

The past decade has seen the emergence of a growing body of research literature on the learning of Portuguese by Spanish speakers. Starting in 2003, a series of symposia on Portuguese for Spanish speakers have taken place, followed by the publication of selected papers from these symposia (Simões, Carvalho & Wiedemann, 2004; Wiedemann & Scaramucci, 2008). Some of this research has focused on transfer patterns between the two languages and on specific difficulties that Spanish speakers experience in learning Portuguese. Researchers have attempted to situate Portuguese for Spanish speakers in the context of research on third language (L3) learning, examining the influence not only of transfer from Spanish, but also factors such as the order of acquisition of the languages, amount of experience with the L3, age, proficiency in the L3, and degree of metalinguistic awareness. In general, these studies have concluded that the typological similarity between Spanish and Portuguese overrides other factors, meaning that for Spanish speakers learning Portuguese, the fact that they speak Spanish at all plays a greater role than factors such as their age or their background or proficiency in Spanish.

Although some of the abovementioned studies have discussed the pedagogical implications of the results, to my knowledge no systematic attempt has been made to synthesize the findings of different studies and their implications for the classroom. This chapter aims to bring together what is known about Spanish speakers who enroll in Portuguese courses and their characteristics as language learners, with an eye toward helping instructors plan courses to meet the needs of these students.

Who Are "Spanish Speakers"?

Spanish-speaking students of Portuguese consist of at least three groups, each with distinct characteristics. The first group consists of native English speakers who have learned Spanish as a foreign or second language and are studying Portuguese as a third language. These students, although their

Spanish is often far from native-like, have the advantage of having explicitly studied the grammar rules of Spanish, and thus possess a relatively high degree of metalinguistic awareness that allows them to readily understand similar rules in Portuguese, such as the contrast between *ser* and *estar* or *por* and *para.*

The second group of students consists of native Spanish speakers who are international students or have immigrated to the U.S. These students have generally received a formal education in Spanish in their home country. They enjoy a number of advantages in learning Portuguese: they can read and write in Spanish at the ACTFL Advanced to Superior level, unlike some native English speaking students; they have a native command of Spanish grammar; they have a broad Spanish vocabulary encompassing a wide variety of concrete and abstract topics; and they have an insider's knowledge of at least one Hispanic culture.

The third group consists of heritage speakers of Spanish – students who have grown up in Spanish-speaking households in the U.S. but have received all or most of their formal education in English. These students vary widely in their mastery of Spanish: some are confident in speaking and understanding the language in informal contexts but less so in academic contexts, whereas others have relatively strong listening skills but lack confidence in speaking. Many of these students lack literacy skills in Spanish and have a range of vocabulary that is limited to everyday, concrete topics. Nevertheless, having grown up in Spanish-speaking homes, these students are generally quite familiar with Hispanic cultural customs and perspectives.

Research has revealed differences among these three groups of students in terms of their acquisition of certain Portuguese grammatical structures, vocabulary items, and social pragmatics, with the three groups of students exhibiting different patterns in their learning of Portuguese and committing different types of errors (Simões et al., 2004; Wiedemann & Scaramucci, 2008). Additional research is needed to further pinpoint differences among these groups. Throughout this chapter I have attempted to address these differences in terms of their implications for pedagogical approaches; however, it is probably safe to assume that the three groups have more in common with each other than they do with non-Spanish speaking students of Portuguese.

Why Offer Separate Classes for Spanish Speakers?

There are a number of reasons why it makes sense to offer separate Portuguese classes for Spanish speakers. The most obvious reason is that these students learn the language much more quickly than do non-Spanish speakers, due largely to lexical and grammatical similarities between the two languages. The receptive skills of these students in particular are much stronger than those of other students: research has shown that depending on the context and topic, Spanish speakers can understand as much as 50% of spoken Portuguese, and over 90% of written Portuguese (Henriques, 2000; Jensen, 1989).

Spanish-speaking students may also differ from other students of Portuguese in terms of their motivation for learning the language. It has long been recognized that traditional Portuguese students often have personal reasons for studying the language, such as the influence of family and friends or interest in cultural phenomena such as soccer or *capoeira.* In contrast, at least one study (Bateman & Oliveira, 2014) has found that Spanish speakers tend to enroll in Portuguese courses not only due to the relative facility of learning the language, but also because many of these students plan to use Portuguese in their careers, recognizing that if they speak Portuguese, Spanish, and English, they can function in professional contexts throughout North and South America as well as much of Europe.

The remainder of this article will focus on four general topics related to the teaching of Portuguese to Spanish speakers: teaching specific features of Portuguese that differ from Spanish; capitalizing on the receptive skills of students; capitalizing on students' cultural knowledge; and assessing students' Portuguese skills.

Teaching Specific Features of Portuguese that Differ from Spanish

There are at least four types of differences between Spanish and Portuguese that instructors need to address: lexical differences, phonological differences, orthographic differences, and grammatical differences. The following sections will address each of these topics in turn.

Lexical Differences

Spanish speakers learning Portuguese enjoy an enormous advantage due to lexical similarities between the two languages. The website Ethnologue.com estimates that 89% of Spanish and Portuguese words share similar characteristics and origins. Nevertheless, there also exist many lexical differences between the two languages, as well as a number of false cognates that can cause trouble for Spanish speakers. Figure 1 lists some of the most common of these false cognates. I find it helpful to give students a copy of this list and refer to it periodically throughout the course. (This and subsequent figures are adapted from my textbook *Perspectivas: Português para falantes de espanhol,* forthcoming from Linus Learning.)

Figure 1 *False Cognates of Spanish and Portuguese*

Español	***English***	**Português**	***English***
acordarse	*to remember*	acordar	*to awake*
el apellido	*surname*	o apelido	*nickname*
borracho/a	*drunk*	a borracha	*eraser*

botar	*to throw away*	botar	*to put*
la cadera	*hip*	a cadeira	*chair*
embarazada	*pregnant*	embaraçado/a	*embarrassed*
el escritorio	*desk*	o escritório	*office*
esquisito/a	*exquisite*	esquisito/a	*strange*
largo/a	*long*	largo/a	*wide*
la oficina	*office*	a oficina	*workshop*
el oso	*bear*	o osso	*bone*
pegar	*to hit*	pegar	*to get*
raro	*strange*	raro	*rare*
reparar	*to repair*	reparar (em)	*to notice*
el sobrenombre	*nickname*	o sobrenome	*surname*
tirar	*to throw*	tirar	*to remove*
el vaso	*drinking glass*	o vaso	*vase*

There also exist a number of cognates that have different genders in Spanish and Portuguese; some of these are listed in Figure 2. For the most part, students will need to memorize these differences.

Figure 2 *Nouns with Different Genders in Spanish and Portuguese*

Español	**Português**
la nariz	o nariz
la leche	o leite
la sal	o sal
la crema	o creme
la miel	o mel
la sangre	o sangue
la sonrisa	o sorriso
el árbol	a árvore
el color	a cor
el puente	a ponte
el dolor	a dor
el origen	a origem
el equipo	a equipe *(Br.)* a equipa *(Pt.)*

Words ending in Spanish *–umbre* / Portuguese *–ume:*	
Español	**Português**
la costumbre	o costume
la legumbre	o legume
la lumbre	o lume

Words ending in Spanish *–aje* and Portuguese *-agem:*	
Espanhol	**Português**
el mensaje	a mensagem
el coraje	a coragem
el garaje	a garagem
el masaje	a massagem
el pasaje	a passagem
The same pattern applies to other nouns with the endings *-aje*/*-agem* (there are about 60 of them).	

One helpful technique for Spanish speakers is to learn the Portuguese counterparts for common Spanish suffixes. For example, Spanish *-dad* or *-tad* usually corresponds to Portuguese *–dade*; Spanish *–ción* corresponds to Portuguese *-ção*; Spanish *-ble* corresponds to Portuguese *-vel*; and Spanish *-ud* corresponds to Portuguese *-ude*. Nouns ending with these suffixes nearly always have the same gender in both languages. One exception is the Spanish suffix –*aje*, which is associated with masculine nouns in Spanish (*el garaje, el mensage*), and corresponds to the Portuguese –*gem,* associated with feminine nouns (*a garagem, a mensagem*).

Phonological Differences

Portuguese pronunciation is often challenging to learn for speakers of other languages, but it presents unique challenges for speakers of Spanish. There are multiple reasons for these challenges, including the following: (a) the correspondence between spelling and pronunciation is closer in Spanish than in Portuguese; (b) the same letters and combinations of letters sometimes produce different sounds in Portuguese than they do in Spanish; and (c) Portuguese possesses some sounds that do not exist at all in Spanish.

The following section briefly discusses some of the differences in pronunciation between the consonants and vowels of the two languages. I have attempted to explain these differences in terms that students can understand, avoiding phonetic symbols and complex linguistic terminology, and taking advantage of the fact that students who know both Spanish and English can make comparisons with both languages. In cases where the Brazilian pronunciation differs from the European, I have emphasized the former; however, teachers of European Portuguese could easily adapt these explanations. (For a more detailed presentation of this topic, see Chapter 13).

Consonants. In general, Portuguese consonants cause fewer difficulties for Spanish speakers than do vowels, as most of the consonants have approximate equivalents in either Spanish or English; thus, learning the consonants becomes mainly a question of learning which sounds are associated with which letters. I find it useful to give students a handout like the one in Figure 3 that associates Portuguese consonants with familiar sounds in Spanish, English, or both, depending on which language contains sounds that most closely approximate those of Portuguese. If the instructor is not a native Portuguese speaker, it is helpful to have a native record these examples and make the recording available for student practice.

Figure 3 *Portuguese Consonants with Pronunciation that Differs from Spanish*

Consonant	Pronunciation	Examples
b	As in English (no "soft" sound as it may have in Spanish)	*bolo, lobo, saber*
ç	Like *c* of Spanish "cita"	*maço, praça, almoçar*
ch	Like *sh* of English "**ship**"	*chamar, chuva, acho*
d	Before *a, o,* or stressed *e,* pronounced similarly to English (no "soft" sound as it may have in Spanish)	*dá, dedo, nada, comida*
	Before *i* or unstressed final *e*, pronounced like *j* of English "**jeep**" in most of Brazil	*dia, disse, medicina, tarde, pode*

g	Before *a, e, or o*, pronounced as in English (no "soft" sound as it may have in Spanish)	*gato, pago, entregar*
	Before *e* or *i*, pronounced like *s* of English "plea**s**ure"	*gelo, giz, página, mágica*
j	Like *s* of English "plea**s**ure"	*já, viajar, jogar, justo*
l	At start of word or syllable, pronounced as in Spanish	*lado, lama, falar*
	At end of word or syllable, pronounced similarly to *w* of English "fe**w**" in Brazilian Portuguese	*sal, Brasil, fácil, alto*
lh	Like Spanish *ll* in some dialects; roughly similar to *li* of English "mi**lli**on"	*olho, folha, trabalhar*
m	At start of word or syllable, pronounced as in Spanish	*mala, moça, cama*
	At end of word or syllable, **not pronounced;** simply indicates that the preceding vowel is nasalized	*um, bom, tem, também*
nh	Similar to Spanish *ñ*, but without touching tip of tongue; also similar to a nazalized English *y*	*senhor, tenho, banhar, vinho, unha*
r	At start of word, or at end of word or syllable, pronounced similarly to *j* of Spanish "**j**ota"	*rato, rio, falar, comer, carta, corpo*
	Between vowels, pronounced as in Spanish	*cara, coro, barato*
rr	Similar to *j* of Spanish "**j**ota"	*carro, correr, erro, morro*
s	At start of word or syllable, pronounced as in Spanish	*sala, solto, sábado*
	Between vowels, voiced like English *z*	*casa, mesa, coisa, vaso*
t	Before *a, o,* or stressed *e*, pronounced as in Spanish	*taça, tela, torta*
	Before *i* or untressed final *e*, pronounced like *ch* of English "**ch**eese" in most of Brazil	*tio, mentir, noite, dente*
v	As in English (never sounds like *b* as in Spanish)	*vaso, vai, levar, palavra*
x	Four possible pronunciations: • Like *sh* of English "**sh**e" (most common) • Like *z* of English "**z**ero" • Like *x* of "ta**x**i" • Like *s* of "**s**olo"	*caixa, bruxa, puxar* *exame, exemplo, êxito* *táxi, fixo, sexo* *trouxe, próximo, máximo*
z	Voiced like English *z*	*zero, azul, azar, vizinho*

Spanish speakers frequently need to be reminded that *-m* at the end of words is merely a spelling convention, not a consonant that is pronounced. One way to address this issue is to suggest that students write words ending in *-m* as *um, bom, tem, também*, etc. until they become accustomed to the correct pronunciation. Using humor can also help; students find it amusing to learn that if they pronounce the *-m* in ***um** hotel,* Portuguese speakers will interpret it as *um motel*, which in Brazil is an establishment that rents rooms by the hour.

Vowels. Portuguese vowels present a challenge for Spanish speakers, partly because there are more of them: Portuguese has seven oral vowels and five nasal vowels, as compared with only five (oral) vowels in Spanish. Furthermore, some Portuguese vowels vary in pronunciation depending on whether they occur in a stressed or unstressed position in a word.

Oral vowels. Of all the sounds of Portuguese, the semi-open *e* and *o* probably cause the most trouble for Spanish speakers. Native Spanish speakers seem to struggle with these sounds more than native English speakers do, perhaps because English contains roughly similar sounds whereas Spanish does not.

A traditional linguistic approach to teaching oral vowels is to show students a diagram depicting the position of the tongue and lips in forming each vowel. Although this approach is undoubtedly helpful for some students, it fails to consider that adult and adolescent learners generally rely on the written language rather than the spoken language as a point of departure: they see a printed word and want to know how to pronounce it. For this reason, I also give students a handout showing the written vowels and the possible pronunciations of each vowel (see Figure 4).

Figure 4 *Oral Vowels*

Vowel	Pronunciation	Examples
a	In stressed syllables, similar to Spanish	*h**á**, l**á**, h**á**bito, r**á**pido*
	In an unstressed final syllable, similar to "schwa" sound in English "sof**a**"	*nad**a**, fal**a**, sal**a**, fulan**a***
e	In stressed syllables, can be either *close* or *open.*	
	• Close *e:* Pronounced similarly to Spanish *e*	Close *e:* ***pê**, **e**le, p**e**so, beb**ê***
	• Open *e:* No equivalent in Spanish; somewhere between *e* of English "b**e**t" and *a* of "b**a**t"	Open *e:* ***pé**, **e**la, jan**e**la, at**é***
	In an unstressed final syllable, similar to *i* in Spanish "cas**i**"	*fal**e**, tard**e**, noit**e**, padr**e***
i	As in Spanish	*v**i**, l**i**, v**i**da, s**i**do*
	• When a word ends in *i* preceded by a consonant, that syllable is stressed; no accent mark is needed	*com**i**, beb**i**, aqu**i**, abacax**i***

o	In stressed syllables, can be either *close* or *open*. • Close *o*: Pronunced similarly to Spanish *o*	Close *o: avô, pôde, doze, boca*
	• Open *o*: No equivalent in Spanish; similar to *a* in English "call," but with lips rounded as in British English	Open *o*: *avó, pode, nós, óculos*
	In an unstressed final syllable, similar to *u in* Spanish "tribu"	*falo, canto, passo, sábado*
u	As in Spanish	*tu, tudo, pulo, último*
	• When a word ends in *u* preceded by a consonant, that syllable is stressed; no accent mark is needed	*tatu, urubu, peru, xampu*

Instructors can provide students with practice listening to and pronouncing minimal pairs with open and close vowels, such as *pê/pé, avô/avó,* and *pôde/pode,* including pairs consisting of a noun and a verb, such as *o começo/eu começo* and *o gosto/eu gosto.*

One additional hint for Spanish speakers is that Spanish words with the diphthong *ie* often correspond to Portuguese words with open *e* (e.g., *diez – dez, fiesta – festa, piedra – pedra*), and Spanish words with the diphthong *ue* often correspond to Portuguese words with open *o* (e.g., *nueve – nove, puede – pode, escuela – escola*).

Nasal vowels. Nasal vowels are also challenging for Spanish speakers, especially when they occur at the end of a word. Instructors can give students opportunities to practice listening to and pronouncing minimal pairs with nasal and non-nasal vowels, such as *mudo/mundo, cato/canto,* and *tuba/tumba,* reminding learners once again that the *–m* or *–n* at the end of words or syllables is not pronounced.

Diphthongs. Portuguese has many more diphthongs than does Spanish; some of them also exist in Spanish, but many do not. Open diphthongs and nasal diphthongs will be especially new to Spanish-speaking students. Again, it is helpful for students to practice listening to and pronouncing minimal pairs, such as *mais/mães, pais/pães, pau/pão, mal/mão, sal/são, sei/sem, amei/amém*, etc.

Orthographic Differences

Spelling is another area that presents challenges for Spanish speakers, since there are many words that are pronounced similarly in the two languages but spelled somewhat differently. Instructors can show students a list of some of the most common spelling differences between Spanish and Portuguese like that in Figure 5, and then simply remind students of these differences when necessary. It can also be helpful to inform students that they will be expected to spell these words correctly on tests and writing assignments, and that a (small) number of points will be deducted for incorrect spelling.

Figure 5 Some Spelling Differences of Spanish and Portuguese

Español	Ejemplos	Português	Examplos
e	madera, primero, canté, cantaré	*ei*	madeira, primeiro, cantei, cantarei
o	ropa, poco, loco, cantó	*ou*	roupa, pouco, louco, cantou
s	asado, asistir, profesor	*ss*	assado, assistir, professor
cua	cuatro, cuando, cuál	*qua*	quatro, quando, qual
z	brazo, azúcar, cabeza	*ç*	braço, açúcar, cabeça

Portuguese words ending in *–ia* and *–io* present a special challenge, since most of these words are pronounced similarly in both languages but follow different rules for written accent marks. Rather than attempting to explain the rules, it is often easier to simply show examples like those in Figure 6 and guide students to induce patterns themselves.

Figure 6 *Examples of Words with the Same Stress but Different Spellings in Spanish and Portuguese*

Español	Português	Español	Português
existencia	existência /z/	alegría	alegria
importancia	importância	economía	economia
memoria	memória	filosofía	filosofia
miseria	miséria	María	Maria
noticia	notícia	(él) bebía	(ele) bebia
secretaria	secretária	(él) comía	(ele) comia
colegio	colégio	(él) sería	(ele) seria
necesario	necessário	río	rio
negocio	negócio	tío	tio
palacio	palácio	desafío	desafio
principio	princípio	navío	navio
silencio	silêncio	frío	frio
premio	prêmio	sombrío	sombrio

There also exist a handful of cognate words between Spanish and Portuguese that are *not* stressed on the same syllable. Figure 7 shows some of the most common of these words. Again, it will be necessary for students to memorize these differences.

Figure 7 *Some Words Stressed on Different Syllables in Spanish and Portuguese*

Español	Português	Español	Português
a**néc**dota	ane**d*o***ta /ó/	aca**de**mia	acade**mi**a
at**mós**fera	atmos**fe**ra /é/	a**ne**mia	ane**mi**a
bu**ró**crata	buro**cra**ta	buro**cra**cia	burocra**ci**a
ce**re**bro	**cé**rebro	demo**cra**cia	democra**ci**a
de**mó**crata	demo**cra**ta	epi**de**mia	epide**mi**a
estereo**ti**po	estere**ó**tipo	his**te**ria	histe**ri**a
gaucho	ga**ú**cho (ga-**ú**-cho)	nos**tal**gia	nostal**gi**a
héroe	her**ói**	te**ra**pia	tera**pi**a
i**mán**	**í**mã		
límite	li**mi**te	poli**cí**a	po**lí**cia
medi**o**cre	me**dí**ocre		
mi**cró**fono	micro**fo**ne		
régimen	re**gi**me		
síntoma	sin**to**ma		
tel**é**fono	tele**fo**ne		

Grammatical Differences

Spanish speakers learning Portuguese enjoy an enormous advantage over non-Spanish speakers in that Portuguese grammar is overwhelmingly similar to Spanish. Furthermore, many of the differences between the two languages are relatively easy for Spanish speakers to understand, even if they take time to master. These differences include the existence of gender-inflected forms for the number *dois/duas* and for the possessives *meu/minha, teu/tua,* and *seu/sua*; the contractions of prepositions with articles, such as *ao, no,* and *pelo*; the difference between the adjective *todo(s)*and the adverb *tudo;* the absence of the preposition *a* in expressing the future with *ir* and when using direct objects referring to people; and the use of *gostar de* as opposed to Spanish *gustarle a uno.*

Much more challenging for Spanish speakers are a handful of verb forms that differ from Spanish, including the present perfect tense, the future subjunctive, and the personal infinitive. In terms of syntax, Spanish speakers tend to struggle most with word order in questions and the use of object pronouns. These students can benefit from a contrastive approach that features examples of parallel structures in Portuguese, Spanish, and (possibly) English. Figure 8 shows an example of such an approach for teaching the future subjunctive.

Figure 8 *Examples for Teaching the Future Subjunctive Inductively*

Español	Português
Mis hermanos viven lejos de mí, pero este año tenemos planes para reunirnos para la Navidad. Tan pronto como **llegue** mi hermano mayor, Roberto, vamos a comprar un árbol de Navidad. Cuando **venga** mi hermana Ana, ella va a preparar un *panettone* especial. Después de que **llegue** mi hermana Sofía, vamos a decorar la casa y cantar villancicos. Mientras que **cantemos**, vamos a tomar chocolate caliente. Luego que **terminemos**, vamos a leer la historia de la Navidad en la Biblia. Si nieva, podremos hacer un hombre de nieve y luego esperar la llegada de Papá Noel.	Meus irmãos moram longe de mim, mas este ano temos planos para nos reunirmos para o Natal. Assim que meu irmão mais velho Roberto **chegar**, vamos comprar uma árvore de Natal. Quando minha irmã Ana **vier**, ela vai preparar um panettone especial. Depois que minha irmã Sofia **chegar**, vamos decorar a casa e cantar canções natalinas. Enquanto **cantarmos**, vamos tomar chocolate quente. Logo que terminarmos, vamos ler a história de Natal da Bíblia. Se **nevar**, poderemos fazer um boneco de neve e depois esperar a chegada do Papai Noel.

After studying the examples in the two (or three) languages, students can be guided inductively to formulate rules explaining similarities and differences among languages. Instructors can pose questions such as *Qual é a função comunicativa desta estrutura em português? Como a estrutura é formada? Em que circunstâncias é usada? Que estruturas são usadas para expressar as mesmas funções comunicativas no espanhol?* This type of inductive approach has the potential to improve both students' understanding of the structures in question and their retention of these structures.

General Hints for Teaching the Linguistic Features of Portuguese

Address important differences between Portuguese and Spanish early in the course. Most Portuguese textbooks, which are not designed with Spanish speakers in mind, sequence grammatical topics according to an assumed hierarchy of difficulty. They typically begin with the present indicative, the preterit and the imperfect, leaving concepts that are thought to be more challenging, such as the future subjunctive and the personal infinitive, for the final chapters of the book. Such an approach does not serve Spanish speakers well, as they need much less practice with the present indicative than with the future subjunctive and other Portuguese structures that differ from Spanish. A better approach is to introduce such structures early in the course so that students can attend to these unique aspects of Portuguese as they occur in oral and written input, and can practice them while speaking and writing in the language.

Address similarities as well as differences between languages. Although students will need more work with Portuguese structures that diverge from Spanish, at least one study (Child, 2013) has shown that many students prefer a systematic approach to grammar that addresses similarities as well as differences between the two languages. While the bulk of time should be devoted to practicing divergent structures, it is also important to give at least a nod to structures that are similar. Such an approach is especially important for native and heritage speakers of Spanish, who often lack familiarity with grammatical concepts and terminology.

Emphasize grammatical accuracy. It has been well documented that a purely communicative approach to learning Portuguese is inadequate for Spanish speakers (e.g., Carvalho, 2002). If students are pushed early on to communicate in Portuguese without an accompanying emphasis on grammatical accuracy, there is a tendency for their errors to fossilize, making these errors extremely difficult to correct. For this reason it is important to help students develop metalinguistic awareness in order to minimize negative transfer from Spanish.

Teach "chunks" of language. Certain Portuguese words tend to occur in conjunction with other words in patterns or collocations that may not be intuitive to language learners. Spanish speakers are likely to assume that such word patterns are the same in Portuguese as they are in Spanish; in cases where they are not, it is helpful to teach these patterns as memorized "chunks." Examples include formulaic social expressions (*muito prazer em conhecê-lo/la, com licença, sinto muito*), verb-noun collocations (*atender o telefone, preencher um formulário*), verb-preposition collocations (*aproximar-se de, gostar de, votar em*), and general idiomatic expressions (*bater um papo, puxar conversa, dar o braço a torcer*). Such "chunks" can help learners acquire a feel for the language and produce utterances that sound natural to native speakers (Silveira, 2013).

Expect transfer from Spanish, but work to decrease it. Despite their best efforts to separate the two languages mentally, students will inevitably mix some elements of Spanish vocabulary, grammar, spelling, and pronunciation as they begin to speak and write in Portuguese. Even students who have reached the Intermediate High proficiency level in Portuguese occasionally throw in common Spanish words such as *pero* instead of *mas*. This may be especially true of heritage speakers of Spanish, who are accustomed to functioning in bilingual environments where code switching is common. Although it is unrealistic for instructors to expect perfection in this respect, they should make clear to students that one of the goals of the course is to develop the ability to separate Portuguese from Spanish. One colleague of mine addresses this issue by drawing a box in the corner of the blackboard and labeling it *caixa de espanhol*. Whenever a student uses a Spanish word, she says, *Isso é espanhol. Vamos guardar todas as palavras do espanhol na caixa, e vocês poderão retirá-las depois da aula.* She then writes the Spanish word in the box, and writes the corresponding Portuguese word in the center of the board.

Capitalizing on Students' Receptive Skills

In order to capitalize on the receptive skills of Spanish speakers, instructors should expose students to authentic written and oral texts from the outset of instruction. In addition to providing the input that students need in order to further their acquisition of Portuguese, such texts can also be highly motivating to students as they realize they can understand materials that were designed for native Portuguese speakers. Following are some general tips for incorporating authentic oral and written texts in Portuguese for Spanish Speakers courses.

Expose students to a variety of text types

Among the many types of authentic print materials are informative, journalistic, and literary texts, as well as written messages of a more interpersonal nature such as emails and posts on blogs or social media. Literary texts may be more challenging for students than other types of printed texts since they tend to incorporate a wider range of vocabulary, which may include colloquial language, regionalisms, or cultural references. Introducing a variety of different text types is the best way to provide essential linguistic input while at the same time catering to the diverse interests and needs of students.

In terms of oral texts, an Internet search can quickly provide audio and video recordings on practically any theme, including news broadcasts, clips of television programs, commercials, and even homemade YouTube videos. Again, the greater the variety of text types, the better.

Pay attention to pre-reading and pre-listening activities

Research on reading and listening comprehension indicates that carefully-planned pre-reading and pre-listening activities can significantly improve students' comprehension of oral or written texts (e.g., Aebersold & Field, 1997; Grabe, 2009). Possibly the most important purpose of pre-reading or listening activities is to activate students' background knowledge about the topic of the text. In addition, such activities can introduce key vocabulary and cultural concepts, provide a purpose for reading or listening, and motivate students to interact with the text at hand.

By way of example, in preparation for reading a *crônica* about a child's birthday party in Brazil, the class could brainstorm a semantic map similar to that in Figure 9, with translations (or better yet, images) provided for words such as *bolo* that differ significantly from Spanish. The instructor could then ask students what they know about how birthday parties in Spanish-speaking countries differ from those in the U.S., and draw comparisons with Brazilian culture. Depending on the content of the *crônica*, it may be helpful to point out that the notion of hosting a birthday party for a child to which only children are invited, but not the child's adult relatives, is completely foreign to Brazilian culture, as is the idea of dropping a child off for a party at another child's house and arranging to pick the child up at a given hour. Such activities can help students get started on the right track in comprehending the story and avoid the need for lengthy vocabulary lists.

Figure 9 *Example of Pre-Reading Semantic Map*

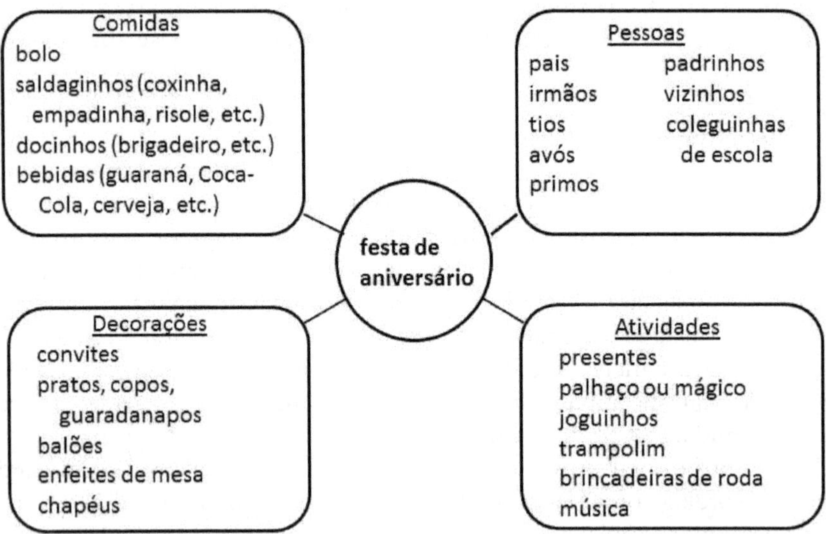

Make use of vocabulary glosses or video subtitles, but only when necessary

Research has shown that glossing unfamiliar vocabulary in printed texts, or providing access to subtitles for videos, can aid students' comprehension in certain circumstances (Vandergrift & Goh, 2011); however, these tools should be used sparingly so as not to deprive students of the chance to figure out meaning on their own. In the case of written texts, obviously the only words that need glossing are those that differ significantly from Spanish. Even so, if these words are related to the theme of the text, it is preferable to introduce them in context during pre-reading activities. When it is necessary to gloss words in the margin of the text, wherever possible the glosses should be in Portuguese; for example, the noun *pulo* could be glossed as *salto*, which is the same in Spanish. When none of these alternatives is possible, and when an explanation of the unfamiliar word in Portuguese would be prohibitively long, glosses can be provided in Spanish, English, or both.

In the case of videos, research suggests that subtitles are best reserved for the second or third viewing, with students using the subtitles to verify their understanding and fill in any gaps (Vandergrift & Goh, 2011). Many DVDs offer the option of viewing subtitles in multiple languages; if they are available in Portuguese, students can view the subtitles while watching the film, thus using reading to reinforce listening skills.

Capitalizing on Students' Cultural Knowledge

It goes without saying that culture is an integral part of language teaching and learning. The *World-Readiness Standards for Learning Languages,* explained in the chapter "Planning a Portuguese Course," include two standards under the Cultures goal area:

Relating Cultural Practices to Perspectives: Learners use the language to investigate, explain, and reflect on the relationship between the practices and perspectives of the cultures studied.

Relating Cultural Products to Perspectives: Learners use the language to investigate, explain, and reflect on the relationship between the products and perspectives of the cultures studied.

The Comparisons goal area of the Standards also addresses culture learning:

Cultural Comparisons: Learners use the language to investigate, explain, and reflect on the concept of culture through comparisons of the cultures studied and their own.

Spanish-speaking learners of Portuguese, including those who have learned Spanish as a second language, already have experience in crossing cultural boundaries, and thus bring a considerable degree of cultural insight to the Portuguese classroom. Just as third language learners have already developed skills in approaching language learning, third culture learners bring with them insights gleaned from experience with multiple cultures. Following are some tips for taking advantage of these students' cultural awareness.

Address cultural practices as well as products

Although many foreign language textbooks incorporate information about cultural products such as foods or music, they often tend to neglect information about cultural practices, such as when the foods or music are eaten or listened to, by whom, with whom, and under what circumstances. Such information can enhance students' understanding of and interest in the target culture. To cite just one example, a discussion of the Brazilian concept of *salgadinhos* would be incomplete without considering where and when these foods are eaten – for example, as a mid-morning or late-afternoon snack in a bar, *lanchonete,* or *padaria,* or at a birthday party – as well as the fact that snacking on a *salgadinho* would rarely be considered a substitute for eating a full meal at lunch or dinnertime.

Invite students to make cross-cultural comparisons

As explained in the *Standards*, involving students in making comparisons across cultures increases their awareness of the concept of culture and of similarities and differences among cultures. *Salgadinhos*, for example, have no real counterpart in American culture, but they do in many Latin American cultures, and they even share some similarities with *tapas* in Spain. Students enjoy playing the role of cultural "experts" when they are invited to make comparisons among Portuguese-speaking cultures and the Hispanic cultures with which they are familiar, as well as with English-speaking cultures. To cite another example, in a unit on work and the economy, native English-speaking students may be surprised to learn that in preparing a résumé for a job application, native Portuguese speakers may include information on their age and marital status, and job interviewers may ask about these topics, or may even solicit candidates of a specific gender or age group. Natives of Spanish-speaking countries, on the other hand, are less likely to be surprised by these facts, since similar practices may be commonplace in their own country. Engaging students in a discussion of these differences can help develop their awareness of multiple cultures, including their own.

Provide opportunities for interaction with native speakers

Interacting with native Portuguese speakers not only gives students a chance to practice their Portuguese; it also provides opportunities to discuss cultural issues. Native Portuguese speakers are easily locatable in many communities throughout the United States; even if they are not, they are readily accessible online. An Internet search for "international keypals" or "international classroom exchange" can help instructors locate classes of native Portuguese speakers who want to practice their English. In addition, sites such as WeSpeke or Livemocha can match students with individual native speakers across the globe.

In these interactions with natives, students should be encouraged to discuss whatever cultural topics are the current focus of instruction. In a unit on work and the economy, for example, students could ask native speakers what types of jobs they have held; how they went about applying for these jobs; how the types of jobs that people hold in their country are influenced by factors such as gender, age, or socioeconomic status; and what differences they have observed among different cultures in terms of economic and employment opportunities. Students could then be asked to report back to the class on what they have learned, providing a springboard for discussion of similarities and differences in cultural practices.

Encourage reflection on cultural perspectives

As defined by the *Standards*, cultural perspectives reflect the beliefs, priorities, attitudes, and values of the members of a given culture. They help explain *why* the members of that culture create certain products or engage in certain practices. An understanding of cultural perspectives can help students develop the type of awareness that leads to true appreciation of other cultures on their own terms. Again, Spanish speakers, due to their previous experience with other cultures, are ideally positioned to appreciate the cultural perspectives of Portuguese-speaking countries.

Returning to the example of *salgadinhos,* a discussion of this cultural product and the associated practices could lead to a cross-cultural comparison of eating habits. For example, students may observe that whereas a *coxinha* would not normally be considered a substitute for lunch in Brazil, Americans may get by with just a muffin or bagel for lunch. Furthermore, students may notice that Americans tend to grab lunch from a vending machine or drive-thru and eat it in their cubicle or car, whereas Brazilians generally take time to eat a full lunch in a restaurant or at home, with family or colleagues. Students could then compare these practices with eating habits in Spanish-speaking countries. This could lead to a discussion of differing cultural priorities: for example, students might conclude that Americans tend to value work, speed, and convenience, whereas Latin Americans tend to prioritize eating complete meals and socializing while eating. The actual hypotheses that students come up with are less important than the process of considering why members of different cultures behave as they do, and how this can reflect cultural differences in world views.

Assessing Students' Portuguese Skills

Assessing the Portuguese skills of Spanish speakers can be problematic due to the fact that these students are often quite fluent and can handle a wide range of communicative tasks, but they tend to mix the two languages, raising the question of how proficient they really are in Portuguese. In the ACTFL Proficiency Guidelines, this issue is addressed by the *accuracy* criterion: in order to reach the Advanced level, for example, students must be easily understandable to native speakers who are not accustomed to interacting with language learners. After one semester of Portuguese, it is relatively common for Spanish speakers to reach the Intermediate High level, but they often do not reach the Advanced level because they still incorporate Spanish words and constructions that native Portuguese speakers would probably not understand unless they speak Spanish.

The same principle can be applied in classroom assessments: instructors can base a portion of students' grade on their accuracy in the use of Portuguese. Written exams can include sections that focus specifically on grammar, encouraging students to attend to grammatical correctness. Oral exams, presentations, and compositions can be graded with rubrics that include criteria such as pronunciation, grammar, and vocabulary, with points awarded for accuracy in the use of Portuguese and the avoidance of Spanish.

In grading writing assignments and written exams, points can be given (or subtracted) for accuracy in spelling, including written accent marks. These procedures do not preclude a communicative approach to assessing language learning; rather, they enhance it by encouraging students to develop metalinguistic awareness and avoid the fossilization of errors.

Conclusion

In many respects, Spanish speakers constitute ideal candidates for learning Portuguese: they are already proficient in a similar language, thus enabling them to master Portuguese grammar and vocabulary relatively quickly; they are able to understand spoken and written texts in Portuguese almost from the outset of instruction; and they possess a considerable degree of cultural awareness that comes from experience in crossing cultural boundaries. In addition, many of them have learned a second language as adolescents or adults, and have developed strategies and skills for language learning. By capitalizing on these students' strengths, instructors can enable them to develop a considerable degree of proficiency in Portuguese in a relatively short time. Such an approach has the added benefit of helping students develop confidence in their Portuguese skills and in themselves as language learners. In light of these facts, it is to be hoped that the availability of Portuguese for Spanish Speakers courses will continue to increase in the coming years.

References

Aebersold, J. A., & Field, M. L. (1997). *From reader to reading teacher: Issues and strategies for second language classrooms* (Cambridge Language Education Series). Cambridge, UK: Cambridge University Press.

Bateman, B., & Oliveira, D. (2014). Students' motivations for choosing (or not) to study Portuguese: A survey of beginning-level university classes. *Hispania, 97,* 264-280.

Carvalho, A. M. (2002). Português para falantes de espanhol: Perspectivas de um campo de pesquisa. *Hispania, 85,* 597-608.

Child, M. W. (2013). Language learning perceptions: The role of Spanish in L3 Portuguese acquisition. *Portuguese Language Journal, 7.* Retrieved from www.ensinoportugues.org

Grabe, W. (2009). *Reading in a second language: Moving from theory to practice* (Cambridge Applied Linguistics Series). Cambridge, UK: Cambridge University Press.

Henriques, E. R. (2000). Intercompreensão de texto escrito por falantes nativos de português e de espanhol. *D.E.L.T.A., 16,* 263-295.

Jensen, J. B. (1989). On the mutual intelligibility of Spanish and Portuguese. *Hispania, 72,* 848-852.

Milleret, M. (2012). Portuguese study in higher education in the United States.

Hispania, 95, 135-150.

Silveira, A. S. (2013). *Précis* to the use of constructions in the teaching of Portuguese as a third language. *Portguese Language Journal, 13*. Available at http://www.ensinoportugues.org/

Simões, R. M., Carvalho, A. M., & Wiedemann, L. (Eds.). (2004). *Português para falantes de espanhol: Artigos selecionados escritos em português e inglês.* Campinas, Brazil: Pontes Editores.

Vandergrift, L., & Goh, C. C. M. (2011). *Teaching and learning second language listening: Metacognition in action.* London: Routledge.

Wiedemann, L., & Scaramucci, M. V. R. (Eds.). (2008). *Português para Falantes de Espanhol: Ensino e Aquisição.* Campinas, Brazil: Pontes Editores.

3.3 BRAZILIAN PORTUGUESE PRONUNCIATION FOR SPEAKERS OF SPANISH, LEARNERS OF PORTUGUESE

Antônio Roberto Monteiro Simões
University of Kansas

This chapter contrasts the basic and most relevant pronunciation features of Spanish and Brazilian Portuguese. It is designed for speakers of Spanish who wish to learn Portuguese as well as for teachers with an interest in Portuguese for speakers of Spanish. Given its bilingual nature, it can also be useful for other audiences, such as speakers of Portuguese who are learners of Spanish and, as pointed out by Beaudrie, Ducar and Potowski (2014 212), to heritage speakers. I will focus only on the pronunciation features that are most relevant for these audiences.

I have chosen to avoid certain phonetic details because they are more useful to linguists, especially to phoneticians and phonologists. It is obvious that it is completely impractical for teachers and learners of Portuguese to try to correct every detail of pronunciation. For a more detailed historical and synchronic description of the sounds of Spanish and Portuguese, I recommend the recent study by Ferreira and Holt (2014).

This chapter focuses on the pronunciation of Brazilian Portuguese. Note that the terms "second language" and "foreign language" are not used, as I prefer the term **additional language**. Although this chapter highlights Spanish and Portuguese, examples from English will be used as needed, to more fully illustrate some of the pronunciation features discussed.

All discussions of pronunciation features within this study are based on a general and idealized pronunciation of national television speakers. In the case of Spanish, these idealized speakers are from the regions frequently referred to as the "high-lands" of Latin America, which are former colonial viceroyalties of Spain (e.g. Mexico, D.F., Guadalajara, Bogotá, La Paz, Lima (although this city is at sea level), Quito, to mention some; in the case of Brazilian Portuguese, these idealized speakers are the national television broadcasters within Brazil. Finally, such idealized registers require that these idealized speakers have a college training or higher or the equivalent in their speaking techniques. It may be helpful to know that there is no "standard" or "general" Portuguese spoken in Brazil.

It may be pedagogically helpful to use the speech of speakers of news anchors as the register of reference in the Spanish or Portuguese classrooms. There are many advantages to this approach. One of them is that both teachers and students can easily refer to this register of reference, given the relative accessibility of national televisions broadcasts in any region, through the Internet, a common tool in today's classrooms. Furthermore, the register of a national news anchor tends to be closer to the formality of the written language while still sounding natural. In other words, we may sometimes find native speakers who are excessively concerned with maintaining a "pure speaking style," and wind up speaking in a pedantic or artificial manner. Usually, that is not the case with national news anchors

Therefore, the goal of this contrastive description of Spanish and Brazilian Portuguese is to provide key practical information about the sound systems of Spanish and Brazilian Portuguese that will help speakers of Spanish to learn the sound system of Portuguese. The contrastive description of how pronunciation patterns operate in these two languages is intended to be a user-friendly reference.

This chapter is organized into three parts. Part I explores the basic pronunciation differences of vowel and consonant segments, as well as some of the most common and productive phonological processes in Brazilian Portuguese.

It must be noted that the first section is intended for readers with little or no background in Linguistics. Part II provides a practical application for the discussion in Part I. It proposes ideas for creating strategies to learn and teach Brazilian Portuguese to speakers of Spanish. Part III expands on Part 1 by discussing additional contrasts between Spanish and Portuguese, especially in terms of language prosody, i.e. suprasegmentals; therefore, it requires some background in linguistics.

How the Sounds of Portuguese and Spanish Work: A Basic Contrast

Table 1 explains the symbols used in this study. Please refer to it as needed. It also lists common conventions for transcribing speech.

Table 1. *Phonetic symbols for Brazilian Portuguese.*

Alphabet Letter	Phonetic Symbol	Alphabet Letter	Phonetic Symbol	Alphabet Letter	Phonetic Symbol
a	[a] **a**to	i	[i] c**i**sco [^{i}] se**i**s	r	[ɾ] ra**r**o, t**r**ês, ve**r**
ã, an am	[ã] l**ã**, **an**tes [ã^{ʊ}] fal**am**	im in	[ĩ] or [ĩ^{ĩ}] s**im** [ĩ] s**in**to	r	/R/ [x] **r**aro, ve**r** [h] **r**aro, ve**r** [χ] **r**aro, ve**r** [ʁ] **r**aro, ve**r** [Ø] mute ve**r**
b	[b] **b**oto	j	[ʒ] **j**ogo		
c	[s] **c**ito, **c**éu [k] **c**ama, **c**om, **c**ulpa	k	[k] **k**art	rr	/R/ [x], [h], [ʁ], [χ] [r] ca**rr**o
ç	[s] dan**ç**a, la**ç**o, a**çú**car	l	[l] brasi**l**eiro [^{u}] Brasi**l**	s	/S/ [s] trê**s**, [z] de**s**de [ʃ] trê**s**, [ʒ] de**s**de
ch	[ʃ] **Ch**ico	lh	[l^{i}y] or [λ] fi**lh**o	s	[z] a**s**a

d	[d] **de**sde, **d**ar, **d**o, **d**uas [ʤ] **di**go, bo**de**, des**de**	m	[m] **m**ais [~] ca**m**po, bo**m**	ss	[s] a**ss**a
e	[e] s**e**ja [ɛ] s**e**te [i] set**e** [^{i}] pass**e**ar	n	[n] ca**n**a [~] ca**n**to, ze**n**	t	[t] **t**eve, **t**al, **t**om, **t**una [ʧ] **t**ime, par**t**e
é ê	[ɛ] Z**é** [e] z**ê**	nh	[^{i}ỹ] or [ŋ] te**nh**o	u	[u] **ú**v**u**la, [^{u}] esto**u**
em en	[ɛ̃^{ɪ}] b**em** [ɛ̃] b**en**to	o	[o] am**o**r [ɔ] m**o**do [u] mod**o** [^{u}] enjo**o**	um un	[ũ] or [ũ^{ɯ}] b**um**! [ũ] n**un**ca
f	[f] **f**oto			v	[v] **v**oto
g+o,a,u g+i,e	[g] **g**ol, **g**ala, **g**ula [ʒ] **g**iz, **g**ê	ó ô	[ɔ] d**ó** [o] av**ô**	w	[v] Os**w**ald [^{u}] **w**att
gu+e,i	[g] pa**gu**e, se**gu**inte	om õ, on	[õ] or [ã^{ɯ}] b**om** [õ] p**õ**e, t**on**to	x	[s] trou**x**e [z] e**x**ato [ks] ne**x**o [š] Te**x**aco
		p	[p] **p**ato		
gu+e,i	[g^{u}] a**gu**entar, ar**gu**ir	q	[k] par**qu**e, a**qu**ilo	y	[i] Lis**y** [^{i}] Ble**y** [ʒ] **j**arda
h	[Ø] mute: **h**otel	qu	[k^{u}] elo**qu**ente, tran**qu**ilo	z	[z] fa**z**er

These symbols reflect an approximation of the pronunciation of national news anchors. The symbol [~] indicates nasality. The variant pronunciations of <r, rr>, [χ] and [ʁ] are less common. The capital letters /S/ and /R/ represent a range of pronunciations, which depend on factors such as personal preferences, language varieties, and others. This table shows only isolated changes. It does not take into account changes made by the surrounding sounds or contexts. For instance, the examples for <s> in the words <tres> and <desde> do not show an [i] that may or not surface in the presence of /s/ as in [tɾes, tɾe^{i}s, dezde, de^{i}zde, tɾe^{i}ʃ, deʒde, de^{i}ʒde].

Segments: Vowels. This study assumes that Brazilian Portuguese has seven oral vowels and five nasal vowels. Regardless of how we approach the description of the Portuguese vowel system, there are more vowels in Portuguese than in Spanish. Furthermore, among the college-educated Spanish population, the Spanish vowels are relatively more stable than in Portuguese, meaning that the vowels in Spanish do not change their features (or qualities) as much as Portuguese or English do.

Interestingly, native speakers of Portuguese understand a good deal of spoken Spanish, whereas native speakers of Spanish frequently have more difficulty understanding basic spoken Portuguese. It is often attributed to the late Brazilian linguist Mattoso Câmara, Jr. the explanation that the main reason for this was due to the difference in the number of vowels within the two languages. However, there are other reasons, vowel instability in Portuguese being one of them. Jensen (1989) empirically observed and described this phenomenon of mutual intelligibility in his study.

Changes in vowel quality permeate Portuguese and this vowel instability has characterized the language throughout its evolution. Vowels in Portuguese change depending on their context. The vowels <e> and <o>, for example, in the word <**e**scrit**o**> are commonly pronounced [i] and [u], [iS.ˈkri.tu], because of contexts or factors such as their position in the word, the degree of stress, the register, to mention some. On the other hand, at the end of the word <escritor> the vowel <o> does not change, it is pronounced [o], [iS.kri.ˈtoR], because of another factor, i.e. the [o] is in a strong position, a stressed position. Spanish, *relative* to Portuguese or English, tends to mirror, although not perfectly, what is written, in the register of spoken Spanish just referred to in this study.

In addition to coming to grips with vowel instability in Portuguese, Spanish speakers will have to learn seven more vowels to become proficient in Brazilian Portuguese. Although the Portuguese alphabet contains five letters to represent its vowels, <a, e, i, o, u>, these letter symbols are not sufficient to represent the actual number of 12 vowel phonemes.

Among the vowels of Brazilian Portuguese, the narrow-mid oral vowels in Brazilian Portuguese, Table 2, are probably the greatest challenge to speakers of Spanish who are learners of Brazilian Portuguese and also to speakers of English learning Portuguese.

A common way of describing the Portuguese vowel phonemes is presented in Table 2. The ones that occur only in strong position are the ones in the boxes with a darker background. Note that the central vowel, referred to as *schwa* (/ə/), has an "only in EP" under it. This is to indicate that it is a vowel phoneme that normally appears only in European Portuguese. Maybe there is a recent trend of production of schwas in Brazilian Portuguese, but if it is the case, the trend may be limited to some regions and in limited contexts. In American English, all unstressed vowels in spontaneous discourse tend to centralize, i.e. to reduce to a schwa. The underlined vowels of the English words <about> and <southern> are examples of schwas in unstressed and stressed syllables[28] respectively. Spanish, perhaps with the exception of some varieties of Spanish spoken in the US, normally does not have schwas in the register we use as reference in this study.

---

[28] The Merriam-Webster dictionary defines schwa as "an unstressed mid-central vowel." This is also a common definition among some linguists. But it is common to have schwas in stressed position (e.g. S**ou**thern). Hence, I have adopted the definition of schwa as "a reduced and mid-central vowel."

Table 2. *The vowel system of Portuguese, based on Simões (2008)*

Front	Central	Back or Velar	
/ i / m**i**to / ĩ /m**in**to, p**in**tura		/ ũ / m**un**do, m**un**dano / u / m**u**do	"Close" or **High/Wide**
/ e / c**e**do / ẽ /s**en**do, ac**en**dendo	/ ə / only in EP	/ õ / b**on**de, **bon**dade / o / p**ô**de	**High/Wide-mid**
/ ɛ / Z**e**ca / ɛ̃ /s**en**do	/ ɐ̃ / m**an**ta	/ ɔ / p**o**de	**Low/Narrow-mid**
	/ a / m**a**ta		"Open" or **Low/Narrow**
Retracted Round	Round	Retracted Round	

Boxes with a darker background show vowels that appear only in strong position, namely stressed syllables. The tilde (~) over a vowel means that the vowel is nasal. Note that this table indicates that the nasal vowel in *sendo* is either front, high/wide-mid (*semi-fechada*), or front low/narrow-mid (*semi-aberta*). Traditionally, this vowel has been described as high/wide-mid or *semi-fechada.*

Spanish speakers, learners of Portuguese will need to learn the Portuguese vowel phonemes not present in Spanish, in addition to learning or perceiving the changes in vowel quality, because these phonemes and their changes in quality are very productive in Portuguese. English and French, for example, have narrow-mid or low mid-vowels that do not correspond exactly to the Portuguese ones. Hence the difficulty that English and French speaker have as well, and Spanish speakers even more, to produce oral narrow-mid vowels in Portuguese, traditionally called "open vowels."

The nasal vowel phonemes may pose some difficulties, but not as much as the open vowels. Finally, some Spanish speakers who speak English as native or near-native language often find the features or terms **lax** and **tense** more helpful than the terms used here, **narrow-mid** or **open**. The narrow-mid or open oral vowels in English are usually described as lax vowels.

Therefore, vowel instability is most likely one of the main factors if not the main factor that makes the intelligibility of Portuguese harder for native speakers of Spanish than the intelligibility of Spanish for native speakers of Portuguese (Simões, 2008).

Given the information in the preceding paragraphs, unstressed vowels in Portuguese change in quality. These changes may result in other phonological processes or phonological rules. In Brazilian Portuguese, a person who changes /e/ to [i] will also change the pronunciation of /t/ and /d/, when these consonants appear before [i], as in

Source	Intermediate Step	Final Output
futebol (soccer): /fu.**te**.ˈbɔl/	→ [fu.**ti**.ˈbɔ^{u}]	[fu.**tʃi**.ˈbɔ^{u}]
cor-de-rosa (pink (color)): /ˈkoR.**de**.ˈRɔ.za/	→ [ˈkox.**di**.ˈxɔ.zɐ]	[ˈkox.**dʒi**.ˈxɔ.zɐ]

Note that the unstressed vowel [ɐ] is used here, instead of the schwa seen in other transcriptions. The symbol [ɐ] represents an unstressed vowel allophone, but not a schwa. With respect to the [e] and [i] alternations, if the person's pronunciation does not change the /e/ to [i], then /t/ and /d/ will remain as they are, alveolar [t] and [d] and, in this person's pronunciation, that is to say the output will be [fu.te.ˈbɔ^{u}] and [ˈkox.de.ˈxɔ.zɐ]. Note that in <cor-de-rosa> I used [x] for the <r> because it is a very common pronunciation. Obviously, there are other possibilities, as shown in Table 2.

With respect to diphthongs, speakers of Spanish, as well as speakers of English, should not have difficulties saying diphthongs in Portuguese. The only obstacle may be to remember their forms, especially in the forms of the verbs in the Preterit verbal aspect of the Indicative mode, e.g. <falou> (Span. <habló>), <amanheceu> (Span. <amaneció>), <saiu> (<Span. <salió>).

Comparison of Oral Vowels in Spanish and Brazilian Portuguese, Using English Vowels When Spanish Lacks the Equivalent

(Male speaker, *capixaba-colatinense* from Espírito Santo)

Spanish	Brazilian Portuguese	English closer equivalents
/i/ Brasilia	/i/ Brasília	
/e/ (el) peso	/e/ (o) peso	/e:/bait; (also /ɩ/ as in bit)
No equivalent	/ɛ/ (eu) peso	/ɛ/ pet; (also /æ/ as in Pat)
/a/ Machado	/a/ Machado	
No equivalent	/ɔ/ posso	/ɔ/ bought, awe
/o/ pozo	/o/ poço	/o:/ boat
/u/ Hugo	/u/ Hugo	

Segments: The Nasal Vowels of Brazilian Portuguese

In general, neither Spanish nor English have nasal vowels that change the meaning of a word when replaced by a corresponding oral vowel. English speakers may have a slight advantage here because English does have the interjection "uh-huh" (/ã-ˈhã/), which can be regarded for teaching purposes as a very close equivalent of Brazilian Portuguese /ã/, as in *cantando*. A special challenge for speakers of Spanish and English as well will be the **nasal sounds at the end of a word**. In addition to *hearing* how these sounds are produced in Brazilian Portuguese, they also have to take into account their misleading spelling. For instance, Brazilian Portuguese words like <um, bem, sim, Cancun, porém, festim, garçom, som, nenhum, assim, falam, vem, porém, aparecem> and many others that end in *–n* or *–m*, are pronounced with a nasal vowel or diphthong. The written *–n* and *–m* are not pronounced.

The visual image of words spelled with a final *–n* or *–m* tends to mislead non-native speakers. Despite the spelling, *–n* and *–m* are mute, but where they appear, they generally make the preceding vowel letter a spoken nasal vowel or a nasal diphthong.

Therefore, the nasal consonant *letters*, *–n* and *–m*, are written but not normally pronounced. The student must *hear* the different nasal feature of these vowels in word final position and produce them accordingly (Simões 2008; 2013). The table below provides a summary of the nasal vowels.

Spanish closer equivalents	Brazilian Portuguese	English closer equivalents
tinto	/ĩ/ assim	No equivalent
centro	/ẽ/ centro	No equivalent
zanja	/ã/ rã	uh-uh
tonto	/õ/ tom	No equivalent
mundo	/ũ/ atum	No equivalent

Note that Spanish speakers should not have difficulties using Portuguese nasal vowels **inside a word**.

Segments: Consonants. In Brazilian Portuguese, in the speech of national television speakers, the consonants tend to be well articulated. For example, a stop consonant, voiceless or voiced, is realized as such. Thus, speakers of English should have no problems pronouncing most of them, whereas speakers of Spanish will need to make an extra articulatory effort to avoid the approximant trait of most Spanish consonants in actual discourse.

Table 3. *The consonants of Portuguese, compared to English and Spanish. Adapted from Simões (2008).*

Comparison of Spanish and Brazilian Portuguese Consonants, Using Some of the English Consonants as Interface		
Closest sound correspondences, in Spanish	**(Brazilian) Portuguese**	**English**
/p/ **p**ura	/p/ **p**ura	/p/ spot
/b/ [b] in sentence initial position, as in *¡Vaya!*, in México, D.F. or Madrid, but not soft [β] as in *a**b**uelo*, everywhere.	/b/ **b**otar (in Span. = *poner*)	/b/ boy
/t/ **t**aco	/t/ **t**aco	/t/ stop
/d/ [d] in sentence initial position, as in *¡Dale!* in México, D.F. or Madrid, but not [ð] as in *na**d**a*, everywhere.	/d/ A**d**a	/d/ day
/k/ **c**asa	/k/ **c**asa	/k/ sky

/g/ [g] in sentence initial position, as in *¡Gooolll!* in México, D.F. or Madrid, but not [ɣ] as in *pago*, everywhere.	/g/ a **g**ata	/g/ goal
/m/ **ma**pa	/m/ **ma**pa	/m/ me
/n/ **n**ada	/n/ **n**ada	/n/ no
/ɲ/ or <ñ> mañana (in Spanish it is a palatal phoneme)	/ŋ/ [ʲỹ] ma**nh**ã **Note:** The use of velar symbol /ŋ/ is not ideal, but it helps avoiding Spanish /ɲ/. Spanish "ñ" and Portuguese "nh" are very different. Spanish "ñ" is more of an anterior articulation; Portuguese "nh" is posterior, a tongue feature that pushes the palatal contact further back in Portuguese, closer to the velar area. The symbol [ỹ] or [ʲỹ] may be the best solution to represent "nh" in BP.	No equivalent; but using **ni** as in o**ni**on helps
/f/ **f**é	/f/ **f**é	/f/ **f**ault
No equivalent	/v/ **v**otar	/v/ **v**ault
/s/ **s**é	/s/ **s**ei, ca**ç**a, ca**ss**a	/s/ **s**ea
No equivalent	/z/ fa**z**er, ca**s**a	/z/ **z**oo
No equivalent *phoneme*	/ʃ//š/ a**ch**o	/ʃ/ mi**ss**ion, fi**sh**
No equivalent *phoneme*	/ʒ//ž/ ajo, garage	/ʒ/ vi**s**ion
/x/ **j**ota	[x] **r**ota, ca**rr**o, gen**r**o, des**r**espeito; Other variants: [h], [ʁ], [χ], [r]	The h-sound, as in "**h**ope" is fine
/r/ or <rr> que**rr**ía, ca**rr**o; softer than BP [rr]	[r] or <rr> **r**ota, ca**rr**o, gen**r**o, des**r**espeito; harder than in Spanish;	No equivalent
/ɾ/ que**r**ía, p**r**áctica, ca**r**o	/ɾ/ que**r**ia, p**r**áctica, ca**r**o	[ɾ] ba**tt**er, be**tt**er in American English
/l/ **l**ata	/l/ **l**ata	/l/ **l**ow
/ʎ/ or <ll> caba**ll**ero, still used (although less than before) in the center and north of Spain	/ʎ// cava**lh**eiro or [ka.va.ˈʎeⁱ.ɾu]	no equivalent phoneme, but English sequence ***lli*** in *million* is similar.

Taking into account the preceding comments and the sound comparisons in Table 3, there are two sets of consonants containing significant phonetic differences that need special attention and pronunciation drills. The first of these sets is <b, d, g>, and the second one is formed with the two sounds spelled <ll> and <ñ> in Spanish and <lh> and <nh> in Portuguese.

Comparison of Spanish and Brazilian Portuguese <b d g>, and the Insertion of [i] and [e] in Brazilian Portuguese. The most obvious differences between this set of sounds in Spanish and Brazilian Portuguese is that in Spanish these sounds are produced as soft or approximant consonants most of the time, especially when they appear between vowels, in *actual discourse*. Relative to Spanish, Brazilian Portuguese, like English, produces these sounds as hard, i.e. stop consonants. In other words, in the production of <b d g> the articulators, i.e. lips, tongue, jaw, soft and hard palates, will either approximate each other without full contact (approximants or soft consonants) or they will touch each other (hard or stop consonants). Generally in Spanish, the articulators do not come into contact. Speakers of Spanish must make sure that these articulators come into contact when speaking Brazilian Portuguese. There are some varieties of Spanish that may have actual stop consonants, especially in the register of some news anchors. In general, however, native speakers of Spanish makes these <b d g> sounds soft, i.e. approximants. As an illustration, the pronunciation of the word <abogado> can be represented in a series of gradual phonetic variations, which we summarize here with three common representations, <abogado>, <a^{b}o^{g}a^{d}o>, <aoao>, to reflect the different degrees of variation of <b d g>. In this summary of gradual variations, the first representation, <abogado>, is what may be expected in the speech of a news anchor. The smaller sizes of the fonts are intended to show the different degrees of variations or reduction, from very slight reduction to complete reduction (deletion) of these sounds, depending on the situation or contexts such as geographical area, social class, register, to mention some. In another illustration, in the sentence the highlighted consonants have varying degrees of reduction, e.g. <a^{b}uelita, auelita; cansa^{d}a, cansaa, cansá; a^{g}uanta, auanta>.

*Mi a**b**uelita está cansa**d**a, ya no a**g**uanta más,*

There is also the case of the consonant **<d>**, which is dental in Spanish and alveolar or alveopalatal for the majority of Brazilian population. In Portugal, and in some areas of Brazil, there are dental **<d>**s. However, there are general descriptions of Brazilian Portuguese (Silva 2005) that describe **<d>** and **<t>** as dentals, as if this feature were the most common realizations of **<d>** and **<t>**, in Brazilian Portuguese. I think this is misinterpretation can be explained. In Brazilian Portuguese, the tip of the tongue is not the point of contact with the alveolar region. The alveolar region is the area of the root of the front upper teeth. In the pronunciation of **<d>** and **<t>,** the front or blade of the tongue, not the tip of the tongue, touches the alveolar area, in Brazilian Portuguese. If **<t>** and **<d>** were dental consonants in Brazilian

Portuguese in general, they would simply sound like Spanish **<t>** and **<d>**, or even Latin **<t>** and **<d>**. That is clearly not the case. Anyone can easily verify these differences by asking native speakers of both languages to say words with these sounds to easily see the difference. Spanish has well attested dentals **<t>** and **<d>**, for comparison.

The Insertion of a Supporting Vowel in Contexts that Include Mostly Stop Consonants. A common phonological process in Brazilian Portuguese is to insert a supporting vowel [i] or [e] after a "dangling" consonant, to repair illegal structures. This insertion of a supporting vowel after a dangling consonant creates new **open syllables**, which are the most common type of syllable in Brazilian Portuguese and also in Spanish. I am using the term "dangling consonant" to refer to consonants that are not tolerated in a given position of a syllable structure. These consonants undergo phonological processes in order to fit into the language system.

In Brazilian Portuguese, these dangling consonants normally come from two sets of consonants, the stops / p t k **b d g** (m n ŋ (ŋ=ỹ)) / and the fricatives / s z f v s ʃ ʒ /. I am listing the complete sets of consonants, although some of these consonants are not part of the process of vowel insertion, simply to show the group of consonants to which they belong. The consonants (m n ŋ or ỹ) are inside parentheses because they are traditionally listed as nasals, outside the group of stops. I include them with the stops, because they behave like stops.

The examples below will help understand how vowel insertion after a dangling consonant works.

Spelling Approximation	Dictionary Orthography (Entry)	Spelling Approximation	Dictionary Orthography (Entry)
rí.ti.mu	<rit.mo>	ró.ti-dó.gui	In English <hot-dog>
pi.si.co.lo.gía	<psi.co.lo.gia>	fí.ki.su	<fi.xo>
a.di.vo.gá.du	<ad.vo.ga.do>	pi.néu	<pneu>
a.de.vo.gá.du	<ad.vo.ga.do>	pe.néu	<pneu>
va.rí.zi	<va.riz>	pĩ´.gui-põ´.gui	<pin.gue-pon.gue>
tí.mi	<ti.me> English <team>	á.fi.ta	<af.ta>
Di.ja.vã´	<Dja.van>	Prá.vi.da	In English <Pravda>

As the words above show, the i/e-insertion creates a common type of syllable made of a consonant and a vowel, i.e. **CV syllables. Open syllables** are syllables ending in one or more vowels, as in <sou>, <a>, <ai>, <é>, <pa.ra.le.le.pí.pe.do>. Open syllables or CV syllables constitute more than

70% of the syllable types in Brazilian Portuguese and Spanish. This can be easily attested by checking or counting randomly the syllable types of words in any page of a dictionary or on an internet newspaper written in these languages. Therefore, most words in Brazilian Portuguese and Spanish are made of CV sequences in the orthography of both languages and this trend increases in spoken language. As a result of this inherent pressure for CV syllables, the language system will fix the syllables with dangling consonants (a **resyllabification** process), by deleting or replacing the dangling consonant in favor of open syllables.

In Spanish, the dangling syllable is usually deleted or replaced: <psicología> becomes *sicología*, <ping-pong> becomes *pimpón*, <ciudad> in general becomes *ciudá*. In cases like *ciudá*, there are exceptions in some varieties and registers where final <d> may either be pronounced like the <th> sound of English as in <wi**th**> or pronounced noticeably with varying degrees of <d> reduction. There are other details involving these phonological processes which can be found in the literature. In sum, there are similarities in both languages in their tendencies to simplify their syllable structures, but there are differences as well. What speakers of Spanish should remember mostly is that in Brazilian Portuguese, the trend towards a preference for CV sequences results in the insertion of a supporting vowel in between consonant sequences (ritmo → rítimo), in word final position (hot-dog → roti-dogui), and in the deletion of the dangling consonant (Kim → kĩ).

Comparison of the Spanish <ll> and <ñ> with the Portuguese <lh> and <nh>. Pronouncing the sounds <lh> and <nh> in Brazilian Portuguese with Spanish features will not in general hinder communication, but sometimes it may disturb communication or create a strong accent for the speaker who pronounces them as in Spanish. Figure 1 suggests the position of the vocal-tract articulators when producing these sounds in both languages. I borrowed a helpful figure from my own work (Simoes 2008), to illustrate these relevant differences.

Figure 1. *Comparison of Spanish <ll> and <ñ> with Brazilian Portuguese counterparts <lh> and <nh>.*

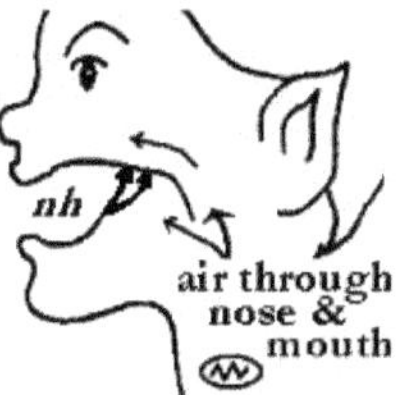

The symbol indicates voiced sounds. The arrows show roughly the areas **targeted** by the tip, blade or center (dorsum) of the tongue as well as the air flow from the lungs through the mouth and nose. These are impressionistic observations, based on the author's intuition.

In Figure 1, the arrow lines indicate the varying positions of the tongue when it approaches the palate. Spanish <ñ>, for example, is pronounced as if there were a little <^{i}> after <n>, as in <man^{i}ana>. In Brazilian Portuguese, using this little <^{i}> is an illegal pronunciation. This <^{i}> can work if placed before <nh>, as in <ma^{i} **.nh**ã> or yet, <mãe+^{i}ỹã>. The symbol **ỹ** represents a sound similar to <y> in Spanish (as in the general pronunciation of <va**y**a>) or in American English (as in <**y**es>), with nasality. The <^{i}> may, however, follow <lh> as in <cava**lh**^{i}eiro>, in Brazilian Portuguese. Note that the pronunciation of Spanish <ll>, especially outside the center and north of Spain, is indistinguishable from Spanish <y>, namely most Spanish speakers pronounce <calle> and <caye> in the same way. Nowadays, this distinction is disappearing in Spain as well. Speakers of Spanish will ideally produce the Brazilian Portuguese sounds <lh> /ʎ/ and <nh> /ỹ/ farther back in the mouth than their Spanish counterparts.

In the case of /ỹ/, there are varying degrees of tongue approximation or contact with the palate, depending on factors like speech registers, speakers, words said in isolation, in discourse, and other factors. The more clearly one intends to be in terms of diction, the closer the articulators tend to get to each other.

On the other hand, for speakers of Portuguese learners of Spanish, there is relatively lesser challenge, in terms of **sound segments** in general. There are areas of Spanish pronunciation that may require attention of speakers of Portuguese, such as rhythm, vowel stability, the <r, rr, j, g> in Spanish words like <Jorge>, <rojo>, <rígido>, etc. and how Spanish consonants in general are "softer" in Spanish than in Brazilian Portuguese. The sound <-rr-> inside a word or <r-> in word initial position has a "harder" version in some southern varieties of Brazilian Portuguese as a variant of the /R/ sound. The rhythm features of Spanish are clearly different than in Brazilian Portuguese. Vowel raising, so common in Brazilian Portuguese (e.g. *fot**o***, *padr**e***, pronounced *fótu*, *pádri*), and discussed in the next section, is not common in the Spanish of national television speakers. Speakers of Brazilian Portuguese may have a tendency to vowel raising when they speak Spanish, which they need to eliminate in their Spanish.

Phonological Processes: Vowel Raising, Palatalization of /t/ and /d/, and Vocalization of /l/.

Among the many phonological processes in Portuguese, this section focuses on four common ones that can be observed in the speech of Brazilian national television speakers. In the many regional variations of Brazil, we can find other important processes, but they would be more of interest to an audience interested in the full spectrum of regional varieties. Similarly, the regional variations in Portugal and other Lusophone regions are also very interesting to study, but they are beyond the scope of this chapter. For example, the palatalization of /s/ in syllable final position characterizes the pronunciation of Rio and Recife, but normally it does not characterize the speech of national television speakers.

Vowel rising interacts with the palatalization of /t/ and /d/. This is a productive process in Brazilian Portuguese. Vowel rising happens when a lower vowel moves up in the phonetic space or diagram shown in Figure 1. In other words, the mid vowels /e/ and /o/ can move to a higher position, becoming respectively high vowels [i] and [u]. When this happens after the alveolar consonants /t/ and /d/, these consonants become respectively palatals [ʧ] and [ʤ]. Examples are abundant in Brazilian Portuguese, as we saw earlier in this study: <escritor> becomes <[i]scritor>, <tango> becomes <tang[u]>. Palatalization requires vowel raising, e.g. <universidade> becomes <universida[ʤi]>, <quente> becomes <quen[ʧi], and so forth. Obviously, if the word has an inherent /i/ phoneme, palatalization happens without vowel raising: <distinto> becomes <[ʤ]is[ʧ]into>.

With respect to vocalization, this is simply the change of /l/ to a semi-vowel [^{u}], in syllable-final position. It happens regularly throughout Brazil, e.g. <Portugal> becomes <Portuga[^{u}]>, <fil.me> becomes <fi[^{u}].me>, <azul> becomes <azu[^{u}]>.

Final Remarks on the Basic Contrasts of Spanish and Brazilian Portuguese

Although I often think of sound segments as having a priority over some areas of prosody (i.e. intonation, rhythm, stress) in terms of teaching pronunciation in a classroom, I also realize that both segments and prosody should be taught and learned in parallel, just like we do when we learn our first language. Looking into the overall differences between Spanish and Brazilian Portuguese, it is striking but easy to see that consonants and vowels are very different in both languages. While Spanish is characterized by relatively unstable consonants and stable vowels, Brazilian Portuguese has stable consonants in the sense that they do not reduce as much as in Spanish. On the other hand, vowels in Brazilian Portuguese are unstable, which means that they change in quality in weak (usually unstressed) position much more than in Spanish. As stated in the beginning of this study, this comparison and all statements I have made rely on the register of national television speakers in Brazil, and on the registers of national television speakers in the centers of colonial viceroyalties of Latin America, often labeled as highlands (México, D.F., La Paz, Lima, Bogotá, etc.), and on the register of speakers with school training in college or higher or the equivalent.

The preceding paragraph helps understand why Brazilians learning Spanish produce consonants that are harder or more articulated than the corresponding ones in Spanish. Likewise, it is easily noticed when Brazilian novice or intermediate learners of Spanish change Spanish post-stressed vowels just as they do in Portuguese. In their incorrect pronunciation, Spanish words like <pronto>, <periódico>, <compadre>, <espionaje>, and others will most likely become "prontu," "periódicu," "cumpadri," "ispionaji."

They may pronounce the consonants <b d g> harder when speaking Spanish, instead of the legal pronunciation of approximants in Spanish. The double -rr- is also softer in Spanish. Brazilians tend to make Spanish -rr- hard, like the trilled-r in some dialects of Brazilian Portuguese.

When looking at Table 4, which depicts a summary of the segmental differences between Spanish and Portuguese, keep in mind that Spanish consonants are in general "softer" than in Brazilian Portuguese.

Table 4. *Thirteen phonemes in Brazilian Portuguese that Spanish in general does not have.*

Oral Vowels	**Nasal Vowels**	**Consonants**
/ɛ/ (eu) peso /ø/ posso	/ĩ/ minto, assim /ẽ/ comenta /ã/ cantando, rã, /õ/ respondo, tom /ũ/ mundo, atum	/v/ **v**otar /z/ ca**s**a /š/ a**ch**o /ž/ a**j**o $[l^{i}y]$ cava**lh**eiro $[^{i}\tilde{y}]$ ma**nh**ã

Pedagogical Strategies

This section contains suggestions for the development of pedagogical applications to teach Portuguese to speakers of Spanish and other interested audiences, such as heritage speakers of both languages. The following suggestions take into account the preceding descriptive comparisons between Spanish and Portuguese. They should provide teachers a point of departure in the preparation of their classes and curricula. There are many more strategic alternatives, though. The ones below are intended to illustrate how to go from the preceding descriptions to an endless variety of applications. The suggestions below address speakers of Spanish learners of Portuguese with an Advanced Low level of language proficiency (using the ACTFL scale) in Brazilian Portuguese, since teaching materials seldom targets these. Teaching materials for novice and intermediate levels are more common. Furthermore, speakers of Spanish in general tend to move faster from novice and intermediate into advanced levels. These suggestions are also intended to help improve the sophistication of their linguistic skills. In other words, students in general, and especially students of additional languages typologically close to the first language, progress very fast through basic instructions, in their first two years, but tend to slow considerably once they reach advanced levels of proficiency. This is a common pattern in language learning. The suggestions below aim at helping advanced students, by training them to continue their language gains. It is assumed that these materials, given their bilingual nature, are of interest to heritage speakers of both languages as well. Therefore, such materials should be presented mostly as a top-down teaching strategy although often a bottom-up strategy could be used, depending on the goals of the class activity.

In the Classroom

The classroom is not expected to be the only source for the learning of an additional language. On the other hand, the classroom can be the reference for all other activities that extend beyond the classroom.

General Goals

Students of languages in general must become aware about regional varieties or dialects, registers, standard language, languages in contact, and language shift. These notions must be studied in conjunction with the notions of culture, social behavior and sociolinguistic factors such as the context of sociolects, i.e. the basolect, mesolect and acrolect. This is valid to all audiences of language learners. Here, the concept of a register of speakers of national television is once again very useful, because we can more easily see how sound changes relative to this register.

Developing Listening and Speaking Skills

Auditory comprehension is essential to the development of speaking skills. There are many ways to develop auditory comprehension. A practical one that does not require a lot of training or special technology is illustrated below for classroom activity.

Auditory Comprehension

1. You will hear four short readings in sequence. Decide if one of the readings is different or if the four of them are the same.[29]

[29] Some of the forms used in these exercises are illegal in Portuguese. Teachers may find them pedagogically flawed because students are exposed to illegal forms. This author does

A B C D All the same

The teacher will read four times, <A. dois hinos; B. dois hinos; C. dois hinos; D. dois hinos>, with one of them different. This is the representation of the voice of a teacher:

A. [doi´zi.nus]
B. [doi´si.nus]
C. [doi´si.nus]
D. [doi´si.nus]   The students are expected to chose A

Some variations can be used in this drill. One is to have only three items (A, B and C); the other is use four items, but make two of them the same, instead of only one as in the example, and so on.

A B C All the same

The teacher will read three times, <A. dois hinos – B. dois hinos – C. dois hinos>, in the same way. For example:

A. [doi´zi.nus]
B. [doi´zi.nus]
C. **[doi´zi.nus]**   The correct answer is All the same

A B C D All the same

The teacher will read <A. Preciso de um hotel; B. Preciso de um hotel; C. Preciso de um hotel; D. Preciso de um hotel>, with two of them the same, with respect to the pronunciation of the letter <-m> in <um>, which is normally not pronounced in Brazilian Portuguese. For example:

A. [pri.´si.zu.dʒ^{i}ũ.o´tɛ^{u}]
B. [pri.´si.zu.dʒ^{i}ũ.mo´tɛ^{u}]
C. [pri.´si.zu.dʒ^{i}ũ.o´tɛ^{u}]
D. [pri.´si.zu.dʒ^{i}ũ.mo´tɛ^{u}]   The correct answer is either A and C or B and D

A B C All the same

The teacher will read <A. mais ou menos – B. mais ou menos – C. mais ou menos>, with the pronunciation of one of them different, with an illegal [s] instead of the legal [z]. For example:

A. [´ma^{i}.zo´mɛ̃.nus]
B. [´ma^{i}.zo´mɛ̃.nus]
C. [´ma^{i}.so´mɛ̃.nus]   The correct answer is C

2. The teacher will read one of the two questions below. With a circle around the letters A or B, indicate the one read by the teacher.

A. O senhor já foi casado?

---

not agree with this view, especially in the cases illustrated in these exercises, given that these cases are very common mistakes made by Spanish speakers, learners of Portuguese. Therefore, I leave it to the reader's discretion to use them or not.

B. O senhor já foi cassado?

3. In Part III of this chapter, we discuss some basic notions of word stress. The drill below is based on this notion of stress. Teachers of Portuguese normally know the terms oxytone, paroxytone and proparoxytone, used in this drill. I hope that including this drill before discussing the basic notions behind it is not a problem to understand its usefulness. In any case, one can always read about stress in Part III, if needed.

Indicate if the words read aloud are proparoxytones, paroxytones or oxytones.

A. proparoxytone paroxytone oxytone
B. proparoxytone paroxytone oxytone
C. proparoxytone paroxytone oxytone

The teacher can choose words to read aloud. For example, if the teacher says

"- A. - Difícil!" the student should circle the word in the second column of item A, that is <paroxytone>. Then, the second word, item B, can be <"- Oficial"> and the correct answer will be to circle the word in the third column, <oxytone>. The third reading could be <"- Parágrafo"> and the answer should be the third word from the right, in item C, <proparoxytone>. This activity may last anywhere between 5 to 20 minutes.

These are some of the possibilities for aural training, taking into account the descriptions of the differences between Spanish and Portuguese. Teachers can create many other variations for aural training that will help make the speakers of Spanish aware of these differences between Spanish and Portuguese. Therefore, a teacher can read aloud isolated words, expressions or preferably short sentences that contain differences in authentic contexts with the sound targeted for the audiences of interest.

Another way of improving auditory comprehension and consequently pronunciation is through self-analysis of their own pronunciation, using recordings of their voices. In self-analysis, students can be given tasks for recording their voices and then listen to themselves. One task, for example, can be the interview of a native speaker of Portuguese. In this interview, they will dialogue with natives for 10-30 minutes. Then, they rewind the interview and listen carefully to the dialogues with the native, stopping the recording as needed, and taking notes of what they notice. Instructions on how they could direct such activities are shown below. This suggestion is intended for a semester program.

Recording Assignments

Students will conduct two 15-20 minute interviews this semester. These interviews must be made with native speakers of Portuguese about current events in his/her country of origin. For both recordings, students will turn in a well written and organized analysis of their own pronunciation and the pronunciation of their interviewee. Students are allowed to add information about their recording experience, but their analyses must include comments about the vowels, consonants, and prosodic elements of Portuguese pronunciation. The model of presentation below illustrates a way of making these analyses. Students will present these analyses in class, orally, and the written presentation is intended to help them with their oral presentation. But do not rely too much on the written presentation, because the oral presentation must sound as spontaneous as possible. Make sure you provide examples of words from your recording, and avoid over-emphasizing vague comments like, "tenho que trabalhar muito para melhorar minha pronúncia," "Gostei muito de ter feito esta gravação," among others. Such comments are fine, but they are not the most important ones in these analyses, because they are superficial, they do not discuss specific patterns of pronunciation. For the length of this self-analysis, one to two solid pages is sufficient.

Presentation #1, made by [name of the student]

Na minha primeira apresentação, entrevistei uma brasileira de São Paulo e conversamos sobre as músicas de Gilberto Gil e Rita Lee. Depois de terminar esta gravação, passei a ouvi-la e observei o seguinte:

1. A entrevistada, não pronuncia o <t> e <d> como eu esperava. Ela pronuncia o <t> em certas palavras como <tivesse>, <batida> com o <t> mais parecido com o <t> do espanhol e não como o <t> do locutor da TV Globo. O <l> de <palco> é como a vogal <u>.

2. Estes são os comentários sobre a minha pronúncia:

Minha pronúncia em geral está bem, apesar do meu sotaque. Por isso me daria a nota 7/10, de uma maneira geral. Em áreas específicas, isso foi o que notei:

Vogais: minhas vogais estão bem, mas não mudo muito a qualidade das vogais como costumam fazer os brasileiros e, ainda mais que os brasileiros, os portugueses. Digo <Chic[o]> em lugar de <Chic[u]>, etc. Minhas vogais ainda lembram muito as vogais do espanhol, mas me entendem muito bem quando falo e por isso me daria a nota 8/10, em relação às vogais. (10/10 = falante nativo)

Consoantes: Ainda não consigo falar o /z/ conforme tenho que fazer. Quando disse as palavras <abusar> e <presidente>, notei que sairam sem o /z/, como <abu[s]ar> e <pre[s]idente>, e não como <abu[z]ar> e <pre[z]idente>. Nesta parte a minha nota poderia ser 6/10.

Acento de palavra: Comentários sobre o lugar do acento nas palavras, etc. (...) 9/10
Prosódia em geral: Explicar como está a entoação, o ritmo, os enlaces e outros processos fonológicos semelhantes, etc. 8/10
Total: ____/ 100

After the student turns in her/his self-analysis, the teacher should meet with the student and listen together to the recording, then provide the student with further comments on her/his pronunciation.

Dictations are still a helpful, user-friendly and practical way to develop auditory comprehension. For students with advanced level of language proficiency, the teacher can use authentic 10-20 seconds passages from audio and video interviews on the internet, and ask them to simply write down what they heard, using normal handwriting. It is important to check their understanding, too, after they write down what they have heard.

Movies are also excellent for not only improving their pronunciation, but also understanding the culture and current events in a Luso-Brazilian region. This can be done with an accompanying list of movie terminology in Portuguese to help their presentations. There are increasing resources on the internet. A key-word that will produce good results is <terminologia de cinema em português>. Most movies can be easily found on campus existing resources, or through Netflix.

Students should watch the movies outside class. But the teacher may select 30 minutes of passages of one movie to show in class, and make one presentation of this selected movie, which will serve as a model presentation for the students. In each presentation, students should prepare themselves according to a set of criteria, a rubric that the teacher will use to evaluate their presentation.

Below I suggest two of the many rubrics that can be created, which was prepared for speakers of English, intermediate and advanced learners of Spanish, in my undergraduate and graduate classes.

Maximum number of points: 24 (6*4). All components on the leftmost column weigh the same.

	4 =Highest			
CONTENT Organization and flow of ideas	Engages in conversation in a participatory manner, in the major time frames of past, present, and future, when appropriate; has coherence and cohesion; articulated and easy flow of ideas		Communicates short messages on highly predictable, everyday topics. Inadequate handling of conversational subjects; not easy flow of ideas.	
	4	3	2	1
SOCIO-LINGUISTIC COMPETENCE	Shows awareness of socio-linguistic and cultural rules, formal vs. informal register		Does not show a clear awareness of socio-linguistic and cultural rules, formal vs. informal register	
	4	3	2	1
MORPHO-SYNTAX: Use of syntax and the appropriate forms of pronouns, i.e. "grammar" in general: word order, mode, tense, etc. (This area does not include general agreement (*concordancia*).	Uses relatively more complex grammar structures; use of implicit SUBJECT pronouns adequately; uses object pronouns adequately. Uses structural patterns, but not with consistent accuracy		Uses basic grammar structure; excessive/unnecessary use of subject pronouns; prefers the use of nouns instead of pronouns, i.e. avoids pronouns.	
	4	3	2	1
AGREEMENT (***concordancia***) in general: Gender, number and subject-verb	Relatively fewer mistakes in agreement in general		Does not show a clear mastery of agreement	
	4	3	2	1
PRONUNCIATION Overall	Native or near-native pronunciation; or speaks with strong accent, but clearly. Pronunciation flows without hindering communication.		Misuse of speech sounds affects communication; requires repetition to be understood.	
	4	3	2	1
VOCABULARY	Uses a variety of vocabulary, without excessive use of repeated vocabulary.		Speaks with limited vocabulary, i.e. excessive repetition of frequent words (*entonces, también*, *gustar*, *ser*, *estar*, etc.), vague or "lazy" vocabulary (imprecise words like *cosa*, *interesante*, depending on context, and the like.)	
	4	3	2	1

Sugestões para guias de avaliacão das apresentações orais

Significado dos símbolos utilizados	Símbolos	Peso
Seguiram-se ou não as instruções. A apresentação se fez ou não dentro do tempo permitido? Houve falta de preparação?	I	0-10
Competência socio-linguística: uso in/adequado de regras socio-linguïsticas e culturais, registro formal e informal.	SL	0-5
Uso de **sintaxes** ou "gramática" em geral: ordem das palavras, modo, tempo e aspecto verbal, etc. Aqui não se inclui a *concordância* (agreement).	S	0-10
Concordância em geral: gênero, número e desinência verbal.	C	0-10
Vocabulário: repetição excessiva de palavras de uso frequente tais como *então, também, ser, estar, gostar,* etc.), vocabulário vago, impreciso como *coisa, interessante.*	V	0-20
Organização das ideias: Deve-se anunciar claramente o que vai ser a apresentação, seguir uma progressão lógica das ideias através de uma introdução clara, um desenvolvimento e uma conclusão; coerência e coesão.	O	0-20
Pronúncia: uso in/correto de fonemas e uso exagerado de sons do espanhol, especialmente as consoantes aproximantes; acento de palavra.	P	0-20
PESO TOTAL	**100**	

Short 5 minute individual presentations of the movies

Students should not summarize or present an analysis of the film or its characters. Rather, students must relate the film to other issues—cultural, historical, political, economic, social, etc. — and present this context to the class. The presentation should include information about the director, awards won, to mention some, so that you will become familiar with the new vocabulary. Students may be as creative as they would like in the way that they present — via an interview, a dramatized scene, visual aids, YouTube clips (3 minutes maximum), etc.

In order to optimize class work, students should present to each other, all at the same time, while the teacher goes around verifying their interactions, and moderating as needed. Their 200-400 word written text that they will prepare for their oral presentation is to be used as a supporting element for the spoken presentation. They should follow their text as a guide, as they present their analyses of the movie, so that their pronunciation is natural. In other words, instead of reading mechanically the text that they write, they should become used to speaking with only short glances at their written presentation and make more eye contact with their classmates and instructor.

Otherwise, they will not disconnect their eyes from their paper and will likely present in a boring mechanical manner.

Developing Cultural Proficiency

The development of cultural proficiency through pronunciation can also be realized through an array of possibilities. One of them would be for the teacher to identify what characterizes the pronunciation of a region. For example, the Spanish sound for the letter <ñ> as well as the letter itself is probably what most characterizes the Spanish culture throughout the world. Is there any sound or letter that characterizes the Portuguese world? Maybe the nasal vowels, but specially the nasal marker <~>, as in <Camões>. But maybe there is another trait and teachers may want to think about it. If we go into more regional traits, Spanish and Portuguese have plenty to offer. For instance, the word final palatal /s/ of Rio de Janeiro's, as in <rapa[^{i}ʃ]> (<rapaz>), or the nasal diphthong in the City of São Paulo, as in <set[ẽ $^{\tilde{\imath}}$]bro>, for <setembro>. Another social and regional trait throughout Brazil is the r-caipira, which can also be explained and explored in many ways such as skits where the characters are *caipiras*.

All languages have some clearly noticeable cultural traits reflected in the way native speakers interact. The question tag <..., né?>, short for <não é?> in Brazilian Portuguese, is a Brazilian trait that my students notice the most among native speakers of Brazilian Portuguese. Furthermore, why do I know that a person abroad whom I have never seen before is Brazilian just by catching some of their milliseconds of voice gestures like <hmmm>, interjections or even the way the laugh, in a shopping mall, for example? What is there in these very brief sounds, not actual words, that is inherent to a Brazilian? The French *mou*, for example, is a typical trait probably limited to Metropolitan France. It is a facial-lips-sound gesture that expresses their *je m'en fous*, disagreements, doubts, disbeliefs, and similar meanings. The French also expect of everyone speaking French a full greeting when they meet someone they know. A Frenchman must say confidently to the other <Bonjour, Monsieur/Madame Untel. Comment-allez vous>, or something similar. A monotone greeting as it is common among Americans, like <Hi!>, or a shy handshake or head movement instead of a full salutation is considered rude or bizarre among the French. This is so typical of the culture that it can cause a lot of misunderstanding when a foreigner does not apply this cultural trait when in France. We, instructors of Brazilian Portuguese, should identify these patterns of linguistic and behavioral traits, not only to make our classes more appealing to our students, but also to increase our awareness of our own language and culture.

As we can see, many interesting patterns of linguistic and cultural traits of a nation can easily enliven classroom discussions. These traits can be identified either by asking ourselves which ones they are, or in discussions with other colleagues, or yet through internet groups as these groups continue to grow on the internet.

Outside the Classroom

All the activities proposed here have rich and easily accessible resources that can help teachers planning their classes, and students to continue learning additional languages outside the class room. Below I list a few of the ones I use regularly, all visited normally in spring 2015. Most are free, but some will cost around $10 dollars a month.

- Mango: http://lib.ku.edu/databases/database/2871 Usually available in US Public Libraries and in most campuses.
- Kansas City Public Library: http://www.kclibrary.org/languages-literature, then click on <Languages>.
- iLove languages: http://www.ilovelanguages.com/ at the New York Public Library;
- Duolingo: https://www.duolingo.com/;
- BBC languages: http://www.bbc.co.uk/languages/spanish/;
- Google translate: https://translate.google.com/
- Yabla: https://www.yabla.com/ This one is not for free. It costs c. $10/mo.

In other words, nunca parem de aprender! The internet can complement our classroom work. Therefore, teachers may consider this type of work outside class as part of their student grades. In this case, teachers may want to ask their students to prepare either a journal written in Portuguese, or a portfolio of their outside classroom activities.

Further Reading on the Differing Functions of Portuguese and Spanish

Table 5 adds another set of common conventions to the ones already used in this study.

Tab*le 5. Some conventions for symbols used in phonemic (phonological) and phonetic transcriptions*

Symbol	**Meaning**
< >	Orthographic transcription; it encloses regular writing.
/ /	Phonemic or phonological transcription; it indicates what is expected.
[ ]	Phonetic or physical transcription; it indicates what the speaker actually says.

<table>
<tr><td>→</td><td>It indicates a current sound change; it reads as “becomes;” it also represents a flat intonation contour (see below in this table).</td></tr>
<tr><td>/</td><td>It means “in the context,” or some equivalent expressions like “when…” and alike.</td></tr>
<tr><td>#</td><td>Word boundary</td></tr>
<tr><td>.</td><td>Syllable boundary</td></tr>
<tr><td>|</td><td>Short pause</td></tr>
<tr><td>||</td><td>Longer pause</td></tr>
<tr><td>ˊ</td><td>Word stress, place before the stressed syllable.</td></tr>
<tr><td>↑, ↓, →</td><td>Rising, falling and flat intonation, respectively; there are other possibilities not included here.</td></tr>
</table>

As stated previously, the goal of this contrastive description of Spanish and Portuguese is to provide key information about the Spanish and Portuguese sound systems that will help speakers of Spanish who are learners of Portuguese to improve their pronunciation and hopefully to find fast and friendly access to information regarding how these two languages work, in terms of pronunciation. Pronunciation can be divided into two major areas of study, Phonetics and Phonology. Phonetics is essentially the study of the sound output, i.e. the physical features of sounds, what is measurable, what is tangible. Phonology (or Phonemics) belongs more in the domain of abstractions. Phonology describes how sounds form patterns as they form syllables, morphemes, words and other language units. The key concepts in these areas are the **phoneme**, i.e. the smallest linguistics unit that changes the meaning of a word when replaced by another linguistic unit, and the allophone, which is the materialization of a phoneme.

A speech sound is a phoneme if it changes the meaning of a word, when replaced by another sound in a pair of words that contain the same sequence of sounds, except in one spot where the sounds being compared appear. Such pairs of words are called **minimal pairs**.

The Portuguese names <Célia> (/ˈsɛ.lia/) and <Zélia> (/ˈzɛ.lia/) form a minimal pair. In Portuguese, if we replace /z/ of the word <Zélia> or /ˈzɛ.lia/, with the /s/ of <Célia> or /ˈsɛ.lia/, we refer to two different persons, i.e. we change the meaning of these words by alternating /z/ and /s/. Therefore, /z/ and /s/ are **phonemes** in Portuguese. These same sounds are also phonemes in English. In English we find similar pairs, as in <zeal> and <seal>. Normally, we do not find such pairs contrasting /z/ and /s/ in Spanish, although there are <z> and <s> **letters** in Spanish. In the center and north of Spain there is no /z/ phoneme, either. The letter <z> in some areas of Spain has a different sound, which is like the <th> sound of the English word <with>, and usually represented with the symbol /θ/. In Spain only, the sound of the letters <s> and <z> are in contrast, in minimal pairs, and therefore their sounds constitute different phonemes, because they change the meaning of words when they replace each other, e.g. <ves> vs. <vez> or /bes/ vs. /beθ/. In other words, orthographic <z> and <s> exist in Spanish, but /z/ is not a **phoneme**. In most of the Hispanic World, <z> is an **allophone** of Spanish, because the [z] sound appears *predictably*, that is to say, it appears before voiced consonants, as in <mismo>. Therefore, Spanish only has the sound [z] as an allophone, not as a phoneme. Phonemes appear unpredictably.

To illustrate further the notions of phoneme and allophone, we can use the word used earlier in this study, <tango>, which in Portuguese has five phonemes, /ˊtan.go/. Since the phoneme is an abstraction, we can think of these five phonemes as "ideas" that form the word, and the word itself is another "idea." This phonological "idea," /ˊtan.go/, materializes with five allophones in Portuguese, [ˊtãŋ.gu]. It is useful to represent these "ideas" with three types of representations.

Orthographic representation: <tango>

Phonemic or phonological representation: /ˊtan.go /

Phonetic representation: [ˊtãŋ.gu]

Although the orthographic representation is very close to the actual pronunciation of this word, the orthography is not always so close to the actual pronunciation. The orthography is not an efficient representation of speech sounds or phonemes, because it does not always represent a one-to-one correspondence of symbols and speech sounds or phonemes. For example, in Portuguese the word <argentino> has the consonant graphemes or letters <g> and <t> pronounced in a way that is different in other words; for example, <tango>. Likewise, the <r> in <argentino> has different pronunciations depending on personal preferences, regional variation and other factors. The same letter, however, is used for different pronunciations. That is not the case with phonological and phonetic representations, because in these representations the correspondences are one-to-one. The phonological and phonetic symbols for language sounds will change if the phonemes or sounds change. For instance, <tango argentino> is represented phonologically or phonemically as /ˊtan.go#aR.ʒen.ˊti.no/ and phonetically as [ˊtãŋ.gwar.ʒen.ˊʧi.nu].

Notice that the symbol /R/ represents several varieties already introduced in Table 1:

[x] **r**aro, ve**r**

[h] **r**aro, ve**r**

[χ] **r**aro, ve**r**

[ʁ] **r**aro, ve**r**

[Ø] mute ve**r**

I picked the [x] realization in <argentino> because it is the most common pronunciation in Brazil and among speakers of national television.

In order to study the sound system of any human language, we need to distinguish between "sound segments" and what is not a sound segment, that is to say the melody of languages. **Prosody** (or suprasegmentals) is the melody of a language. **Prosody** *envelops* intonation, rhythm, stress, accent, sound quality, duration and phonological processes.

Sound segments are basically raw vowels and consonants. They were discussed in Part I.

Sound segments in Portuguese are relatively easier to teach and to learn. The melody demands more work on the part of the teacher and students, because language studies still need improvements in this area. We still have difficulties in making generalizations about prosodic patterns in Portuguese as well as in Spanish, although we have probably all the information we need to teach sound segments. It is very difficult to implement in the teaching of additional languages what we know about the melody of a language. Regardless of the drills one uses to implement these teachings, mechanic or contextualized drills, it is difficult for students to internalize the prosodic patterns that we know through classroom teaching. But it is important to teach what we know, because somehow some students will learn and internalize prosodic patterns and it is helpful to simply become aware of them.

The English term "language," has two equivalents in Portuguese and Spanish, namely *língua* and *linguagem*, *lengua* and *lenguaje*, respectively. A general view of these notions is summarized below. The symbol "=" indicates a direct relation.

> Language (*língua* or *lengua*) = Phonology or Phonemics = Phoneme, enclosed in / /
> Speech act (*fala* or *habla*) = Phonetics = speech sounds or allophones, enclosed in [ ]

To illustrate a **phonological rule** and the use of the symbols and conventions in Tables 1 and 5, we can use the same word <tango>. Below there is a **phonological rule** called Assimilation Rule, which describes one of the changes in the word <tango>, from the abstraction of a phoneme to a concrete allophone, that is to say from abstraction to materialization. This rule states that "/n/ changes from alveolar nasal to the velar nasal represented as [ŋ], before the velar consonant [g]."

Assimilation Rule: /n/ → [ŋ] / __ [g]

As one can see, this phonological rule is a short and more efficient way of describing the change that took place. This is a very simple rule, but very common and productive in human languages. A **phonological rule**, which is the same as phonological principle or phonological process, describes language changes in pronunciation, especially when changes are repeated or predictable, i.e. when they form patterns. Phonological rules can clarify many changes that occur with the phonemes of Portuguese. For instance, they tell us why in Brazilian Portuguese <t> is sometimes pronounced with a sound like the <ch> in the English word <church> and sometimes almost like

English <t> in <stop>.

Below there are examples of typical transcriptions in the three representations considered here: orthographic transcription (regular writing, graphemes or letters), phonemic transcription (anticipatory representation of sound targets, phonemes, abstraction) and phonetic transcription (the result or the output of what had been anticipated, i.e. the allophones). The phonological representation is intended to reflect the general voice of speakers of national television in cities like Lima, Bogotá, La Paz, México, D.F. and cities alike where the spoken language is closest to the written language. The national television variety of Spanish and Portuguese makes it difficult or impossible to tell where the speaker is from in the country where s/he comes from.

Here, the arrows represent the directions of the main intonational inflexions. Note that in Mexican Spanish, the two arrows represent a typical Mexican intonation contour, known as *circumflex* intonation, often represented with a caret (^). In this type of contour, the intonation goes up and down in the last or nuclear word of a sentence or phonological unit.

American English

Orthographic (graphemes):

< - Did you eat yet? >

Phonemic/phonological (phonemes, abstractions mostly):

/ˈdid#ju#ˈit#jɛt ↑ /

Phonetic (allophones, physical):

[ˈʤi^{ʔ}jɛ^{ʔ} ↑]

Note: This American English example is adapted from Ladefoged and Johnson (2014 142). The physical/phonetic representation follows exactly what a speaker of American English actually says. The phonetic transcription here is one among several possibilities.

Brazilian Portuguese, Vitória, Espírito Santo

Orthographic (graphemes):

< - Sim… Mais ou menos. > (Yes… more or less.)

Phonemic/phonological (phonemes, abstractions mostly):

/sĩ → | ˈmais#ou#ˈmɛ.noS ↓ /

Phonetic (allophones, physical):

[sĩ → | ˈma^{i}.zoˈmɛ̃.nus ↓]

Note: The physical/phonetic representation follows exactly what a speaker of BP says. The phonetic transcription here is one among several possibilities.

Mexican Spanish, D.F.:

Orthographic (graphemes): -

<Sí… Más o menos.> (Yes… more or less.)

Phonemic/phonological (phonemes, abstractions mostly):

/ ˈsi → | ˈmas#o#ˈme.nos ↓] /

Phonetic (allophones, physical):

[ˈsi → | ˈma.so.ˈme.nos ↑↓]

Note: The physical/phonetic representation follows exactly what a speaker of Mexican Spanish actually says. The phonetic transcription here is one among several possibilities.

Transcriptions are helpful tools to help language learners master pronunciation. The preceding discussion was intended as a refresher for some teachers and as a helpful discussion for teachers without a background in Phonetics and Phonology to prepare their own class activities for pronunciation drills.

Prosody: Intonation and Rhythm

Either intonation or rhythm can be described in details, but we will not get into these interesting details here. This discussion focuses on simple and general descriptions of both languages. In such a scope, some universal or common patterns can be helpful.

The general patterns of intonation in Spanish and Portuguese follow common patterns of intonation in world languages.

Falling intonation, a **toneme** represented as /↓/, usually indicates the **conclusion of an idea**, usually at the end of a sentence. This falling intonation usually appears as the last inflexion movement at the end of declarative sentences, linked to the last "content" word, as the word <Santo>, in <Sou de Vitória, Espírito Santo>. In Spanish, it is generally similar, as in the word <Perú> or <México>, in <Soy de Lima, Perú > or <Soy de Chihuahua, México>.

Tonemes that are either **Flat** /→/ or **slightly raising in intonation** /↗/ can indicate **continuity**. An example would be the intonation of the underlined words in <Meu filho, passe no mercado e compre farinha de trigo, manteiga, café e pão> (Eng. Son, go to the market and buy flour, butter, coffee and bread). Usually, the word before the last in this list, <café>, will carry a relatively slightly higher rising intonation, in anticipation of the last word in the list, <pão>, which concludes the idea, and as a result carries a falling intonation.

A **rising intonation** /↑/ usually means in Portuguese, Spanish, English and other languages a **yes-no question**, and in a way it also means **continuity**, because a question requires an answer, i.e. a continuity. If the parent in the preceding paragraph asked his son, <Você trouxe o café?> (Eng. Did you bring the coffee?), the answer will be either <sim> (yes) or <não> (no). The word <café> usually has a rising intonation. This is what is common and expected, but since intonation also reflects the **attitude** of the speaker, <café> may sometimes have a falling intonation, just as in Spanish. A falling intonation may signify a concern on the part of the parent, or other subtle meanings, e.g. a double check on what his/her son did, because s/he knows that the son is sometimes absent minded.

Likewise, some people, especially teachers who try to put students at ease when speaking with them, may try to make them feel comfortable, not threatened, by using different rising intonations where a flat or falling intonation would be expected. This is possible in Portuguese, Spanish or English, and it can be labelled as part of a **social prosody**.

As seen above, intonation in languages like Portuguese, Spanish and English is relatively simple in its limited contrastive meanings. There are, however, some interesting intonation patterns still being studied in these languages, which are not in the scope of this study and rarely discussed in an additional language classroom. Although this discussion called attention to the difficulty that some language students may find to learn the prosody of an additional language, speech prosody should not be an obstacle to Spanish speakers learners of Portuguese, because native speakers tend to intuitively accept and filter false prosodic notes of non-natives.

Stress Assignment in Portuguese

Stress assignment also contributes to create rhythmic patterns in a language. In general, words in Portuguese fall into a three-syllable window as follows (the little squares represent the syllable in words):

... □.□.□.□́ – oxytones, *por.tu.guês*;

... □.□.□́.□ – paroxytones, *di.fí.cil*;

... □.□́.□.□ – proparoxytones, *pa.ra.le.le.pí.pe.do.*

Similar to Spanish, paroxytone words in Brazilian Portuguese are considered the most common pattern. If we subscribe to this claim, we can consider paroxytones **unmarked**, and the two others as marked. This would explain why in the Portuguese and in Spanish orthography paraxytones do not have as many stress markers as much as proparoxytones and oxytones, the marked ones, do. It is also noteworthy that there are some unusual cases of stress in the 4th syllable in Portuguese, but these are limited to a couple cases of lexicon borrowings like "técnica", i.e. [té.ki.ni.ka].

Scholars (e.g. Mateus 1975; 1983; Bisol 1994; Cagliari 1999; Lee 2007) have tried to explain stress assignment in Portuguese with a single rule, based on the high occurrence of paroxytone words. These attempts, usually influenced by the generativist tradition in US linguistics, are still inconclusive. These explanations in Portuguese require excessive abstraction and solutions that create artifacts. Maybe the ongoing changes in Brazilian Portuguese nowadays (Roberts 1993, Tarallo 1993) are behind the difficulties one finds to describe stress assignment in a predictable manner. After all the efforts so far, it may be the case that stress assignment is not predictable in Portuguese as Câmara Jr. (1970 1972) already claimed many years ago.

Rhythm, Timing

The late Kenneth Pike (Pike 1945) and later Abercrombie (1967), used an explanation about rhythm, which can be very useful pedagogically, although it may face some challenges if this explanation is attempted to be tested empirically. Pike's goal, to his credit, was to provide a useful explanation about rhythm for teachers and language learners.

In this view, there are essentially two main types of rhythm, **stress-timed** and **syllable-timed** rhythms. English and Spanish are usually taken as references to best illustrate these timing notions. **English** is a typical **stress-timed** language, and **Spanish** is a typical **syllable-timed** language. According to this notion, we can use a metronome to time the reading out loud of prose by a native speaker of American English. A native speaker of English can read out loud a text stressing or beating the most proeminent syllables in a sentence, following a metronome. In Spanish, it would be harder for a native speaker to read a text aloud, following a metronome. In the classic example below, from Pike, these beats are indicated with the marker <'> on the most prominent syllables. Thus, the sentence

If 'Tom will 'I will

keeps the same timing, even if we add other syllables, as in

If 'Tom'll do it 'I will.

Notice that the number of syllables increased, but the number of beats are the same. In other words, the number of syllable feet are the same. In order to fit into this interstressed sequences, English reduces the number of sounds, reduces some sounds and lengthens others as needed, to fit the syllables in between stresses or beats. In this example, with the addition of <do it>, <will> becomes <ll>.

In Spanish, if the number of syllables increases, the tendency is to keep the sounds, increasing the length of the sentences, without segment reductions or lengthening as in English.

Si 'va a tocar 'Tom, i'remos.

Si 'va a to'car Tom Jo'bim, i'remos.

Pike claimed that is because Spanish is syllable-timed. There is a tendency among native speakers of Spanish to beat on as many syllables as possible and still maintain the sentence beats. Spanish strikes (or focuses on) primarily the syllables, whereas in English the beats are primarily at sentence level.

The interstress beats in English give the impression of a "chopping" rhythm. Hence the difficulty English speakers find in saying long words in Spanish, because they will attempt to cut long words into two or more words, causing vowel reduction, among other consequences, and a strong foreign accent. Brazilian Portuguese can be placed between these two prototypical types of rhythm depending on the regional variety. Peninsular Portuguese in general, tends to be more of a stress-timed variety, and this may explain why there are more vowel reduction in Peninsular Portuguese than in Brazilian Portuguese, especially in the production of schwas. In Brazilian Portuguese, we can find different rhythmic patterns, but in terms of the notions discussed here, it makes more sense to expect Brazilian Portuguese to oscillate between stress- and syllable-timed rhythms. The illustration below, may help to compare with English and Spanish. In Brazilian Portuguese, if we add one syllable, in the idiolect of the author, the number of syllables increases.

Se o ′Tom Jo′bim to′car eu ′vou.

Se o ′Tom Jo′bim for to′car eu ′vou.

Compare the poem by Robert Frost (1874-1963) below, and see how the number of feet is the same, whereas the number of syllables change.

Nothing gold can stay[30]
N**á**ture's first gr**ée**n is g**ó**ld, (6 syllables)
Her h**á**rdest h**ú**e to h**ó**ld. (6 syllables)
Her **éa**rly l**éa**f's a fl**ó**wer (7 syllables)
But **ó**nly s**ó** an h**ó**ur. (7 syllables)
Then l**éa**f subs**í**des to l**éa**f. (6 syllables)
So **É**den s**á**nk to gr**íe**f. (6 syllables)
So d**á**wn g**ó**es d**ó**wn to d**á**y. (6 syllables)
N**ó**thing g**ó**ld can st**á**y." (5 syllables)

In music, we find similar illustrations. Consider the tempo or timing in Tom Jobim's popular song "Garota de Ipanema." Notice that the words whose meanings are easier to understand, the so called "content words," are the ones that usually carry the sentence beats, but not necessarily always.

′O.lha, que ′coi.sa mais ′lin.da
Mais ′cheia de ′gra.ça
É ′e.la me′ni.na que ′vem e que ′pa.ssa
Num ′do.ce ba′lan.ço ca′mi.nho do ′mar.

In Brazilian Portuguese, we can tap on prominent syllables at the sentence level and also on the syllables.

The preceding discussion is based on Pike's view of rhythm in natural languages, and it is provided here because it is a useful approach in language teaching. However, current empirical work that I have been conducting (Simões and Meireles, forthcoming) shows that **both** syllable-timed and stressed-timed rhythms exist not only in Spanish, but also in Portuguese, English, French and Italian, depending on the situation or on the intent of the speaker.

Phonological Processes: Linking

A very common phonological process in Portuguese and in Spanish is the

[30] I thank my colleague, Jonathan Mayhew, for the suggestion to use Frost's poem.

linking of the last consonant of a word with the following vowel of the next word, as follows.

Portuguese

- Sim... Mais ou menos. (Yes... more or less.)

/sĩ → | ˈmais#ou#ˈmɛ.noS ↓ /

[sĩ → | ˈma^{i}.zoˈmẽ.nus ↓]

Spanish

- Sí... Más o menos. (Yes... more or less.)

/ˈsi → | ˈmas#o#ˈme.nos ↓ /

[ˈsi → | ˈma.so.ˈme.nos ↑↓]

The /s/ after <mais> in Portuguese, and <más> in Spanish links to the following vowel. Note that in Portuguese it changes to [z], a common process in intervocalic context. In Spanish, the /s/ remains [s], after linking happens. In this case, if Spanish speakers do not change /s/ to [z], s/he will have a strong accent, although it does not affect the meaning in this case. However, sometimes surfacing an illegal [s] in Portuguese, in a linking, can disturb communication and sometimes change the meaning of the message. For example, in the sequence <dois hinos> (two hymns) already referred to earlier in this chapter, if one does not change the /s/ to [z] as [ˈdo^{i}.ˈzi.nus], the meaning is different, that is to say, <dois sinos> (two bells), [ˈdo^{i}.ˈsi.nus].

Concluding Remarks

This chapter compared basic elements of pronunciation in Spanish and Brazilian Portuguese. Although it is based on current theoretical descriptions of Spanish and Brazilian Portuguese, these descriptions were simplified to facilitate the development of pedagogical tools for learners of Brazilian Portuguese. Given its bilingual nature, this study may also be of interest to heritage speakers of both languages as noted in Beaudrie, Ducar and Potowski (2014 212). Furthermore, parts of this study can serve as preliminary materials to teach speakers of BP learning Spanish, if one understands that the strategy discussed here will follow a reverse path. For instance, if a speaker of Spanish learning BP is instructed to pronounce Portuguese stops <b d g> with more articulatory effort, a speaker of BP learning Spanish will be instructed to make these consonants less effort. In principle, once we undertand how the sound patterns of Brazilian Portuguese work in comparison with Spanish, it should not be difficult to follow the reverse path to discover how Spanish works for speakers of Brazilian Portuguese. This chapter did not go into the specifics of this strategy, because it was not the goal of this book project.

This chapter dealt with pronunciation only, because this is most likely the first step a Spanish speaker needs to take to learn Portuguese. Obviously, there are other language components of interest for the speaker of Spanish, such as morpho-syntax, as seen in other materials (e.g. Simoes 2008). I hope that teachers and students will find this chapter useful for their teaching and learning of Brazilian Portuguese.

References

Azeredo, José, et al. (2011), *Gramática comparativa Houaiss: Quatro línguas românicas*, São Paulo, Editora Publifolha.

Azevedo, Milton M. (2005), *Portuguese: a Linguistic Introduction*, Cambridge, Cambridge University Press.

Beaudrie, Sara, Cynthia Ducar and Kim Potowski. 2014. *Heritage Language Teaching: Research and Practice – McGraw-Hill second language professional series: Directions in second language learning*. New York, NY: McGraw-Hill Education.

Bisol, Leda (1994), *O acento e o pé métrico binário*, Letras de Hoje 98, 25-36.

Bisol, Leda (org.) (2005), *Introdução a estudos de fonologia do português brasileiro*, Porto Alegre, EDIPCURS.

Cagliari, Luiz Carlos (1999), *O acento em português*, Campinas, Editora do Autor.

Câmara, Jr., Joaquim Mattoso (1970), *Estrutura da língua portuguesa*, Petrópolis, RJ, Vozes.

——. (1972), *The Portuguese Language*, Chicago, University of Chicago Press.

Domahs, U., I. Plag and R. Carroll. (2014) Word stress assignment in German, English and Dutch: Quantity-sensitivity and extrametricality revisited. In *Journal of Comparative Germanic* Linguistics, 17, 1, 59-96.

Ferreira, Letânia and D. Eric Holt (2014). On the partially divergent phonology of Spanish, Portuguese and points in between, in *Portuguese-Spanish Interfaces: Diachrony, synchrony, and contact*, in Patrícia Amaral and Ana Maria Carvalho, editors. John Benjamins Publishing Company

Jensen, John B. (1989), *On the Mutual Intelligibility of Spanish and Portuguese*, Hispania 72, 848-852.

Lee, Seung-Hwa (2007), *O acento primário no português: Uma análise unificada na Teoria da Otimalidade*, in: Gabriel Antunes de Araújo (ed.), *O acento em português: Abordagens fonológicas*, São Paulo, Parábola Editorial, 121-143.

Ladefoged, Peter and Keith Johnson (2014), *A course in Phonetics*, 7th Edition, Stamford, CT, Cengage Learning.

Landercy, Albert, and Raymond Renard (1977), *Éléments de phonétique*, Bruxelles, Belgium, Didier.

Mateus, Maria Helena Mira Mira (1975), *Aspectos da fonologia portuguesa*, Lisboa, Centro de Estudos Fonológicos.

——. (1983), *O acento de palavra em português: Uma nova proposta*, Boletim de Filologia 27, 211-229.

Molczanow, J., Domahs, U., Knaus, J. & Wiese, R. (2013) The lexical representation of word stress in Russian: Evidence from event-related potentials. *The Mental Lexicon*, 8, 164- 194.

Núnez Cedeño, Rafael A. and Morales-Front, Alfonso. *Fonología generativa contemporánea de la lengua española.* Washington, D.C.: Georgetown University Press, 1998.

Pike, Kenneth (1945), *The intonation of American English*, University of Michigan Publications in Linguistics 1. Ann Arbor: University of Michigan Press.

Plag, Ingo. (2006) The variability of compound stress in English: structural, semantic, and analogical factors. *English Language and Linguistics* Volume 10 Issue 01 / May 2006, 143-172.

Roberts, Ian (1993), *Pósfácio*, in: Ian Roberts/Mary A. Kato (edd.), *Português brasileiro: Uma viagem diacrônica*, 2a edição, Campinas, SP, Editora da UNICAMP, 409-425.

Roberts, Ian/Kato, Mary A. (1993), *Português brasileiro: Uma viagem diacrônica*, 2a edição, Campinas, SP, Editora da UNICAMP.

Roca, Iggy M. (1990) "Diachrony and synchrony in Spanish stress", *Journal of Linguistics* 26: 133–164.

——. (1999), *Stress in the Romance Languages*, in: Harry van der Hulst (ed.), *Word Prosodic Systems in the Languages of Europe*, Berlin, Mouton de Gruyter, 659-811.

——. (2006) "The Spanish stress window", in F. Martínez-Gil & S. Colina (eds.), *Optimality-theoretic advances in Spanish phonology*, Amsterdam: John Benjamins. 239-77.

Silva, Thaïs Cristófaro (2005), *Fonética e fonologia do português*, 8a edição, São Paulo, Editora Contexto.

Simões, Antônio R.M. (2008), *Pois não: Brazilian Portuguese Course for Spanish Speakers, with Basic Reference Grammar*, Austin, University of Texas Press.

——. (2013), *Baticum! E-Curso avançado de português para estrangeiros através da MPB*, Creative Commons, in: http://www.merlot.org/merlot/viewMaterial.htm;jsessionid=3E5CC8A19295C1135AFC4636A34EC343?id=732260, (10.07.2013).

——. 2014. Lexical Stress in Brazilian Portuguese in Contrast with Spanish. In Campbell, Nick, Dafydd Gibbon and Daniel Hirst, editors, *Annals of the Speech Prosody Conference # 7*. Dublin, Ireland, Trinity College: 251-255. http://www.speechprosody2014.org/

——. 2016 (in print). Stress assignment contrasted in Spanish and Brazilian Portuguese prosodic non-verbal words. Chapter Three, in *Courses on Speech Prosody*, Alexsandro Rodrigues Meireles, editor. London: Cambridge University Press, 33-51.

Simões, Antônio R.M. and Alexsandro R. Meireles. (in progress). Speech

Prosody in Musical Notation: Spanish, Portuguese and English.

Sosa, Juan Manuel. (1999) *La entonación del español: su estructura fónica, variabilidad y dialectología.* Madrid: Cátedra.

Tarallo, Fernando (1993), *Diagnosticando uma gramática brasileira: o português d'aquém e d'além mar ao final do século XIX*, in: Ian Roberts/Marx A. Kato (edd.), *Português brasileiro: Uma viagem diacrônica*, 2a edição, Campinas, SP, Editora da UNICAMP, 69-106.

CONTRIBUTORS

THE EDITORIAL BOARD:

AUTHORS:

Blair Bateman holds a Ph.D. in Second Languages and Cultures Education from the University of Minnesota. He has worked for over 25 years as an instructor of Spanish and Portuguese at the university and high school levels. He is currently an Associate Professor of Spanish and Portuguese Pedagogy at Brigham Young University, where he designs and supervises first through third-year Portuguese language courses and teaches undergraduate and graduate-level courses for language teachers, including a methods course specifically for Portuguese instructors. He has published several articles on the teaching of Portuguese and is currently co-authoring a textbook for teaching Portuguese to Spanish speakers.

Ligia Bezerra recently joined Arizona State University an Assistant Professor of Portuguese. She also taught at Spelman College in Atlanta, GA, where she worked on program and curriculum development in Portuguese. She received training on the ACTFL Oral Proficiency Interview (OPI) and the Interagency Language Roundtable (ILR) scale for reading and listening. She is also one of the co-founding members of the Georgia Portuguese Programs Association (GAPPA). Throughout her career, she has taught Portuguese, Spanish, and English as a foreign language in various institutions in Brazil and in the United States, including courses on teaching methodology of the Portuguese and English languages. She has also provided training on English as a Foreign Language to high school teachers from the state of Ceará, Brazil, in addition to having given conference presentations and workshops on language teaching.

Ivian Destro Boruchowski, MEd, is a Ph.D. student in Curriculum and Instruction at FIU dedicated to research on and discussion of bilingual education. She received an award as "World Ahead Student" from Florida International University for her MA thesis. She currently teaches Portuguese as a heritage language in Miami. She is also actively involved with Portuguese speakering communities all over the world raising awareness about heritage language education. She participates in the Advisory Committee of ABRACE (Associação Brasileira de Cultura e Educação), in Washington; American Organization of Teachers of Portuguese (AOTP); and Portuguese International Parents Association, PIPA (Miami). Before coming to the U.S., Ivian worked in Brazil as a Portuguese and Brazilian Literature teacher and coordinator, as well as a textbook author.

Orlando R. Kelm is an Associate Professor of Hispanic Linguistics at the University of Texas at Austin where he teaches courses in Portuguese and Spanish, focusing mainly on business language and the cultural aspects of international business communication. His most recent online materials development projects are entitled "*Conversa Brasileira*" and "*Língua da Gente.*" He co-authored with Mary E. Risner a book about Brazilian perceptions regarding their work with North Americans, "*Brazilians Working with Americans.*" His next book with co-author David A. Victor is entitled "*The Seven Keys to Communicating in Brazil: An Intercultural Approach.*" It will be published through Georgetown University Press in 2016.

Megwen May Loveless has been teaching Portuguese and developing curricula for the Portuguese classroom for over thirteen years. She has taught at Harvard and Princeton universities and is currently the Director of the Basic Portuguese Language Program at Tulane University. Her pedagogy emphasizes the use of music, popular culture and new media, as well as innovative teaching methods and expansion of the language program outside of the traditional classroom. Additional interests include: telecollaboration, community-based learning, mentoring of teaching assistants, games and play in the language classroom, development of strategic competence, oral proficiency/pronunciation, extracurricular program development, literacy in L2/L3, African diaspora in Latin America, ethnomusicology and Afro-Brazilian religion/dance/music.

Celeste Dolores Mann is Lecturer in Spanish at Georgian Court University in New Jersey. Previously, she was Coordinator of Portuguese at Villanova University, where she taught Spanish and Portuguese for six years. Celeste participated in the STARTALK Portuguese program at the Concordia Languages Villages in 2011, STARTALK Portuguese at Boston University, in 2012, and won an AATSP scholarship to study PLE (Português como Língua Estrangeira) at Torre de Babel Idiomas in São Paulo in 2014. She earned a B.A. in Spanish with Distinction from Yale University, her M.A. in Spanish from the University of Iowa, and also studied in the Masters program in Letras at PUC-Rio early in her studies for the doctorate. Celeste has frequently presented on Portuguese teaching pedagogy She performs the music and researches the life of Brazilian composer/conductor Chiquinha

Margo Milleret taught Portuguese language, culture and literature at several institutions for almost thirty years before retiring from the University of New Mexico in June of 2015. While at UNM, she mentored graduate teaching assistants, evaluated the Portuguese curriculum and developed new courses and assessments. She also served as editor of the *Portuguese Language Journal.* She has published on the topics of program evaluation and development, Portuguese enrollment growth, and the future of Portuguese study in the U.S.

Mary Risner is Associate Director of Outreach at the Center for Latin American Studies at the University of Florida where she develops and manages initiatives that integrate world language and area studies across the K-16 curriculum. She has taught language at a variety of levels and has organized educational programs abroad. Among her Portuguese language projects are a co-authored collection of bilingual case studies, a series of online interviews and materials on the cultural aspects of doing business in Brazil, and an advocacy clip on "Why Study Portuguese?" In 2006 she founded the peer-reviewed online publication the *Portuguese Language Journal* and started a monthly electronic Portuguese newsletter. She is an avid user of social media to connect with and share resources among educators promoting the study of Spanish and Portuguese languages and culture skills.

Cecília Rodrigues is an Assistant Professor of Portuguese at the University of Georgia and the Curriculum Coordinator of the Portuguese Flagship Program. In addition to fifteen years of experience as a foreign language instructor, she has extensive knowledge of program development through organizing cultural events, implementing recruiting strategies, proposing new courses, and redesigning curricula. As well as supervising a Portuguese language program, she co-authored a series of workbooks for the foreign language classroom in Brazil and is currently co-writing instructional material for Portuguese conversation courses.

Gláucia V. Silva has been working with heritage speakers since 2005, when she joined the Department of Portuguese at the University of Massachusetts Dartmouth. She has presented and published several papers on Portuguese as a heritage language. She has also facilitated a number of workshops and teacher training series on the topic. Furthermore, Gláucia developed the Portuguese for Heritage Speakers course sequence at UMass Dartmouth, which has been offered since 2009.

Antônio Roberto Monteiro Simões is an Associate Professor of Spanish and Portuguese Applied Linguistics at the University of Kansas, Lawrence.

He studied in Brazil, France and United States, and concluded his doctoral studies in Ibero-Romance Linguistics at the University of Texas at Austin (1987). His current research and teaching focus on Phonetics and Phonology of Spanish and Portuguese, especially in language prosody. Professor Simões has authored books and articles on Portuguese for speakers of Spanish. He has been teaching and working on language curricula in several campuses in the United States, Brazil, Spain, Buenos Aires and China.

Robert Simon is Professor of Spanish and Portuguese, as well as the Coordinator of the Portuguese Program and the Minor in Lusophone Studies, both of which he founded, in the Department of Foreign Languages at Kennesaw State University. He has instructed courses in Hispanic and Lusophone Languages, Literatures, and Cultures since 2000. Simon has worked in program development for a variety of new programs at Kennesaw State and has mentored (formally and informally) graduate students and junior faculty on professional development and the job market. Simon is also a founding member of the Greater Atlanta Portuguese Program Association, or GAPPA, in 2014.

Ana Catarina Teixeira completed her PhD in Portuguese and Brazilian Studies at Brown University (2014). Prior to joining the faculty at Emory in 2014, Prof. Teixeira taught at the Massachusetts Institute of Technology, the University of North Carolina at Asheville, the University of Rhode Island, and Brigham Young University. At Emory University, she directs the Portuguese language program, the Emory Study Abroad Summer Program in São Paulo, and is affiliated faculty in African Studies. Teixeira is interested in best practices for second-language acquisition.

Naomi Pueo Wood is an Assistant Professor of Spanish and Portuguese at Colorado College. She founded the Portuguese language program in 2011 and since then has developed a language and culture curriculum, founded a Luso-Brazilian Studies minor, and initiated a summer study abroad program. She has also worked to understand the particular needs of students and affiliate faculty in the Liberal Arts College context.

BOAVISTA PRESS

www.ingramcontent.com/pod-product-compliance
Lightning Source LLC
Chambersburg PA
CBHW052034090426
42739CB00010B/1909

* 9 7 8 0 9 9 6 0 5 1 1 8 7 *